REFUGE AND REALITY

Feuchtwanger and the
European Émigrés in California

GERMAN MONITOR No. 61
General Editor: Ian Wallace

REFUGE AND REALITY

Feuchtwanger and the
European Émigrés in California

Edited by

Pól O'Dochartaigh and Alexander Stephan

Amsterdam - New York, NY 2005

The paper on which this book is printed meets the requirements of "ISO 9706:1994, Information and documentation - Paper for documents - Requirements for permanence".

ISBN: 90-420-1945-X
©Editions Rodopi B.V., Amsterdam - New York, NY 2005
Printed in the Netherlands

Table of Contents

Foreword

In July 2001 a number of scholars from the USA and Europe came together at the Villa Aurora in Pacific Palisades and at the University of Southern California to found the International Feuchtwanger Society. This meeting was held at the instigation of Ian Wallace (University of Bath). It was sponsored by the University of Southern California and facilitated by Marje Schuetze-Coburn who directs the Feuchtwanger Memorial Library at USC. The Society, which elected Ian Wallace as its first chair, aims to hold biennial conferences that should alternate between the USA and Europe. The papers in this volume are a selection from the first conference, which took place at the Villa Aurora in April 2003.

The Society determined that it wants to promote research both on Lion and Marta Feuchtwanger and on wider issues related to their lives and works, including, *inter alia*, anti-Semitism, the exile experience, and historical novels. The range of contributions to the present volume reflects this goal.

The nine papers offered in *Refuge and Reality: Feuchtwanger and the European Émigrés in California* fall broadly into three categories: literary analyses of Feuchtwanger's works, studies on other exile writers, and examinations of Feuchtwanger's correspondence and activities, all with a focus on the exile community in California. Wulf Koepke interprets *Die Brüder Lautensack* as a novel of self-doubt about the role of the writer and intellectual, but also, via its descriptions of the occult background of Nazism, as a book of revenge against Hitler. Arnold Pistiak's reading of *Jefta und seine Tochter* employs an 'historical-philosophical' method to investigate Feuchtwanger's attempt to interpret the significance of power in the context of historic processes. Pól O'Dochartaigh approaches *Waffen für Amerika* not as a simple analogy between French aid for America in the War of Independence and US aid for Europe against Nazism, but as an ongoing historical metaphor for promoting reason rather than unilateralism through US-European co-operation, a view that Feuchtwanger was able to develop effectively in the light of his own experiences on two continents.

The volume then turns to other exiles in the United States. Engaging in a close analysis of the film *Hangmen also die* while also relying on archive resources, Ian Wallace shows that Bertolt Brecht regarded his input into the film purely as a 'Brotarbeit', whereas Fritz Lang felt that his professional future depended on the commercial success of the movie. David Midgley turns our attention to Alfred Döblin, whose conversion from Judaism to Catholicism in 1941 caused a minor scandal among German exiles.

The four remaining papers of *Refuge and Reality* use various correspondences and archival material to illuminate aspects of Feuchtwanger's relocation to California and his extensive contacts with other exiles. Using unpublished letters from the Feuchtwanger archive in Los Angeles, Marje Schuetze-Coburn traces Lion and Marta's key movements in this period. Alexander Stephan draws on new documents released since the publication of his 1995 volume *Im Visier des FBI*, which told the story of the surveillance of the exile community, including Lion and Marta Feuchtwanger, to illustrate the banality of the FBI activities directed against refugees from Nazi Germany suspected of left-wing sympathies. Daniel Azuélos looks at the relationship between Feuchtwanger and Franz Werfel in light of their contributions to the Jewish newspaper *Aufbau*. The volume closes with an essay by Jeffrey Berlin, who conducted extensive archival research to give us an insight into the collaboration between Feuchtwanger and his New York publisher, Ben Huebsch.

Pól O'Dochartaigh and Alexander Stephan,
February 2005.

NB: With regard to the four contributions in German in this volume, the editors have respected the decision of authors to adhere either to the traditional or re-formed spelling standard.

Wulf Koepke

Hitler in Hollywood.
Lion Feuchtwangers Abschied von Deutschland im Spiegel von
Die Brüder Lautensack

Between his arrival in the United States and his establishment in Pacific Palisades, Lion Feuchtwanger wrote a number of short stories and three larger texts that have been unduly neglected by scholars: *The Devil in France*, *Simone*, and *Double, Double, Toil and Trouble*, in German: *Die Brüder Lautensack*. The protagonist of this novel, published in 1943, is a telepath-magician, modelled after Jan Erik Hanussen, who entered into a close relationship with Adolf Hitler and was murdered in 1933. This is Feuchtwanger's last depiction of contemporary Germany. It centers on the 'occult' background of the Nazi movement. Feuchtwanger sees close similarities between the telepathic swindler, Nazi propaganda, and the illusions created by Hollywood. It is essentially a book of self-doubt and questioning about the role of the writer and intellectual, and a book of 'revenge' against Hitler.

Mit erstaunlicher Hartnäckigkeit setzte sich Lion Feuchtwanger an den Schreibtisch, während er sich 1940 in Marseille beim amerikanischen Vizekonsul Hiram Bingham versteckt hielt und auf eine Gelegenheit zur Flucht aus Frankreich wartete, und schrieb weiter am dritten Band seiner ‚Josephus'-Trilogie *Der Tag wird kommen*. Höchst erstaunlich, denn er hatte gerade die Zeit im Internierungslager Les Milles hinter sich und war körperlich und seelisch erschöpft. Diese Erschöpfung machte sich dann erst richtig bemerkbar, als Feuchtwanger endlich auf dem Dampfer Excalibur von Lissabon nach New York unterwegs war – er verschlief die Überfahrt zum großen Teil.[1] In Marseille hielt ihn die Spannung wach; er war immer noch in Lebensgefahr, weit mehr als die Kollegen Heinrich Mann und Franz Werfel; denn ihn verfolgte Adolf Hitlers persönlicher Haß, er war berühmt und berüchtigt.

    Feuchtwanger hatte seine ‚Wartesaal'-Trilogie mit dem Roman *Exil*, englisch *Paris Gazette*, beendet, der noch 1940 bei Querido in Amsterdam erschien, bevor die deutschen Truppen die Niederlande überfielen. Jetzt sollte unbedingt auch der ‚Josephus', sein Hauptwerk dieses Jahrzehnts und ein persönliches Bekenntnis der Stellung und Aufgaben des jüdischen Schriftstellers in der westlichen Gesellschaft,[2] zu Ende gebracht werden. Das Manuskript erreichte dann die USA mit dem diplomatischen Kurier. Es erschien nach weiteren Revisionen 1942 in englischer Übersetzung und 1945, nach dem Krieg, auf deutsch im Bermann-Fischer Verlag in Stockholm.

    In den USA folgte zunächst eine Zeit der Unruhe, der Umzüge und der Ungewißheit, bis sich die Feuchtwangers Ende 1943 ihr neues Nest am Paseo Miramar in Pacific Palisades einrichten konnten. 1944 begann Feuchtwanger mit der Niederschrift des zweibändigen Romans *Waffen für Amerika* bzw. *Die Füchse im Weinberg*, der 1947 erschien und als erster Roman einer Trilogie über die Voraussetzungen, Hintergründe und Ideen der Französischen Revolution angesehen werden kann, zu der außerdem die Romane über Francisco Goya und Jean-Jacques Rousseau zählen.

In der Zwischenzeit jedoch schrieb Feuchtwanger drei längere Texte und eine Reihe von kürzeren Erzählungen, die die Forschung als 'Nebenwerke' beiseitegelassen hat: den Lager- und Fluchtbericht *Unholdes Frankreich*, späterer Titel *Der Teufel in Frankreich*; den Roman *Die Brüder Lautensack*, in den USA: *Double, Double, Toil and Trouble*, und den Roman *Simone*, hervorgegangen aus der Mitarbeit an Bert Brechts Stück *Die Gesichte der Simone Machard*. *Unholdes Frankreich*, das Brecht besonders schätzte und ‚wahrscheinlich sein schönstes Buch' nannte,[3] wird als Dokument über die französischen Internierungslager zitiert, doch seltener als Selbstaussage Feuchtwangers und gar nicht als literarischer Text gewertet. *Simone* hat die zweifelhafte Funktion, als Kontrast zu Brechts Stück zu dienen, um dessen Qualitäten und Feuchtwangers Mängel herauszustellen.[4] Es dient dabei ebenso wie *Der falsche Nero* als Beweisstück für die ungenügende, weil ‚idealistische' Geschichtsauffassung Feuchtwangers. *Die Brüder Lautensack* ist nahezu unbeachtet geblieben – ein Paradox bei einem Text, der offensichtlich für ein breites Publikum geschrieben ist.[5] Alle drei Texte und einige der gleichzeitig geschriebenen kurzen Erzählungen haben zwei Charakteristika gemeinsam: sie betreffen die aktuelle Situation in Europa, es sind Texte zur Zeit; und sie verraten ein sehr persönliches Engagement mit vielen autobiographischen Elementen, auch in den Romanen. Es sind Texte der Selbstbefragung und der Klärung: sie sollen bestimmen, worum es im antifaschistischen Kampf geht und was der Standpunkt des Autors, des Intellektuellen, sein kann und muß. Sie sind daher bei einer gründlichen Analyse zusammen mit den Essays, Artikeln und Interviews Feuchtwangers aus diesen Jahren zu lesen.

Während *Unholdes Frankreich* durchaus zur rechten Zeit erschien und seine Wirkung ausgeübt hat,[6] war den beiden Romanen eine merkwürdige Erfolglosigkeit beschieden. *Simone* erreichte immerhin seinen kommerziellen Zweck, da der Roman als Film angekauft, wenn auch nie verwirklicht wurde, und das Honorar, das Feuchtwanger mit Brecht teilte, den beiden in einer kritischen Zeit zugute kam. Brecht notierte lakonisch: ‚Kaufe neue Hose'.[7] Die Aktualität von *Simone*, die französische Résistance im Zweiten Weltkrieg, war jedoch bereits so gut wie vorüber, als das Buch erschien, und Brecht hat sein Stück zu Lebzeiten weder aufgeführt noch veröffentlicht. *Die Brüder Lautensack* brachte Feuchtwanger dringend nötiges Geld durch den Vorabdruck in *Collier's Magazine*; aber sein Hitler-Porträt wollte den Entscheidungsträgern in Hollywood nach Chaplins *Great Dictator* und Ernst Lubitschs *To Be or Not To Be* nicht mehr einleuchten, und die amerikanische Buchkritik verhielt sich ebenso kühl wie das deutsche Exil und die spätere Kritik und Wissenschaft.[8]

Es ist an der Zeit, den sich daraus ergebenden Fragen auf den Grund zu gehen. Dafür kann ich hier nur etwas Vorarbeit leisten. Obwohl ich den Lagerbericht zusammen mit *Simone* für besonders aufschlußreich halte, geradezu für

Schlüsseltexte in Feuchtwangers damaliger Situation, die einer der Wende-
punkte seines Lebens war, möchte ich mich auf *Die Brüder Lautensack* konzentrieren, da der Roman zu den besonders vernachlässigten Texten Feuchtwangers
gehört.

Es ist leicht, *Die Brüder Lautensack* abzutun, da man sich auf Feuchtwangers eigene uncharakteristische Skepsis während der Arbeit berufen kann.
Am 21. Januar 1942 schrieb er an Arnold Zweig:

> Ich selber habe jetzt angefangen, einen Roman zu schreiben über einen Hellseher im
> Dritten Reich. Es ist nicht die glücklichste Wahl, die ich getroffen habe. Trotzdem
> glaube ich, daß das Buch glücken wird und mir, à la longue, auch Genugtuung
> bringen wird.[9]

Zwar brachte der Vorabdruck in *Collier's Magazine* Anfang 1943 das nötige
Einkommen, um das Haus am Paseo Miramar, das ‚Schloß am Meer', zu
kaufen, doch ärgerte sich Feuchtwanger über die willkürlich herausgerissenen
Auszüge, die einen schlechten Eindruck vom Buch vermittelten und sicherlich
mit der wenig enthusiastischen Kritik zu tun gehabt haben – eine erste Erfahrung mit dem ‚unliterarischen' Kommerzialismus in den USA.[10]

In Feuchtwangers Briefen von 1942 ist gewöhnlich vom Roman über den
Hellseher die Rede; auch in Bezug auf das Theaterstück, das er vorher mit Leo
Mittler zu schreiben versucht hatte. Als erster Titel war *Der Zauberer* vorgese-
hen. Erst im Brief vom 21. Januar 1943 an Alfred Kantorowicz, in den Ant-
worten auf einen Fragenkatalog für ein halbstündiges Radio-Porträt oder Hör-
bild, schreibt Feuchtwanger: ‚Soeben vollendet habe ich einen Roman, der
Hitlers Wahrsager zum Helden hat und die magischen und abergläubischen Hin-
tergründe des Dritten Reichs zum Gegenstand'.[11] Auch hier fehlt die Erklärung
für den amerikanischen Titel *Double, Double, Toil and Trouble*, also die Problematik des Doppelgängers, die in Chaplins *Great Dictator* und in Heinrich
Manns Roman *Lidice* im Mittelpunkt steht, und Hitlers eigene Rolle im Roman.
Es ist daraus zu entnehmen, daß Feuchtwanger nicht nur, wie so oft bei ihm, der
Stoff während des Schreibens gewachsen ist und sich in ungeplante Richtungen
verzweigt hat, sondern daß Feuchtwanger selbst vor einigen Komplexitäten der
Geschichte zurückschreckte, da er den Roman klar und überschaubar halten
wollte. Bei *Simone* ist ihm das überzeugender gelungen.

Die Brüder Lautensack führen zurück in die letzten Jahre der Weimarer
Republik in Berlin und den Anfang des Dritten Reichs, eine Epoche, die vorher
der Gegenstand von *Die Geschwister Oppermann* gewesen war. Während dort
der Beginn der nationalsozialistischen Diktatur als Ende des deutschjüdischen
Bürgertums geschildert wurde, führt der Roman *Die Brüder Lautensack* ins
Innere der nationalsozialistischen Führungsspitze und schildert Adolf Hitler als
Person, weit näher und intimer als in *Erfolg*. Jetzt tritt Hitler unter seinem
eigenen Namen auf, unverkleidet, ‚Hitler, wie ihn keiner kennt', während seine
Gefolgsleute, wie z. B. Röhm, zwar leicht erkennbar sind, aber romanhafte
Namen tragen. Auch Oskar Lautensack ist erfunden, wenn auch sein Schicksal

Ähnlichkeit mit dem von Hitlers Hellseher Jan Erik Hanussen hat. Feuchtwanger hat in der Tat an das amerikanische Publikum gedacht, dem alle Namen
der deutschen Zeitgeschichte außer Hitler und die historischen Einzelheiten der
Jahre vor und nach 1933 unbekannt waren.

Feuchtwanger macht Lautensack zum Bayern und vermeidet das Paradox
Hanussens, der, obwohl er Jude war, eine solch enge Beziehung zu Hitler hatte.
Feuchtwanger spielt außerdem mit dem Gegensatz von München und Berlin. In
vieler Hinsicht ist das Buch eine Fortsetzung von *Erfolg*, ein Zusatz zur
,Wartesaal'-Trilogie, und vor allem ein Abschied von Deutschland, so wie *Unholdes Frankreich* und *Simone* ein Abschied von Frankreich waren. Feuchtwanger hat nach diesen drei Texten kein Buch mehr geschrieben, das sich mit
dem gegenwärtigen Deutschland und Frankreich befaßte. Er hatte diese Länder
innerlich hinter sich gelassen – trotz des Heimwehs und trotz des unerfüllten
Wunsches, einmal eine Europareise zu machen.

Im Vergleich dazu könnte man auch Thomas Manns *Doktor Faustus*
einen Abschied von Deutschland nennen, der zugleich eine Abrechnung war.
Heinrich Manns Werk in den USA kreist fast ausschließlich um den Abschied
von Europa, den er mit so bewegten Worten in *Ein Zeitalter wird besichtigt*
beschrieben hat. *Empfang bei der Welt* und noch mehr *Der Atem* schildern eher
gespenstisch den Traum vom ,alten Europa'. Zu denken wäre ebenfalls an Anna
Seghers' vielsagende Geschichte *Der Ausflug der toten Mädchen*, die unter
anderem als letzter Abschied von der Heimat verstanden werden kann. Die
Themen ,Abschied' und ,Ende' blieben keinem Exilierten erspart.

Die Komplexe, um die der Roman *Die Brüder Lautensack* kreist, sind das
Phänomen des ,Hellsehens' und die innere Eigenart von Adolf Hitler und seiner
Bewegung. Lion Feuchtwanger hatte schon früh Hitler als eine Gefahr erkannt,
in seiner magischen Wirkung auf die unzufriedenen Massen der Kleinbürger,
und so wird Hitler in *Erfolg* dargestellt, noch dazu als Günstling der baye-
rischen Politiker. Die Nazis vergalten Gleiches mit Gleichem. Feuchtwanger,
der Jude mit Welterfolg, wurde sofort verfolgt: sein Haus wurde durchsucht und
geplündert, sein Vermögen wurde beschlagnahmt, ihm wurden die Staatsange-
hörigkeit und der Doktortitel entzogen, und bei dem Vormarsch der deutschen
Armee durch Frankreich 1940 geriet Feuchtwanger in Lebensgefahr. Als er mit
Mühe und Not und unter falschem Namen entkommen war, mußte er in New
York erfahren, daß ein antisemitischer Hetzfilm, in dem alte Freunde und
Bekannte aus München und Berlin die Hauptrollen spielten, die Geschichte von
Jud Süß, mit der Feuchtwangers Name und Erfolg untrennbar verbunden waren,
pervertiert hatte und gerade in Venedig preisgekrönt wurde. Alles das war
Grund genug, nicht nur mit sich zu Rate zu gehen und zu fragen, wie und
warum das alles so gekommen war, was Feuchtwanger in *Unholdes Frankreich*
begonnen hatte, sondern auch im Zorn an Adolf Hitler, dieses ,Nichts', zu
denken, und an die Deutschen, die sich ihm unterworfen hatten.

Brecht und Feuchtwanger hatten freundschaftliche, aber scharfe Streitgespräche über Hitler, deren Echo im *Arbeitsjournal* zu finden ist. So bereits am 1. November 1941, bezugnehmend auf *Erfolg* und *Der falsche Nero*: ‚Er hatte *Hitler* als ein Nichts dargestellt, als bedeutungsloses Sprachrohr der Reichswehr, einen Schauspieler, der den Führer spielt usw. Kurz, Hitler soll keine „Persönlichkeit" sein. Ich ... lege Wert darauf, daß er eine ist' (22). Wie könne man den Amerikanern klarmachen, daß ‚ein Mann nichts sein könnte, wenn die USA 40 Milliarden zu seiner Vertilgung ausgeben wollen' (22). Noch am 27. Februar 1942 notierte Brecht: ‚Feuchtwanger und andere können mit dem Phänomen *Hitler* nicht fertig werden, weil sie das Phänomen „herrschendes Kleinbürgertum" nicht sehen' (58). Einen Tag später: ‚Thema wieder: *Ist Hitler ein Hampelmann?*' (63)

Dieser Streit stammte nicht nur aus der persönlichen Vertrautheit Hitlers in den Münchener Tagen und aus der bis heute ungelösten Frage, ob und wie Hitler literarisch dargestellt werden könnte, da es keine wirklich adäquate Hitler-Darstellung gibt. Brechts und Feuchtwangers Anstrengungen, dem Phänomen Hitler näherzukommen, sind ein Zeugnis einer sehr persönlichen Betroffenheit. Feuchtwanger, nicht anders als Döblin und Heinrich Mann, erfuhr in Los Angeles-Hollywood, daß er eigentlich in diesem Filmbetrieb ein Nichts war, trotz seiner Popularität bei amerikanischen Lesern, die allerdings mit jedem neuen Buch wieder auf die Probe gestellt wurde. Auch er konnte sich nicht viele Flops erlauben. Der deutsche Schriftsteller, Träger des deutschen bzw. europäischen Geistes, kam in Los Angeles ohne Gepäck an, ohne den Glanz seiner Würde und seines Ranges. Eine Ausnahme, die manchen Neid hervorrief, war der Nobelpreisträger Thomas Mann, der von seinen Ehren lebte, die er dann durch seine Persönlichkeit auszufüllen verstand und durch neue, besonders akademische, Ehren vermehrte. Die anderen Autoren hatten ihre Nützlichkeit durch finanzielle Erfolge und Popularität zu beweisen, also durch ihre Leistungen. Sie waren keine ‚Persönlichkeiten' des öffentlichen Lebens, sondern bestenfalls tüchtige Handwerker, deren Arbeit im Filmbetrieb meistens anonym blieb. Wenn Brecht darauf pochte, eine ‚Persönlichkeit' zu sein und sein geistiges Eigentum bei *Hangmen also die* hartnäckig behaupten wollte, so war er sehr am falschen Platz. Paradoxerweise war Brechts eigene Konzeption des Theaters die einer Gemeinschaftsleistung, auch was den Text betraf, doch die Teamarbeit im Film stieß ihn ab.

Dieses Thema ist hier insofern relevant, als es Feuchtwangers Hitler-Figur betrifft. Feuchtwanger bekam in Hollywood ein neues Verständnis für das Phänomen Hitler, da er hier, wie alle seine Kollegen, mit der amerikanischen Kulturindustrie konfrontiert war, und damit mit dem Entertainment, der Unterhaltung für die Massen. Oskar Lautensack erlebt Hitler zum erstenmal bei einer Rede im Zirkus Krone in München – es ist ein ‚Zirkus' in mehrfacher Bedeutung. Oskar erlebt mit, wie Hitler sich selbst in Trance and Rage redet, und wie er die Zuhörer zu einer Masse macht, die ihm willenlos ergeben ist und allen seinen Gefühlen und Aggressionen folgt. Auch Oskar wird mitgezogen; aber er bleibt sich dessen bewußt, und er fühlt ein besonderes Fluidum zwischen sich und dem Führer. Adolf Hitler, so wird wiederholt vorgeführt, ist unfähig zum Gespräch, zum Dialog, er sitzt stumm da ohne zuzuhören, bis er zu reden anfängt und die Zuhörer mitreißen will. Er ,funktioniert' ausschließlich im Zusammenwirken mit einer Masse, auf die er einredet. Für sich allein ist er wirklich ein Nichts. Er existiert nur als Führer oder Verführer einer Masse.

Diese nichtige Figur, die eine solch ungeheuer faszinierende Wirkung ausübt, ist nur verständlich als Funktion der Massenmedien. Sie ist nicht nur theatralisch, sie ist eine Theaterfigur, die inszeniert werden muß, was man die Ästhetisierung der Politik nennen mag. Sie braucht den Nimbus eines Mediums, und deshalb wird sie übertragen in den Rundfunk und den Film. Es ist nicht Kunst, sondern Künstlichkeit, die ihre Wirkung besiegelt. Der Führer im Film *Triumph des Willens* ist gleichzeitig allgegenwärtig und unerreichbar fern. Brecht sah seinen Arturo Ui als Theaterfigur, Feuchtwangers Hitler ist in den Film entrückt. Wann immer und warum er die Arbeit mit Leo Mittler am Theaterstück *Der Zauberer* abbrach, sein Hitler hätte nicht als lebendiger Schauspieler auf die Bühne kommen dürfen.

Das Massenmedium Film in Hollywood kam Brecht wie eine Lügenfabrik vor. In Feuchtwangers Roman heißt das Schlüsselwort ,Schwindel'. Oskar Lautensacks Bruder Hans, der sich als prominenter Nazi und Propagandachef dann zu ,Hannsjörg' aufnordet, erklärt Oskar im entscheidenden Moment der Handlung, worum es geht:

> Es ist nun einmal nicht möglich, ... den Massen etwas beizubringen ohne Aufmachung, ohne Reklame, ohne Schwindel. Die Menschen sträuben sich gegen alles, was absticht vom Gewöhnlichen. Glaubst du vielleicht, unser Herr Jesus hätte was erreicht, wenn er nicht seine Apostel ausgeschickt hätte, um für seine Wunder Reklame zu machen? Nicht einmal der Führer hätte sich durchgesetzt ohne gewisse Nachhilfen, ohne große Worte, ohne das, was du vorher grob ,Schwindel' genannt hast. Lies doch einmal nach, was er in seinem Buch dargelegt hat über die Notwendigkeit der Propaganda, der Lüge, des Schwindels. Wieviele Meineide, wieviel Selbsterniedrigung hat er auf sich nehmen müssen. Überwinde auch du dich, Oskar. Mach Konzessionen. Das bist du deiner Begabung einfach schuldig.[12]

Diese Logik ist eines Goebbels würdig, und der zu-kurz-geratene Krüppel Hans ist etwas wie eine Mischung von Horst Wessel – nur daß bei Feuchtwanger bei dem Streit um die Hure der Kommunist erschossen wird – und Goebbels, der dann durch den Schwindel seiner Propaganda aus Horst Wessel den Märtyrer der Bewegung schuf. Feuchtwanger etabliert hier die Gleichung von Propaganda, Reklame, Lüge und Schwindel. Das betrifft nicht nur den Propagandachef Hannsjörg (dessen Name Schwindel ist) und Oskar, der aus dem Hellseher zum Schwindler wird, nicht nur den meideidigen Hitler, sondern genauso die amerikanische Reklame und die Szene von Hollywood, wo der Schriftsteller in Brechts Sicht Lügen verkauft. Die Analyse der Kulturindustrie bei Günther Anders und in der *Dialektik der Aufklärung* mag von heute her gesehen problematisch sein; sie konstatiert jedenfalls das System des Schwindels, der Manipulation und der Illusion, von dem die Gesellschaft und die Wirtschaft lebt. Damit ist der ‚Okkultismus', von dem Feuchtwanger sprach, die Verschleierung der Klarheit und Wahrheit, ein grundlegendes Element des Kapitalismus, nicht nur seiner faschistischen Auswüchse.

Dieser Vorwurf des Schwindels trifft nun ebenso den Schriftsteller in der kapitalistischen Gesellschaft. Der Roman *Die Brüder Lautensack* ist genau wie *Unholdes Frankreich* und vorher *Die Geschwister Oppermann*, *Josephus* und *Exil* eine Phase der fortgehenden Selbstbefragung Feuchtwangers im Exil. Genau wie Gustav Oppermann hat der Schriftsteller und Kritiker Paul Cramer in *Die Brüder Lautensack* zu spät angefangen, gegen Hitler zu kämpfen, und obendrein kämpft er mit den falschen Waffen. Wie auch anderswo arbeitet Feuchtwanger in diesem Roman mit Gegensatzpaaren. Neben dem Paar der schon körperlich gegensätzlichen Brüder Lautensack haben wir das Paar Oskar Lautensack-Adolf Hitler und außerdem Oskar Lautensack-Paul Cramer – alles drei Paare, aus deren Beziehungen sich die Handlung entwickelt, die um Oskar Lautensack kreist. Paul Cramer, der Halbjude, ist der Schriftsteller, der der Kritik, der Vernunft, der Klarheit und der Präzision verpflichtet ist. Er schreibt die Kritik am unmöglichen und fehlerhaften Stil von Hitlers *Mein Kampf*, Feuchtwangers eigene Kritik, die ein Grund für Hitlers persönlichen Haß war, und die hier im Roman Paul Cramers Schicksal besiegelt, was Feuchtwanger 1940 so sehr für sich gefürchtet hatte. Auch Oskar Lautensack schreibt. Er soll ein wissenschaftliches Buch über das Hellsehen schreiben; stattdessen wird er Redakteur einer Propagandazeitschrift für die Nazis. Höchst aufschlußreich sind die Szenen, in denen Oskar Käthe Severin, der Halbschwester Paul Cramers, seine Artikel diktiert. Die Schilderung des erotischen Fluidums zwischen Diktierer und Stenografin beruht ohne Zweifel auf eigenen Erlebnissen. Der Inhalt ist allerdings romanspezifisch: ‚Was er zu sagen hat, klingt vag und dunkel. Dafür ist Musik in seinen Sätzen. Käthe hört sie mit Lust' (85-86). Hier versucht Feuchtwanger das zu fassen, was die Deutschen an dieser wirren Weltanschauung so fasziniert:

> Es beschreibt aber der Fremde ein Phänomen, das ihr bisher fernlag und das er bald als Telepathie, bald als Gedankenlesen, bald als Metaphysik bezeichnet. Feste Grenzen scheint der Begriff nicht zu haben, und im Grund ist Käthe, nachdem der Herr eine ganze Weile diktiert hat, nicht klüger geworden. Aber sie spürt hinter seinen unklaren Sätzen eine Größe, die jede unehrerbietige Kritik verscheucht. (86)

Während Käthe Oskar willig folgt und sich schließlich in ihn verliebt, wird sie jetzt von der scharfen Kritik ihres Halbbruders Paul Cramer abgestoßen. ‚Er arbeitet an einem Essay über die Heraufkunft eines neuen magischen Zeitalters' (102). Sie hört und stenografiert seinen Text ‚mit Unlust'. ‚Sie hatte Verständnis für Pauls hellen, scharfen Verstand. Aber was kam heraus bei all dem Theoretisieren? Niemals hatte er etwas Praktisches vorgeschlagen. Alles blieb unfruchtbares Räsonnement' (102).

Hier sind die beiden Extreme, zwischen denen Feuchtwanger für sein eigenes Schreiben einen Weg finden wollte. Oskar ist eigentlich eher Redner als

Schreiber. Das ist noch mehr bei Hitler der Fall, der aus dem Reden und durch das Reden existiert. Doch nicht umsonst hatte ihn Thomas Mann 1939 ‚Bruder Hitler' genannt, den unangenehmen Kollegen, der leider immer noch zur eigenen Zunft gehörte. In dieser Kette Hitler-Hans Lautensack-Oskar Lautensack-Paul Cramer steckt die ganze Skala vom Irrationalismus, von der Widervernunft, bis zur rationalen Kritik und Vernünftigkeit. Hier steckt der Komplex des antifaschistischen Schriftstellers, ob er und wie er in dieser Zeit der falschen Mythen, oder wenn man Adorno/Horkheimer folgt, des Umschlagens der Aufklärung in Mythen, mit dem Wort für die Vernunft kämpfen kann. In seinem Essay von 1935 ‚Vom Sinn und Unsinn des historischen Romans' hatte Feuchtwanger noch optimistisch formuliert: ‚Ich für mein Teil habe mich, seitdem ich schreibe, bemüht, historische Romane für die Vernunft zu schreiben, gegen Dummheit und Gewalt, gegen das, was Marx das Versinken in die Geschichtslosigkeit nennt'.[13] 1943, in ‚Der Schriftsteller im Exil', spürt Feuchtwanger bei den großen Vorgängern im Exil ‚infernalischen Haß' – Dante – ‚blitzende Schärfe' – Victor Hugo – und ‚eleganten und tödlichen Hohn' – Heine.[14] Auch im optimistischen Schluß, daß das Exil Gutes gebracht habe, manche Schriftsteller hätten ‚sich erneuert', kommt er nicht ohne das Wort ‚bitter' aus: ‚Sie sind nicht nur bitterer geworden, sondern auch weiser, gerechter gegen ihre neue Welt, dankbarer und der eigenen Sendung tiefer bewußt' (538). Sind sie auch gerechter gegen die alte Welt? Wohl kaum, wenn man dem Text von *Die Brüder Lautensack* folgt, den Feuchtwanger allerdings zu dieser Zeit bereits fertiggestellt hatte.

Die Schriftsteller im Exil, Dante, Victor Hugo und Heinrich Heine zum Beispiel, haben nicht der Vernunft allein vertraut, sondern mit Worten voll starker und aggressiver Emotionen gekämpft. Paul Cramer hat seinen Artikel über Hitlers Stil mit intensiver Gefühlsbeteiligung geschrieben und daher auch Wirkung erzielt:

> Es war in diesen Tagen, daß Paul Cramer den Artikel über den Schriftsteller Hitler schrieb, jenen Aufsatz, der soviel dazu beigetragen hat, das Bild Hitlers zu zeichnen, wie wir Späteren es sehen. Tief überzeugt, daß sich das Wesen eines Menschen unter allen Umständen spiegle in seinem Stil, zeigte Paul Cramer an Hitlers trüben Sätzen seine trübe Seele auf. Mit klaren Strichen zeichnete er diesen armen Affen Napoleons, Nietzsches und Wagners, diese wildgewordene Null, die, empört über die eigene Minderwertigkeit, sich aufmacht, das eigene Nichts zu rächen an der ganzen Welt. (172)

Wie in *Erfolg* versetzt sich der Erzähler in die Zukunft nach dem Ende Hitlers, aus deren Perspektive der ‚Späteren' er die Gegenwart als vergangene Geschichte erzählt. Der Absatz lebt vom Gegensatz der Adjektive ‚trübe' und ‚klar'. Hitlers tödlicher Haß gegen Paul Cramer (und Feuchtwanger) beruht nicht nur darauf, daß sein Stil als unbeholfen und schlecht abgetan wird, also daß er sich in seiner Würde als Schriftsteller verletzt sieht, sondern daß er sich durchschaut fühlt. Im Stil spiegelt sich sein Charakter, und Cramers Artikel ist ein Spiegel, den er Hitler vorhält. Hitler ist nicht nur ein Nichts, er ist eine ‚wildgewordene Null', seine Aggressivität ist Wut über die eigene Minderwertigkeit, er ist ein armer Nachahmer Napoleons, ein Schauspieler, der glaubt, ein großer Feldherr, ein großer Philosoph und der Schöpfer des deutschen Musiktheaters zu sein.

Das Schauspieler-Motiv durchzieht den gesamten Roman. Der Hofschauspieler, der Hitler – und Oskar Lautensack! – Sprechunterricht gegeben hat, bemerkt, daß Hitlers Leistung als Redner mittelmäßig ist. Doch für das Leben sei das ja genügend; auf der Bühne würde mehr verlangt. Der Theateragent Mautz verbreitet genüßlich, daß Hitler bei ihm vorgesprochen habe, um ein Engagement als Schauspieler zu suchen. Er habe ihn als unbegabt und wegen seines unmöglichen bayerisch-österreichischen Akzents abgelehnt. Später tut ihm das leid, Hitler hätte als Provinzschauspieler so viel weniger Schaden angerichtet denn als Politiker. Hitler rächt sich natürlich an Mautz, der kaum mit dem Leben davonkommt.

In diesen sarkastischen Charakterisierungen spricht sich der Zorn des Autors Feuchtwanger aus, der Hitler mit dem Wort vernichten möchte. *Die Brüder Lautensack* ist im Kern ein Anti-Hitler-Buch. Doch genau wie Paul Cramer hat auch Feuchtwanger gewußt, daß seine Waffen keine Wirkung haben konnten:

> Da hat er also einen guten Aufsatz geschrieben. Ein paar tausend Leute werden ihn lesen, und ein paar hundert werden schmunzeln und mit den gescheiten Köpfen nicken. Und was weiter? Nichts weiter. Ein Dreck. Die Emotionen, welche Hitler und sein Lautensack hervorrufen, kann man nicht mit dem Verstand bekämpfen, sondern wieder nur mit Emotion. Mit ihren eigenen Mitteln müßte man gegen die dumme Schlauheit dieser Leute angehen. Aber das bringen wir nicht über uns. Das können wir nicht. Darum haben wir keine Wirkung auf die Massen. Darum kommen wir nicht auf gegen die Hitler und Lautensack. Sie werden sich betätigen, sie werden uns erledigen. (173)

Paul Cramer wirft in seiner Eifersucht gegenüber Käthe Hitler und Oskar Lautensack zusammen, doch mit einigem Recht; Lautensack ist ein Sprachrohr der Nazis. In dem Namen ‚Lautensack’ stecken die Elemente ‚laut’, ‚Laute’ und ‚Sack’, wie in Dudelsack; abgesehen davon, daß es sich um einen gebräuchlichen Namen handelt, sind es keine präzisen Wortbedeutungen, aber doch Assoziationen, die Oskar zu einem Stimmverstärker, einem Megaphon der Propaganda machen. Wenn Cramer versucht, die Nazis durch das Oxymoron ‚dumme Schlauheit’ zu definieren, so will er die Mischung des Antirationalismus mit dem durch keine moralischen (oder ästhetischen!) Skrupel gehemmten Machtstreben erfassen, das alles zerstört, was ihm in den Weg gerät, und bei diesem Streben durchaus zweckrationalistisch und erfinderisch vorgeht.

Ironischerweise folgt Oskar Lautensacks Sturz von den Höhen der scheinbaren Macht nicht allein auf seine Hybris, die in dem pompösen Gebäude im Nazi-Stil, der Sophienburg, versinnbildlicht ist, dessen ‚Größe’ die Vergeltung der Nazi-Größen herausfordert, sondern auf seine Unfähigkeit, das Leben seines Gegners und Rivalen Paul Cramer zu retten, wodurch er Käthe, und mit ihr sein Kind, verliert. Das Kind als Symbol der besseren Zukunft gegen und nach Hitler, das fast ein Klischee zu nennen ist, steht hier gleichzeitig für die

Existenz und Bedeutung des ‚anderen Deutschlands' im Exil, das in diesem Text so emphatisch mit der Wahrheit verbunden wird.

Oskar Lautensack, der Bayer aus Deggenburg (=Deggendorf), steht vor der Entscheidung zwischen drei Alternativen: er hat eine echte telepathische Begabung, aber das Geschäft geht schlecht. Es sind die Krisenzeiten, in denen Hellseher gefragt sind, also die Jahre des ersten Weltkriegs und der turbulenten Nachkriegszeit, aber nicht während der scheinbaren Stabilitätsperiode ab 1924. Oskar könnte mit einem Stipendium des Professors Hravliczek ein Buch über das Hellsehen, seine Natur und seine Grenzen, schreiben, und damit zur wissenschaftlichen Erkenntnis beitragen. Das wäre höchst verdienstvoll, aber es brächte ihm keinen Ruhm. Er könnte zweitens wie bisher mit seinem Freund Alois Pranner, dem Zauberer, im Varieté auftreten und also ‚ehrlichen' Schwindel bieten, Unterhaltung, die nicht behauptet, tiefe Erkenntnis zu sein. Drittens kann er, und das ist seine Wahl, im Dienst der Nazi-Partei in großem Stil als Hellseher auftreten, der die Zukunft großer Persönlichkeiten und bedeutende Ereignisse, wie den Ausgang von Wahlen, voraussagt. Damit steht er im Rampenlicht der Öffentlichkeit und ist gezwungen, nach dem ersten Schwindel immer weitere zu begehen, bis er am Ende das Licht der Wahrheit und damit sich selbst verliert. Im Hintergrund zieht sich das Motiv der Gesichtsmaske durch den Text, die die Bildhauerin Anna Tirschenreuth in München von ihm verfertigt hatte, ein Idealbild, dem er, wie Oscar Wildes Dorian Gray, immer weniger gerecht wird. Es ist eine Geschichte über die Erkenntnis der Wahrheit, die in der trüben Aura des Nationalsozialismus immer mehr abhanden kommt.

Hellsehen und Zauberei sind dabei scheinbar verwandte, aber eigentlich gegensätzliche Begriffe. Zauberei bedeutet Verwandlung, es kann auch Hypnose bedeuten: der Zauberer Hitler verwandelt die Menschen durch seine hypnotische Rede in eine willenlose, ihm bewußtlos folgende Masse. Thomas Mann hat das Phänomen am Beispiel des italienischen Faschismus in *Mario und der Zauberer* dargestellt. Zauberei bedeutet Macht und führt in dieser politischen Form zu einer sadomasochistischen Beziehung zwischen Herrscher und Massen, zu einer in jeder Hinsicht totalen Beherrschung der Menschen. Die hypnotische Wirkung des Films haben Feuchtwanger und Thomas Mann ebenfalls früh erkannt und in *Erfolg* und dem *Zauberberg* dargestellt. Seit Jahrhunderten haben ebenfalls die moralischen Kritiker der Gattung Roman die hypnotische Wirkung des Romanlesens beklagt. In der deutschen Zweiteilung von ‚Dichtung' und ‚Trivialliteratur' wird diese hypnotische, verführende Wirkung dem Trivialroman zugeschrieben, während der ernste Roman der Erkenntnis der Menschen, der Gesellschaft und der Geschichte verpflichtet ist. Die Vorwürfe von Hans Mayer und Marcel Reich-Ranicki, das Exil und der Weltruhm hätten Feuchtwanger zum Trivialschriftsteller verkommen lassen, haben daher eine moralische und eine politische Pointe.[15] Feuchtwanger selbst war sich dieses Dilemmas voll bewußt. Eine wahre Obsession wurde für ihn die Qualität und Genauigkeit der Übersetzungen, angefangen mit *Unholdes Frankreich*; die Mißverständnisse und den mangelnden Erfolg von *Die Brüder Lautensack* führte er auch auf Übersetzungsprobleme zurück. Dabei hatte er gerade in diesem Buch das getan, was Hans Mayer und Marcel Reich-Ranicki ihm vorgeworfen haben: er hat seine Sprache so präzisiert, daß sie auf Übersetzbarkeit hin geschrieben zu sein scheint. In ,Der Schriftsteller im Exil' betonte er die Präzision im Wortgebrauch, zu der das Exil zwinge, und er sieht darin eine Bereicherung:

> ... daß zum Beispiel auch der erzwungene ständige Kontakt mit der fremden Sprache, über den ich vorhin so laut zu klagen hatte, sich am Ende als Bereicherung erweist. Der im fremden Sprachkreis lebende Autor kontrolliert beinahe automatisch das eigene Wort ständig am fremden. Häufig dann sieht er, daß die fremde Sprache ein treffenderes Wort hat für das, was er ausdrücken will. Er gibt sich dann nicht zufrieden mit dem, was ihm die eigene Sprache darbietet, sondern er schärft, feilt und poliert an dem Vorhandenen so lange, bis es ein Neues geworden ist, bis er der eigenen Sprache das neue, schärfere Wort abgerungen hat. (537-38)

Hier sieht man den Autor Feuchtwanger bei der Arbeit an einem seiner Romane. Man wird diese Beschreibung kaum verallgemeinern können. Von Übersetzbarkeit ist an dieser Stelle nicht die Rede, wohl aber von dem ,schärferen' Wort. Das ist eine besonders gute Charakterisierung für den Stil von *Die Brüder Lautensack*, ein Buch, in dem alles klar und deutlich ausgesagt wird, und dem man den Vorwurf machen kann, daß es weniger schildert als definiert. Doch gerade die Qualität der Begriffe und Attribute, die diesem Buch Rahmen und Sinn geben, ist keineswegs leicht in eine andere Sprache zu übertragen. Man denke zum Beispiel an die zentralen Adjektive ,hell' und ,trübe' – scheinbar problemlos, und doch hat besonders das Wort ,trübe', das Hitler und Oskar Lautensack charakterisiert, seine eigene unnachahmliche Färbung. Die Geschichte des Hellsehers wird im Dialog oder aus der Perspektive der beteiligten Personen erzählt: der Autor faßt in Worte, was sie jeweils fühlen oder für sich selbst denken. Es ist die Geschichte von Menschen, die voreinander auf der Hut sein müssen, die ihre Worte berechnen, und die herauszufinden versuchen, was hinter den Worten, Mienen und Gesten des anderen Menschen steckt. Sie wollen ihr Inneres verstecken. Als Manfred Proell sich von Oskar Lautensack durchschaut fühlt, wird er zu dessen Todfeind. Die Menschen und ihre Worte sind von der Perspektive der Berechnung und Berechenbarkeit aus gesehen; es geht um Geschäft, Vorteil und Macht. Diese Sicht ist von Feuchtwangers Kritikern als flach und ein- oder bestenfalls zweidimensional moniert worden. Ein ,allwissender Erzähler' stelle für das amerikanische Publikum eine unzulässige Vereinfachung komplizierter psychologischer, gesellschaftlicher und politischer Zusammnhänge dar.[16]

Nun geht es in diesem Roman gerade um das Durchschauen der Zusammenhänge und Charaktere, um das ,hell-sehen'. Heinrich Mann tat sich viel darauf zugute, daß er zur Erkenntnis der geschichtlichen Zusammenhänge beigetragen habe und die Zukunft voraussagen könne. Es ist das Modell von Geist und Macht, in dem der Geist das Licht geben muß, um die Macht in die richtige Richtung zu lenken. Heinrich Mann sah in *Ein Zeitalter wird besichtigt* die

alliierten Staatsmänner als Intellektuelle und damit bei Roosevelt, Churchill und
Stalin die einmalige Chance einer Vereinigung von Macht und Geist in einer
Person, eine Transformation der Philosophen auf dem Königsthron, dem Traum
der Aufklärung. Feuchtwanger war sehr viel skeptischer, trotz seiner Illusionen
über Stalin von 1937. Er wußte von dem unüberbrückbaren Gegensatz von
Erkennen und Handeln, den er in *Thomas Wendt* gestaltet hatte. Gerade deshalb
war er kritisch gegen Leon Trotzki, den er als Intellektuellen einschätzte, und er
betrachtete Hitler als verkorksten Künstler und Schriftsteller. In *Die Brüder
Lautensack* ist Hitler alles andere als ein Tatmensch, und er ist besonders emp-
findlich gegen Cramers Kritik seines Stils. Hitler betrachtet sich als Werkzeug
der ‚Vorsehung‘ (ein Wort, das er mit mindestens zwei rr aussprach), er sieht
die Zukunft und führt sein Volk dorthin. Sein Spiegelbild Oskar ist nicht nur
Hellseher, sondern ebenfalls Schriftsteller, und zwar mit einem ‚trüben‘, un-
durchsichtigen, emotionellen und unscharfen Stil. Feuchtwangers alter ego als
Schriftsteller ist zweifellos Paul Cramer. Und doch wurde Feuchtwanger Trivia-
lisierung vorgeworfen, und das bedeutet zumindest auch Unschärfe, billige
Emotionen. Cramer sieht sich wie sein Autor Feuchtwanger unter dem politischen (und finanziellen) Zwang zur Massenwirkung, und damit steht er in Gefahr, seine Botschaft der Aufklärung und Vernunft zu verwässern und zu per-
vertieren. Er steht vor dem Problem der Drehbuchautoren in Hollywood, die
ihren Text und seine kritische Botschaft im Endprodukt, das allein den Gesetzen
der Spannung und Unterhaltung diente und nicht mehr provozieren wollte, nicht
mehr wiederfinden konnten. Der Autor steht, auch abgesehen von der antifaschistischen Kampfsituation, zwischen dem Ideal der Nähe zum Volk oder
‚Volkstümlichkeit‘ und der Gefahr der trivialen Massenunterhaltung. Dabei ist
das Phänomen ‚Volk‘ ohnehin kaum zu bestimmen, wie Brecht bald nach 1933
festgestellt hatte.

Die kontrastierenden Schriftstellerfiguren in *Die Brüder Lautensack* führen die komplexen Beziehungen zwischen Autor und Publikum vor, zusammen
mit den Konsequenzen, die sich daraus für das Schreiben der Wahrheit ergeben.
Wenn der Autor, der geistige Mensch, der Intellektuelle, ein Hellseher ist, der
die Wahrheit jenseits der Ideologien, Propaganda und Reklame erkennt, wie
kann er diese seine Erkenntnis verbreiten, ohne daß das Medium seine Botschaft
verfälscht? Zumal wenn er mehr als ‚the happy few‘ erreichen will. *Die Brüder
Lautensack* gibt keine positive Antwort, sondern beschreibt, wie Oskar, dem die
Wahrheit einmal zugänglich war und einleuchtete, sich immer mehr in den
Schwindel und die Lüge verstrickt, an die er schließlich selbst glauben muß. Die
ganze Handlung ist eine Folge von Rechtfertigungen für seine Kompromisse.
Feuchtwanger selbst bemühte sich, optimistisch zu bleiben. Am Ende seines
Rousseau-Romans wird gesagt, daß zwar von Rousseaus Ideen nur wenige und
sehr vereinfachte ins Volk gedrungen seien, daß jedoch diese wenigen Schlag-
wörter die Französische Revolution begleitet und geleitet hätten und weiter fort-
wirkten. So wollte Feuchtwanger die Langzeitwirkung der Kunst und seiner

Schriften sehen.

Als Feuchtwanger nach Los Angeles kam, kam ihm die Stadt, d.h. ihre Vororte am Meer, wie ein gigantisches Sanary-sur-Mer vor. Ihn sprach die Natur und das Klima an, im Gegensatz zu Brecht, und er war zufrieden, als er dann endlich im eigenen Haus saß, umgeben von einer wachsenden Bibliothek, mit der Möglichkeit zu Gesprächen mit Partnern wie Brecht, aber sonst schon durch die Entfernungen abgeschirmt vor lästigen Besuchern. Damit konnte er, anders als Brecht, sich auch von der sonst allgegenwärtigen Kulturindustrie und Lügenfabrik Hollywoods zurückziehen. Seine um die Französische Revolution kreisenden Romane sprechen nur noch vereinzelt von der aktuellen Wirkung des Schriftstellers, wie im Fall von Beaumarchais; sie befassen sich primär mit der Dauerhaftigkeit des Werks und seiner Erkenntnisse. Der Schriftsteller, der wie in *Unholdes Frankreich* und *Die Brüder Lautensack* in die politischen Kämpfe verstrickt ist und in Lebensgefahr gerät, hat es schwer, seinen Glauben an die Vernunft der Geschichte zu bewahren. Er versteht obendrein, daß es gefährlich und letzten Endes sinnlos ist, auf die Mächtigen und damit auf den Lauf der Ereignisse Einfluß nehmen zu wollen. Er hat vor allem begriffen, daß der vermeintliche Hellseher als Führer, der Schriftsteller als Prophet ein Unding ist. Adolf Hitler ist eine Null, aber eine Null als Künstler, als Träumer, als Intellektueller. Das erst macht ihn so gefährlich. Er kann, im Leben leichter als in der Kunst, zum Zauberer werden, zu einem Schwindler, der die Massen in den Bann schlägt.

Die Handlung von *Die Brüder Lautensack* ist kalkuliert und kalkulierbar; die Figuren haben keine undurchschaubare Tiefenschicht, sie sagen, wer sie sind, wenn es nicht der Erzähler sagt. Davon macht jedoch Oskar Lautensack eine Ausnahme. Wenn auch sein Schicksal nach dem dramatischen Schema eines Aufstiegs, einer Hybris und eines jähen Sturzes – angekündigt durch die Titel der Teile des Buches – verläuft, so bleibt seine erste Entscheidung, sich mit den Nazis einzulassen, genauer: sich an sie zu verkaufen, doch jenseits der gegebenen Erklärungen: midlife crisis, Geldmangel, Erfolglosigkeit, Zweifel an sich selbst und Unzufriedenheit mit sich – alles das sind mitbestimmende Faktoren, doch was Oskar im tieferen Grunde zu Hitler zieht, kann nicht erklärt werden. Oskar wird eine Beispielfigur für die deutschen Intellektuellen, und sein Bruder Hans, eines seiner ‚Double', gibt dazu eine weitere Dimension: er ist wie Joseph Goebbels ein erfolgloser Schriftsteller (Goebbels war außerdem Germanist, genau wie Feuchtwanger!), zu kurz gekommen im Leben, voll Ressentiment, voll Haß auf die Erfolgreichen, voll Bewunderung für seinen massiven und aus seiner Sicht begabten, ja genialen Bruder Oskar. Oskar verschleudert sein Talent, als Hellseher und als Schriftsteller, um Erfolg, Ruhm und Macht zu gewinnen, er ist das Beispiel des im Text zitierten Bibelworts, nämlich dessen, der Schaden an seiner Seele nimmt, um die ganze Welt zu gewinnen. Er ist ein Genießer, er liebt die Frauen, er will schöne und kostbare Gegenstände um sich haben, kurz, er hat allerhand Ähnlichkeit mit seinem Autor Lion

Feuchtwanger. Er ist das warnende Beispiel. Der Autor soll sich nicht für einen Propheten halten.

In der ersten Zeit nach seiner Ankunft in den USA wurde Feuchtwanger ständig interviewt und in den Zeitungen zitiert; aber er trat mit seinen Aussprüchen mehrfach ins Fettnäpfchen. Der Platz des Schreibenden und Betrachtenden ist nicht im Rampenlicht der Öffentlichkeit. Der Autor ist kein Schauspieler. Das könnte auch als Kritik gegen Thomas Mann und seine Vortragsreisen und Reden gewendet werden.

Wenn der Autor Feuchtwanger Gefahr läuft, seine Begabung zu sehr durch die Politik und die Massenwirkung zu vergeuden, wie es der böse Blick von Marcel Reich-Ranicki festgestellt haben will, so hat er sich Oskar Lautensack als warnendes Beispiel vor Augen gestellt. Feuchtwanger kam zwar nicht aus Deggendorf, sondern aus München (seine Familie allerdings aus Feuchtwangen); doch in seinem ‚Buch Bayern' *Erfolg* erscheint auch München als finstere Provinz, die einen Adolf Hitler ausbrütet. Etwas in Oskar Lautensack, was er selbst und sein Autor nicht erklären können, treibt ihn Hitler in die Arme. Adolf Hitler wiederum, dessen innere Gedanken und Beweggründe das Buch uns vorenthält, da er keine ‚Persönlichkeit' sein soll, wird nie ‚erklärt'. Er ist wie er ist; es gibt dafür im Buch weder eine psychologische noch eine gesellschaftliche Begründung. Deshalb wird seine Darstellung als ‚mißraten' angesehen.[17] Hitler ist aber vorhanden, er hat Präsenz; er ist die dunkle, die ‚trübe' Seite des deutschen Geistes. Es ist die gefährliche Seite des Irrationalismus, die hier an die Oberfläche kommt. Hitler, das ist meine Ansicht, ist in diesem Buch nicht allein der gehaßte Gegner, den das sarkastische Porträt bekämpfen will, Hitler ist ‚in uns'. Thomas Mann sprach nicht nur von ‚Bruder Hitler', sondern er sah in seinem so aufschlußreichen Essay ‚Deutschland und die Deutschen' von 1945 das Böse als das ‚fehlgegangene Gute', und das bedeutet, die Untrennbarkeit des Guten und des Bösen. Feuchtwanger stößt auf das Problem, und an dieser Stelle hört er auf weiterzudenken, ob es möglich ist, Hitler als ‚den Anderen' abzutun und sich einfach von ihm loszumachen. Wenn Oskar Lautensack seinem Autor so nahesteht, dann ist auch dieser insgeheim von diesem lächerlichen Nichts fasziniert, vielleicht gerade weil Hitler eine Null ist, die die Welt in Atem hält.

Feuchtwanger hat diese beunruhigenden Vorstellungen nicht weiter verfolgt, sondern sich in die Distanz der Geschichtsbetrachtung zurückgezogen. Brecht hatte es leichter: für ihn war Hitler der zur Macht gekommene Kleinbürger und der typische Gangster. Man könnte die These aufstellen, daß Feuchtwangers Hitlerfigur in *Die Brüder Lautensack* gerade deshalb so unbefriedigend wirkt, weil der Leser spürt, daß hier eine Tiefendimension angerührt ist, die der Autor dann wieder verdeckt, damit ihm sein Buch nicht aus der Hand gleitet und über die gesteckten Grenzen hinausdrängt, wie es nach Feuchtwangers Ansicht bei den Romanen Alfred Döblins zu gehen pflegte. Feuchtwanger hat sich gewiß nicht zuletzt deshalb zurückgehalten, weil der Roman aus Finanzgründen schnell fertigwerden mußte, und weil er auch den Stoff für Hollywood geeignet halten wollte. Ein Film *Die Brüder Lautensack* war 1943 in Hollywood sehr wohl denkbar. Er hätte sich auf Oskar Lautensack konzentrieren und Hitler im Hintergrund halten sollen. Schauspieler wie Charles Laughton oder auch Orson Welles hätten eine faszinierende Darstellung bieten können.

Es ist verständlich, daß Feuchtwangers Vorstellungen, nach dem *Great Dictator* und den Nachrichten von Veit Harlans *Jud Süß*, um die Möglichkeit kreisten, Hitler in seinem Massenmedium, im Film, direkt anzugreifen. Er verlangte aber zu viel von Hollywood. Die Geschichte von *Simone* war sehr viel bescheidener und handgreiflicher und leuchtete daher viel mehr ein.

Alles in allem ist der Roman *Die Brüder Lautensack*, genau wie *Unholdes Frankreich*, ein Dokument des Übergangs, der Unsicherheit, der Selbstbefragung und Selbstkritik, ein Dokument des Zorns auf die Deutschen, der jedoch mit mehr Verständnis für sie gemischt ist als es den Anschein haben mag. Wenn Alfred Döblin bei seiner berühmt-berüchtigten Geburtstagsrede 1943 mit christlicher Geste die Exilanten dazu aufforderte, ihre Mitschuld am Nationalsozialismus zu erkennen und zu bekennen, so zeigt dieser gleichzeitige Text Feuchtwangers, daß auch er etwas vom ‚Hitler in uns' spürte, allerdings nicht gern zugeben wollte. In den folgenden Romanen hat Feuchtwanger dann die positiven Figuren revolutionärer Künstler und Intellektueller in den Mittelpunkt gestellt. Doch auch in diesen Texten spricht sich die Betroffenheit über die Fragwürdigkeit der Existenz dieser Menschen aus. Etwas Neid schwingt in Feuchtwangers Gruß von 1946 zum 75. Geburtstag des von ihm hoch verehrten Heinrich Mann mit, wenn er die Wucht und Wirkung von Heinrich Manns antifaschistischen Artikeln und Reden beschreibt und anschließend das positive Beispiel des *Henri IV* hervorhebt:

> Er hat vielmehr den Fratzen der ‚Führer', die rings um uns aufstanden, die Gestalt eines wahren Führers entgegengestellt, er hat sich nicht nur als der große Hasser, sondern auch als ein großer Verehrer und Liebender erwiesen, er hat in einem weiten und mächtigen Roman-Gobelin das Leben und die Taten eines wahren Führers geschaffen aus der Innigkeit eines großen Herzens und der Leuchtkraft eines überlegenen Verstandes heraus, er hat geschaffen für uns und die Späteren das Bild des Mannes Heinrich IV., Königs von Frankreich, das Bild eines wahren Führers.[18]

Heinrich Mann hat das Bild von Henri IV ‚geschaffen'; es ist keine Geschichtsinterpretation, es ist ein Bild, ein Wandteppich der Geschichte, den die Mitwelt und Nachwelt betrachten soll. Auf diesem Gobelin sieht man im Mittelpunkt den wahren Führer der Menschen. Mit dem Wort ‚Führer' ist das letzte Schlüsselwort gefallen, das zu *Die Brüder Lautensack* gehört. Oskar ist ein Verführter und Verführer, aber Hitler ist das Gegenteil eines Führers. Im ‚Offenen Brief an sieben Berliner Schauspieler' sagt Feuchtwanger sarkastisch, man könne ja auf der Bühne jede Figur als ihr Gegenteil darstellen, nämlich im Lustspiel, zum Beispiel ‚Napoleon als Trottel und Hitler als großen Mann'.[19] Hitler fehlt die Größe von Henri IV und Heinrich Mann; Heinrich Mann, so scheint es nach Feuchtwanger, konnte die Größe eines Führers darstellen, weil er etwas davon in sich hatte. Hitler ist nur die Fratze eines Führers; doch die dunklen Tiefen hinter dieser Fratze wollte Feuchtwanger nicht ausloten. Er sah wie seine Zeitgenossen die Notwendigkeit einer Führung in der Massengesellschaft; auch ihm schien Roosevelt eine positive Führergestalt zu sein, die den richtigen Weg wußte. Dasselbe dachte Feuchtwanger 1937 von Stalin; was er später von ihm hielt, kann hier nicht erörtert werden.

Damit steckt in *Die Brüder Lautensack* zumindest potentiell der Zusammenhang der Erkenntnis, des ‚Hellsehens‘, mit dem Handeln, mit dem ‘Führer’ – alles andere als ein neues Problem bei Feuchtwanger, doch in neuer Gestalt, nämlich angesichts des Phänomens der Manipulation im Massenmedium, also der Gestalt des ‚Zauberers‘, des Lügners und Schwindlers. Nicht vergessen werden sollte dabei ein früherer Roman über Handeln und Nichthandeln, nämlich *Jud Süß*, der Feuchtwanger ja gerade wieder mit Gewalt nahegebracht wurde. Jud Süß Oppenheimer zeigt in seinem Lebenslauf, seinem Aufstieg zur geborgten Macht und seinem Sturz mancherlei Parallelen mit Oskar Lautensack und weist darauf hin, daß im Verhältnis Oskar-Hitler etwas von der Beziehung des Hofjuden zum Herrscher steckt, wobei man dann an das historische Modell für Lautensack, nämlich den Juden Hanussen denken kann. Auch Jud Süß verkauft sich für den Lebensgenuß und die scheinbare Macht mit dem Glanz der Öffentlichkeit; auch bei ihm gibt es die Züge der Hybris. Auch Oskar Lautensack verliert sein (allerdings noch ungeborenes) Kind, wie Oppenheimer. Kurz: es steckt in *Die Brüder Lautensack* auch das unausgesprochene, untergründige Motiv der Verführung der Juden durch die deutsche Kultur, durch die Aussicht, Anteil am deutschen Leben zu haben und in ihm mitbestimmen zu können. Diese ‚Macht‘ hat sich spätestens 1933 als eine Illusion erwiesen, was Feuchtwanger ja bereits in *Die Geschwister Oppermann* dargestellt hatte.

Anmerkungen

[1]   Lothar Kahn, *Insight and Action. The Life and Work of Lion Feuchtwanger*, Rutherford/Madison/Teaneck: Fairleigh Dickinson University Press, 1975, S. 243.

[2]   Vgl. Wulf Köpke, ‚Lion Feuchtwangers Josephus: Ost und West‘, in: Wilhelm von Sternburg, Hg., *Lion Feuchtwanger. Materialien zu Leben und Werk*, Frankfurt am Main: Fischer, 1989, S. 134-50.

[3]   Bertolt Brecht, *Arbeitsjournal*, Werke. Große Berliner und Frankfurter Werkausgabe, Hgg. Werner Hecht, Jan Knopf, Werner Mittenzwei und Klauf-Detlef Müller, Bd. 27: Journale 2, 1941-1955, Berlin/Weimar: Aufbau und Frankfurt: Suhrkamp, 1995, S. 38, Eintragung vom 24.12.1941.

[4]   Vgl. z. B. Reinhold Jaretzky, ‚‚„Der Sieg der Fünften Kolonne“. Frankreich-Kritik in literarischen Werken von Bertolt Brecht und Lion Feuchtwanger‘, in: Helmut F. Pfanner, Hg., *Der Zweite Weltkrieg und die Exilanten. Eine literarische Antwort*, Bonn/Berlin: Bouvier, 1991, S. 73-83. Jaretzky definiert den Gegensatz als die ‚Differenz von historisch-

sozialer und ethisch-idealistischer Deutung und Darstellung der französischen Ereignisse'
(81).

[5] Margot Taureck ('Gespiegelte Zeitgeschichte. Zu Lion Feuchtwangers Romanen Der
falsche Nero, Die Brüder Lautensack und Simone', in: von Sternburg (Hg.), *Lion
Feuchtwanger*, S. 172, Anm. 31) weist darauf hin, es gebe nur eine 'einzige ausführliche
Besprechung des Romans', nämlich Sigrid Schneider, 'Double, Double Toil and Trouble.
Kritisches zu Lion Feuchtwangers Roman *Die Brüder Lautensack*', *Modern Language Notes*,
95 (1980), 641-54. Bezeichnend ist der Titel: 'Kritisches zu ...' Auch Margot Taurecks
Darstellung, S. 159-66, enthält viel Kritik: 'Die Lektüre hinterläßt beim heutigen Leser ein
gewisses Unbehagen' (163); Feuchtwanger habe eben 'in erster Linie für ein amerikanisches
Publikum geschrieben' und sei damit zur 'Vereinfachung' und zur 'Personalisierung gesell-
schaftlicher Konflikte und politischer Phänomene veranlaßt' worden (163). Die 'mißratene
Hitlerdarstellung' (166) verurteilt sie mit den Argumenten Brechts.
Feuchtwanger selbst schrieb am 8. Mai 1942 an seinen Verleger Ben Huebsch: 'Die seltsame
Mischung von Okkultismus, Schwindel und großer Politik muß, glaube ich, auch ein sehr
breites Publikum ansprechen.' Zitiert bei Lothar Kahn, 'Lion Feuchtwanger', in: John M.
Spalek und Joseph Strelka, Hgg., *Deutsche Exilliteratur seit 1933*, Bd. 1: Kalifornien, Bern/
München: Francke, 1976, S. 341. Lothar Kahn selbst sieht *Die Brüder Lautensack* ebenfalls
als verfehlt an.

[6] Obwohl die Rezension der großen Zeitungen genau am Tag des japanischen Überfalls auf
Pearl Harbor erschienen und daher in der Aufregung des Kriegsbeginns unbeachtet blieben,
wie Feuchtwanger, der die Besprechungen genau verfolgte, mehrfach beklagte. So schrieb er
am 6. Januar 1942 an Alfred Kantorowicz: 'Es hat zwar eine ausgezeichnete Presse gehabt,
allein seine Publikation fiel in die Wochen des beginnenden Kriegs, und so scheint das Buch
völlig versunken.' Harold von Hofe und Sigrid Washburn, Hg., *Lion Feuchtwanger: Briefwechsel mit Freunden 1933-1958*, Berlin/Weimar: Aufbau, 1991, Bd. II, S. 193. An Eva van
Hoboken schrieb Feuchtwanger am 14. Januar 1942: 'mein letztes buch, über den sommer 40,
hat einen ausserordentlichen presseerfolg gehabt. leider aber sind die wichtigsten rezensionen
am sonntag des kriegsausbruchs erschienen und völlig untergegangen. immerhin hat das buch
dazu beigetragen, unser aller schicksal hier zu verbessern.' Nortrud Gomringer, Hg., *Lion
Feuchtwanger: Briefe an Eva van Hoboken*, Wien: Edition Splitter, 1996, Bd. I, S. 205. Der
finanzielle Erfolg, der in der ersten Zeit in Los Angeles so wichtig war, kam auch der
Unterstützung und Rettung von Freunden und Kollegen zugute.

[7] Brecht, *Arbeitsjournal*, 11. 11. 1943, S. 183.

[8] Wulf Koepke, 'Die Exilschriftsteller und der amerikanische Buchmarkt', in: Spalek und
Strelka, Hg., *Deutsche Exilliteratur seit 1933*, S. 89-116; zu Feuchtwanger: 102-106. Auf S.
105 bin ich auf *Simone* und *Unholdes Frankreich* eingegangen; aber typischerweise habe ich
Die Brüder Lautensack nicht erwähnt.

[9] Harold von Hofe, Hg., *Lion Feuchtwanger – Arnold Zweig – Briefwechsel 1933-1958*,
Berlin/Weimar: Aufbau, 1984, Bd. I, 249.

[10] Feuchtwanger fällte in einem Brief vom 7. November 1945 an seinen früheren Assistenten
und Sekretär Werner Cahn-Bieker, der den Krieg im Versteck in Holland überlebt hatte, ein
zusammenfassendes negatives Urteil über den Roman: 'Das Buch ist nicht ganz so gekom-

men, wie ich wünschte, weil politische Rücksichten mich veranlaßten, Hanussen zu einem Nichtjuden zu machen.' Er wies ebenfalls auf den verunglückten Vorabdruck in *Collier* hin, der immerhin die Rettung aus der finanziellen Misere bedeutete, und hatte insgesamt keine gute Meinung mehr von dem Buch. Vgl. Lothar Kahn, ,Lion Feuchtwanger', S. 341-42, und Anm. 44, S. 351.

[11] *Briefwechsel mit Freunden*, Bd. II, 204.

[12] Lion Feuchtwanger, *Die Brüder Lautensack*, Berlin: Aufbau, 1996, S. 41. Weitere Zitate mit Seitenangaben nach dieser Ausgabe.

[13] ,Vom Sinn und Unsinn des historischen Romans', zitiert nach Lion Feuchtwanger, *Ein Buch nur für meine Freunde* (vorher *Centum Opuscula*), Frankfurt am Main: Fischer, 1984, S. 501. Vorher hatte er gesagt: ,Sowohl der Historiker wie der Romandichter sieht in der Geschichte den Kampf einer winzigen, urteilsfähigen und zum Urteil entschlossenen Minorität gegen die ungeheure, kompakte Majorität der Blinden, nur vom Instinkt Geführten, Urteilslosen' (500-501). Hier spricht er nicht von der dritten kleinen Gruppe, den Verführern der blinden Masse.

[14] Lion Feuchtwanger, ,Der Schriftsteller im Exil', in L.F., *Ein Buch nur für meine Freunde*, S. 533.

[15] Hans Mayer, ,Lion Feuchtwanger oder Die Folgen des Exils', *Neue Rundschau*, 25 (1965), 120-29; Marcel Reich-Ranicki, 'Lion Feuchtwanger oder Der Weltruhm des Emigranten'. in: Manfred Durzak, Hg., *Die deutsche Exilliteratur 1933-1945*, Stuttgart: Reclam, 1973, S. 443-56.

[16] Taureck, ,Gespiegelte Zeitgeschichte', S. 163, mit Berufung auf Sigrid Schneider, S. 651.

[17] Ebenda, S. 166.

[18] Lion Feuchtwanger, ,Heinrich Mann. Zum 75. Geburtstag (1946)', in: L.F., *Ein Buch nur für meine Freunde*, S. 548.

[19] Lion Feuchtwanger, *Ein Buch nur für meine Freunde*, S. 528.

Arnold Pistiak

Das Vermächtnis des historischen Dichters.
Anmerkungen zu *Jefta und seine Tochter*

This essay offers an historical-philosophical reading of the novel *Jefta und seine Tochter*. At the core of this novel is Feuchtwanger's familiar question: What is history, and specifically: What is the significance of power in the context of historic processes? Making sense of historical events is a fundamental, existential process for Feuchtwanger, an attempt after the events to interpret and re-interpret the original intentions of the historical players. Only by overcoming ambitions to power, by losing ideology and accepting the interests of others does responsible action become possible. Feuchtwanger's last novel thus speaks of the hope not surrendered that the barbaric may be overcome and that power and the intellect may be united.

> *Das ist natürlich kein ‚biblischer' Roman.*
> *Mein Bemühen war, meinem Buch aus dem brei-*
> *teren Wissen unserer Zeit heraus solche Geschicht-*
> *lichkeit zu geben. In diesem Sinne, doch nur in*
> *diesem, sollte* Jefta *ein biblischer Roman sein.*
> *Lion Feuchtwanger*

Mit Blick auf Autoren wie Shakespeare oder Goethe notierte Lion Feucht-wanger wenige Monate vor seinem Tod in der groß angelegten Schrift *Das Haus der Desdemona oder Größe und Grenzen der historischen Dichtung*: ‚Darstellung der Vergangenheit war ihnen niemals Selbstzweck, sondern immer nur Mittel, das Erleben der eigenen Zeit auszudrücken'.[1] In diesem Sinne besteht unser Dichter immer wieder darauf, in seinen Romanen (seien sie zeit- oder vergangenheitsgeschichtlich) die, wenn ich einmal so sagen darf, Dimen-sion des Stoffes streng zu sondern von der des geistigen Rahmens, des ‚Inhalts', des ‚Themas' oder wie immer man das Gedankliche, Geistige bezeichnen möchte. Dabei handelt es sich im Verständnis Feuchtwangers allemal um ‚Gleichnisse': der Autor entwirft das große Bild – an uns ist es, es zu vervoll-ständigen, es mit Leben zu erfüllen und es zu verallgemeinern. Mithin lesen wir *Erfolg* in erster Linie nicht als einen Roman über München, *Waffen für Amerika* nicht als Buch über die Vereinigten Staaten, *Goya* nicht als Werk über einen Maler des 18./19. Jahrhunderts. Und wir würden das Wesen jener Dichtung, die dem Jefta-Roman unmittelbar vorausging und mit ihm mannigfach verzahnt ist – *Die Jüdin von Toledo* – gewiss weitgehend verfehlen, sähen wir in ihr in erster Linie einen Text über die Geschichte der spanischen Juden.

   Während nun aber derlei Feststellungen gleichsam zum Selbstverständnis jener Autoren gehören, die über Feuchtwanger nachdenken, werden sie doch eher selten auf *Jefta und seine Tochter*, den letzten vollendeten Roman unseres Autors, bezogen. Ich möchte dabei an jenen Brief des Aufbau-Verlags erinnern, in dem der Verlag Feuchtwanger bittet, ein Nachwort zu schreiben. Denn die durch Gisela Lüttig überlieferte Begründung jener Bitte lautet, der Roman ‚weiche von dem Grundsatz ab, „daß der Autor, der heute einen historischen Roman schreibe, die Gegenwart darstellen wolle‴.[2]

Nicht die ‚Gegenwart‛ – was dann? Arnold Zweig, der langjährige Brieffreund, teilte die Bedenken des Aufbau-Verlages offenbar. Er bemerkte, nachdem er bewundernde Worte für eine ‚konzentrierte Gestalterleistung‛ Feuchtwangers gefunden hatte, unter anderem:

> Nur Ihr Jefta, liebster Feuchtwanger, vermag uns nicht zu faszinieren. Ganz ausgezeichnet kommt seine Mannhaftigkeit zur Geltung, er wächst vor unseren Augen zum Richter empor [...] – aber, leider, er geht uns nicht sehr viel an (an Feuchtwanger, 31.3.1958).[3]

Jefta ‚geht uns nicht sehr viel an‛! Katia Mann schrieb am 6. August 1958 an Feuchtwanger, sie habe den Roman mit wachsendem Interesse verschlungen, setzt dann aber hinzu: ‚Restlose Sympathie konnte ich aber Ihrem Helden trotz allem nicht entgegenbringen‛.[4]

Diese merkwürdigen Stellungnahmen stehen nicht allein. Bis heute ist Feuchtwangers Roman weder vom Lesepublikum noch von Literaturkritik und Literaturwissenschaft besonders gewürdigt worden. Was die einzelnen Gründe dieses Umstands angeht, so wäre es sicher aufschlussreich, die bei Frank Dietschreit bzw. Wilhelm von Sternburg nachgewiesenen Äußerungen zu *Jefta und seine Tochter* kritisch zu beleuchten – sei es im Hinblick auf Fragen des literarischen Marktes, sei es im Hinblick auf Leserinteressen und Lesererwartungen. Möglicherweise auch hat Feuchtwangers Betonung der identifikatorischen Seiten des Romans – des Erlebens, der Einfühlung – die Leser mehr desorientiert als ihnen geholfen. Sie wurden/werden dadurch vielleicht nicht gerade angeregt, die gleichfalls vorhandenen Distanzierungsmomente aufmerksam zu beachten, etwa die brutale Instrumentalisierung Jemins, die Steinigung des ‚Fremden‛,[5] den Auftrag an Jemin, die Efraimiter zu ermorden (661ff.).

Der Kern der Sache scheint mir jedoch woanders zu liegen: in dem Umstand, dass Feuchtwanger sein Spätwerk in den Jahren des Kalten Krieges schuf. Die DDR und die Sowjetunion – die beiden östlichen Länder, in denen Feuchtwanger am intensivsten rezipiert wurde – hatten keinerlei Interesse, biblisches Gedankengut zu verbreiten. Das erwähnte Schreiben des Aufbau-Verlags ist dafür ein ebenso grotesker wie eindringlicher Beleg. Andererseits dürfte der unkonventionelle Umgang mit biblischer Geschichte einer umfassenden *Jefta*-Rezeption in den USA oder den Ländern Westeuropas nicht eben förderlich gewesen sein. Feuchtwanger zeigt in seinem letzten Roman den Weg in die Barbarei und er benennt den Ausweg, an den er glaubt: einen Neuanfang. In der Zeit der wahnwitzigen Zuspitzung des Kalten Krieges – vergessen wir nicht, dass beispielsweise beide deutsche Staaten feindlichen Militärbündnissen angehörten – geriet er damit ins totale Abseits. Kein Wunder, dass diese Stimme nicht beachtet, dass sie überhört wurde!

Problematisch erscheint mir zudem die in der Sekundärliteratur mehrfach anzutreffende Fokussierung auf das ‚Thema „Judentum‴,[6] auf eine ‚Rückkehr‛

Feuchtwangers ‚in die jüdische Geschichte' beziehungsweise auf eine ‚Darstellung des jüdischen Problems'.[7] Nun liegt es mir natürlich fern zu bestreiten, dass man diesen Text auch mit Blick auf die Geschichte des Staates Israel lesen kann und muss – im Gegenteil. Dass Feuchtwanger mit *Jefta und seine Tochter* seine lebenslange Beschäftigung mit Fragen der Entwicklung der jüdischen Geschichte und Kultur fortsetzt, steht außer Frage. Indem er jedoch als Weltbürger, als ‚internationaliste juif national',[8] auf die Jefta-Erzählungen der Hebräischen Bibel zurückgreift, kommen auch andere, weitergehende Zusammenhänge ins Spiel.

Im Zentrum von *Jefta und seine Tochter* steht, scheint mir, das alte Thema Feuchtwangers: Was ist Geschichte? Und spezieller: welche Bedeutung, welcher Stellenwert kommt der Machtfrage innerhalb des Verlaufs historischer Prozesse zu? Und wie sieht es mit deren ‚Sinn' aus? Das ganze schmale, lehrstückhafte, holzschnittartig komponierte Buch mit den vorgeführten geschichtlichen Verläufen problematisiert diesen Fragenkomplex. Wie ist jenem ‚geheimen Punkt' auf die Spur zu kommen, in dem, in den Worten des jungen Goethe, ‚das Eigentümliche unsres Ichs, die prätendierte Freiheit unsres Wollens, mit dem notwendigen Gang des Ganzen' (Zum Schäkespears Tag) zusammenstößt? Zahlreichen Aspekten könnte hier nachgegangen werden. Ich beschränke mich jedoch auf drei zentrale Figuren des Romans – Ja'ala, Jefta und Elead. Die folgenden Überlegungen seien mithin als ein Versuch verstanden, diese Figuren auf die an ihnen entfaltete Geschichtlichkeit hin zu befragen; als ein Versuch, der Frage nicht auszuweichen, ob denn dieser letzte Roman Feuchtwangers mit uns, den Menschen des sogenannten 21. Jahrhunderts, etwas ‚zu tun' habe.

1

> Mein Untergang vermehrt der Feinde Hauffen,
> Es muß mein Blut zu ihrem Blute lauffen,
> Der Tochter Tod vermehrt der Feinde Schar

klagt die Tochter des Jefta bei Hofmannswaldau;[9] ‚Plorate, filii Israel [...] et Jephte filiam unigenitam in carmine doloris lamentamini' (‚Weint ihr Kinder Israels [...] und beklagt Jephtas einzige Tochter mit Trauergesängen'), singt Jeftas Tochter Filia in dem Oratorium *Jephte* von Giacomo Carissimi,[10] und ein überaus kunstvoll komponierter Schlusschor nimmt ihre Worte auf und stimmt einen Trauergesang an. Klagen dieser Art finden wir in Feuchtwangers Roman jedoch nicht. Mit Ja'ala braucht niemand zu weinen, niemand braucht sie zu trösten. Anders als in der biblischen Vorlage bittet nicht sie ihren Vater um Aufschub, sondern er sie. Und es handelt sich auch nicht um zwei Monate, sondern um zwei Wochen. Ja'ala selbst bewältigt ihren Schmerz, sie selbst tröstet ihre kindlichen Gespielinnen, sie verabschiedet die Mutter, sie bittet den Vater, noch einmal zu lachen, vorher.

Feuchtwangers Ja'ala, so lässt sich vielleicht sagen, die junge Frau, wie sie uns aus den verschiedenen knappen, sorgsam gearbeiteten Passagen des Romans entgegentritt, in denen wir von ihr hören, ist eine starke Persönlichkeit. Körper und Geist befinden sich in harmonischer Einheit. Vielleicht hat Feuchtwanger an Byron's ‚Jephta's Daughter' gedacht?

> I have won the great battle for thee
> And my father and Country are free![11]

Jedenfalls hat Feuchtwanger Ja'ala so angelegt, dass sie die Jefta-Figur in mehrfacher Hinsicht bereichert. Diese Feststellung bezieht sich nur peripher auf die unverzichtbare Übernahme des in der Hebräischen Bibel festgeschriebenen Opfermotivs bzw. auf das hochinteressante Feld quasi-inzestuöser Beziehungen. Hinweisen möchte ich aber auf eine Problematik, die in der Sekundärliteratur vielleicht zu oft ausgeblendet wird: auf Ja'alas Künstlertum. Denn Ja'ala wird für Jefta ja gerade als Künstlerin wichtig – als eine Künstlerin, wohlgemerkt, deren ästhetische Haltungen zu denen des Dichters Feuchtwanger in scharfem Kontrast stehen: nicht Skepsis, Zweifel, distanzierte Beobachtung, Ironie, kühle Vernunft sind für sie wesentlich, sondern Unmittelbarkeit, distanzlos-ungebremste Emotionalität, eine schon fast fanatische Bereitschaft zur Selbstaufgabe.

In diesem Zusammenhang ist der Name von Bedeutung, mit dem Feuchtwanger die Namenlosigkeit der biblischen Tochter des Jefta aufhebt. Seine Mädchenfigur heißt nicht etwa Filia, Iphis oder Mirjam (wie bei Carissimi, Händel, Lissauer), sondern der Autor stellt mit dem Namen Ja'ala eine unmittelbare Beziehung her zu Jaël (der Autor transkribiert, die Ähnlichkeit betonend: Ja'el) – zu jener Frau aus dem Debora-Lied, die dem feindlichen Feldherrn Sissera den Zeltpflock ‚durch seine Schläfe [schlug], daß er in die Erde drang'.[12] Und Jefta kommentiert: ‚Waren Ja'ala und Ja'el *eines*?' (629). – Nun, was die Wildheit, das Ungebärdige des Einsatzes angeht, gewiss. Nicht die frühere häusliche Atmosphäre in Machanajim hatte Ja'ala bestimmend geprägt, sondern das Andere, das Un-Zivilisierte – ‚das freie, unbegrenzte Land Tob war ihre Heimat' (532). Immer wieder interessiert sie die Jagd, immer wieder empfindet sie Freude an der Tötung von Tieren – und identifiziert sich mit deren Leid. Und immer wieder betrachtet sie nicht nur kritiklos, sondern hingerissen ihren löwenhaft-gewalttätigen Vater:

> Ja'ala hatte all die Zeit her auf ihren Vater gestarrt, angeschaut, halboffenen Mundes. Kalt und grausam funkelten ihm die Augen aus dem löwenhaften Gesicht, kleine, grüne Lichter waren in ihnen wie sonst nur in den Augen zorniger Tiere. Ja'ala hatte es ganz deutlich gesehen. So mußte Jahwe ausschauen, wenn er auf der Wolke einherfuhr, Feuer und Grauen unter die Feinde schmetternd (538).

Die Freude an der Gewalt, das Wilde der nomadisch geprägten ‚altheidnischen' Mutter wie des anarchistischen Vaters ist eines – die Übernahme des Jahwe-zentrierten Glaubensansatzes des Vaters ein anderes. Es ist gerade dieser von Jefta vermittelte Jahwe-Glauben, der die Grundlage bildet für die Verschmelzung der Bilder des Vaters und des Gottes (676, 692) – und damit für Ja'alas Bereitschaft, das Gelübde des Vaters zu akzeptieren und alle Rettungsversuche abzulehnen. In beidem – ihrer Freude an der Gewalt wie ihrem Jahwe-Glauben – wurzelt auch Ja'alas Künstlertum; es äußert sich vornehmlich darin, dass sie es vermag, die geheimen Pläne des Vaters zu erfassen und sie in Wort und Ton und Gebärde zum Ausdruck zu bringen. Es ist gerade ihr Lied, ihr ekstatischer, mitreißender, verführerischer Gesang, der die Männer veranlasst, nach der Einsetzung Jeftas zum Richter wild zu schreien ‚Jefta! Jefta! Alle Kraft dem Jefta!' (610).

So stärkt Ja'alas Gesang die Macht des Vaters wie des Feldherren; so befördert sie als ‚Seherin' und ‚Künderin' (618) den Prozess, der zu jenem Krieg führt, in dessen Verlauf Jefta sein Gelübde ‚lautlos' in den Sturm rufen wird (654). Und so bestätigt der weitere Gang der Romanhandlung auch jenes Erschrecken, das Silpa durchfuhr, als sie sah, welche Wirkungen der Gesang der Ja'ala auf die Krieger des Jefta hatte: ‚vielleicht war es nicht ihr [Silpa], sondern dieser Tochter Jeftas bestimmt, dem Volke Gileads zur Debora zu warden' (611). Ja – nicht Silpa, die Etablierte, sondern die Tochter des einst Verjagten wird die Einigung Israels entscheidend voranbringen – wenn auch nicht als Lebende, so doch als Geopferte, wenn auch nicht als die Ja'el aus dem Debora-Lied, so doch als Furcht einflößendes Symbol für die Macht Jahwes und ihres Vaters, ihres Mörders.

Und dann ist da noch die Liebe des Mannes Jefta zu der Frau, von der er sagt, er liebe sie ‚mehr als Ketura, mehr als sich selber, mehr als alle Macht und allen Ruhm der Welt' (674), und die betont erotische Darstellung der Schönheit Ja'alas durch den Erzähler:

> Langsam, ernst, und dennoch leicht stand sie auf. Schritt vor und zurück in strengem Tanzschritt. Holte Töne hervor aus ihrer Zither, aus ihrer Trommel. [...] Es kam vor, daß Ja'ala, wenn sie sang und tanzte, ihre Kleider abwarf; es kam auch vor, daß sie sich in jenes schleierdünne, safranfarbene Kleid kleidete, in welchem sie die scharfe Schwelle überschreiten wird (692).

Zugleich aber lesen wir von der demütigen Hingabe der Frau Ja'ala an den Gott des Vaters; von ihrer sorgsam bewahrten Jungfräulichkeit; von ihrer Liebe zu einem Manne, ihrem Vater:

> Sie sah den Stein, auf dem sie liegen wird, sie sah Jahwes Messer, und ihr schauerte. Gleichzeitig indes spürte sie Stolz und Freude; denn dieses Schauerliche war das höchste Glück, das wahrhafte und für sie das einzig rechte. Sie spürte voraus ihre Vereinigung mit Jahwe, ihr Vater und Jahwe wurden ihr ganz und gar *eines*, sie war voll Frieden (676).

Was geht hier vor? Feuchtwangers *Jefta*-Roman lesend und zugleich an Raquel und ihren Vater Jehuda denkend, wird man sagen dürfen, dass die poetische Gestaltung von Andeutungen eines innig-erotischen Verhältnisses zwischen Jefta und seiner Tochter für den Autor von hohem Interesse gewesen sein muss, dass sie seine Phantasie angeregt, ihn womöglich erregt hat, wer weiß? Herausgekommen ist die Skizze einer höchst poetischen, einer höchst unalltäglichen, einer tragischen, berührenden Liebesgeschichte. Jefta liebt Ja'ala, Ja'ala liebt Jefta. Aber die Wasser waren viel zu tief, wieder einmal.

2

Und doch sind jene Episoden, die von der Liebe zwischen Vater und Tochter sprechen, im wesentlichen auf das fünfte (abschließende) Kapitel des Romans beschränkt, auf die Szenen, die im Zusammenhang mit der Tötung Ja'alas durch Jefta stehen: Nicht sie sind für den Roman konstitutiv, sondern das politisch-militärische Handeln des Jefta. Ja, vielleicht kann man die Konzeption, die hinter der Anlage des Mädchens Ja'ala steht, vereinfacht und zugespitzt mit einem knappen Satz umreißen: Feuchtwanger schuf sich gerade eine solche Kunstfigur, die er brauchte, um *seinen* Jefta vorzuführen. Sein Roman heißt sicherlich nicht zufällig: *Ja'ala und ihr Vater*, sondern: *Jefta und seine Tochter*. Nicht die wie auch immer individualisierte Tochter steht im Mittelpunkt des Geschehens, sondern ihr Vater und die poetische Demonstration, *wie* es zu dessen Opferversprechen kam.

Genauer gesagt: Geradezu gemächlich entfaltet Feuchtwanger in vier der fünf Kapitel des Romans ein großes, multikulturelles Geschichtsbild: Jeftas Machtambitionen, seine ‚löwenhafte' Wildheit, seine Spontaneität, sein Lachen, sein Jähzorn, die Ablehnung einer juristischen Ordnung des Lebens der Sesshaften (‚Mischpat'), seine Liebe zu Ja'ala und Ketura – nichts ändert sich im Verlaufe dieser Kapitel wesentlich. Dann aber spitzt der überlegen arbeitende, souveräne Dichter die Problematik drastisch zu: Jefta opfert die Tochter, er versteinert, er begreift.

Die Opferung der Tochter aber war nichts als die Konsequenz aus all dem, was Jefta zuvor unternommen hatte – und zwar im Interesse seines geradezu ungebremsten Machtstrebens. Denn gerade in dem Streben nach immer größerer Macht liegt das eigentliche Zentrum dieser Figur. Bereits Jeftas erstes Auftreten weist darauf hin: Auf einer ‚hellfarbigen' Eselin reitet er zur Beerdigung seines Vaters – ungeachtet des Umstandes, dadurch ein ‚Ärgernis' auslösen zu können (482). Ist seine Haltung in der Auseinandersetzung mit Silpa und deren Söhnen zunächst einzig darauf gerichtet, die ihm durch den Vater zuerkannten Ansprüche und Rechte durchzusetzen, so verändert sie sich in jenem Moment drastisch, in dem ihm Abijam in Aussicht stellt, Feldhauptmann zu werden ‚nicht nur über Gilead, sondern über alle Sippen und Stämme diesseits des Jordan' (505), und in der Konsequenz das ‚ganze Israel östlich des Jordan' zu einigen (522).

Dieses Ziel wird nun für Jefta wesentlich – und gerade auf dem sich nun entfaltenden Feld lässt Feuchtwanger seine geschichtsphilosophische Souveränität spielen. Indem der Autor die verschiedensten, höchst widersprüchlichen Momente miteinander verknüpft, gelingt es ihm, ein komplexes, ein beeindruckendes Geschichtsbild zu entwerfen. Ein Geschichtsbild, das sich einer simplen Fortschrittsgläubigkeit ebenso entschlägt wie jenen Gut-Böse-Denkmustern, die uns Heutigen so lautstark anempfohlen werden.

So verfehlt etwa Abijam zunächst sein Ziel, Jefta und Ketura zu trennen; vielmehr ist es gerade Ketura, die die vermeintliche Lösung findet: Indem sie den Plan entwickelt, Machanajim zu verlassen, in die Wildnis zu gehen (um, wie sie hofft, sich später an der Silpa-Familie rächen zu können), zerschlägt sie die Alternative, die Abijam dem Jefta hatte aufdrängen wollen: *entweder* Verstoßung der Frau/ Wendung gegen die nicht-israelischen Götter/ gegen das Nomadische/

Reduktion der Fülle des Lebens auf die Unterordnung unter einen engtradierten Lebenskodex, dies alles aber belohnt mit öffentlichem Ansehen und enormer Machtfülle – *oder* Nichtverstoßung der Frau, verbunden mit Machtlosigkeit und Enterbung.

Wie listig ist Keturas Plan! Und doch: welche Täuschung! Denn was Ketura nicht bedenkt, was sie womöglich auch nicht bedenken kann, das ist, dass Jefta eben Jefta ist. Letztlich und ungeachtet aller Geheimverhandlungen und Gedankenspiele kann und will dieser wilde Mensch weder seine Machtambitionen aufgeben, noch die sich auf Israel beziehenden Einigungsbestrebungen, noch sein Selbstverständnis, 'Soldat Jahwes' zu sein und in dessen Sinn zu wirken (550). Es ist ironischerweise Ketura selbst, die – indem sie Jeftas Identität völlig verkennt – ihren Mann auf den Chermon führt und dadurch nicht nur die wachsende Distanz Jeftas zu ihr verstärkt, sondern auch dessen Hoffnung, ganz Israel beherrschen zu können.

Das Angebot des Königs Nachasch war für Jefta ein Schritt auf diesem Weg. Ja'ala freilich würde durch die in Aussicht genommene dynastische Heirat Opfer des politischen Planspiels werden. Und obgleich dieser Umstand Jefta von Anfang an klar ist, obgleich er im Selbstgespräch beschließt, 'sein Geschlecht, sein Volk, seinen Gott' nicht zu verraten (618), entlässt er den Gesandten Nachaschs mit einer zweideutigen Botschaft. Erst im Zusammenhang mit jenem Geheimbrief, den Nachasch ihm hat überbringen lassen, gleichsam in letzter Minute, legt sich Jefta fest: 'Es ist mir leid, daß welche von den Meinen deinem Gott zu nahe getreten sind. Ich will dir die Übeltäter gebunden ausliefern, daß du mit ihnen verfahrest nach Willkür. Aber meine Tochter will ich dir nicht geben' (636).

Wir befinden uns hier an einer der zentralen Stellen des Romans – an einem Punkt, da Abijams Kriegsplan, eine wechselseitigen Interessen dienende Geheimdiplomatie und die Liebe Jeftas zu seiner Tochter zusammenstoßen. Abijam mochte die Zerstörung des Milkom-Heiligtums angezettelt haben, um Jefta und damit Israel in den vaterländischen Einigungskrieg gegen die Ammoniter zu treiben – die eigentliche, die definitive Entscheidung fällt Jefta. Indem er letztlich davor zurückschreckt, Ja'ala nach Rabat zu senden, bekennt er sich zwar zu Israel und zu Jahwe, und nimmt letztlich genau die Rolle ein, die Abijam ihm zugedacht hatte – und doch wäre dessen listiger Plan in sich zusammengefallen, wäre da nicht etwas gewesen, von dem der intrigenspinnende Priester nichts geahnt hatte: die Liebe Jeftas zu Ja'ala. Die Liebe eines Vaters zu seinem Kind wird hier zu dem ausschlaggebenden politischen Faktor, der über Krieg oder Frieden entscheidet.

In tragischer Ironie entscheidet diese Liebe zugleich über die Opferung gerade der Tochter zugunsten des machtpolitischen Kalküls. Denn aus machtpolitischem – nicht aus 'barbarischem' – Denken hatte der Feldherr das Bündnis mit dem westlichen Israel ausgeschlagen, hatte er die Möglichkeit, dass seine eigene geheime Truppenbewegung durchaus erspäht werden könne, nicht einmal bedacht. In jene aussichtslose Lage, in der er sein Gelübde sprach, hatte er sich ja selbst manövriert; in diese Lage geriet er, weil er Abir und Nachasch *allein* besiegen, weil er sie sich unterwerfen, weil *er* Herrscher eines quasi-baby-lonischen Großreiches werden wollte. Gilead sollte das Machtzentrum werden nicht nur für das westliche und östliche Israel, sondern darüber hinaus auch für die angrenzenden östlichen Länder: ‚Und dann wird er der Oberherr sein der östlichen Fürsten, und das ganze Land von Damaschek bis zum ägyptischen Meer soll heißen: Gilead, das Reich des Jefta' (639).

Größenwahnsinnige Weltherrschaftspläne! Dieser Mann weiß – im Gegen-satz zum Jefta der biblischen Richter-Geschichte –, wer ihm in der Regel ent-gegenläuft, wenn er nach Hause kommt, er weiß, wer ihm ‚das Teuerste' ist. Spätestens seit dem Gespräch mit Nachasch ist er bereit, gerade diesem Macht-streben sein ‚Teuerstes' zu opfern – Ja'ala, Ketura. Die Vernichtung seiner Fähig-keit zu lieben, die Austrocknung, Erstarrung, Verhärtung der eigenen Persönlich-keit ist genau der Preis, den er für all das zu zahlen hat. Ja'alas Einfluss auf den geliebten Vater aber reicht nur so weit, den Feldherrn zu bestimmen, sie nicht einem ‚fremden' Gott zu übereignen, sondern stattdessen die von Abijam initiierte nationale Lösung zu wählen.

3

In dem Gespräch zwischen Elead und Jefta wie in den sich daran anschließenden Schlusskapiteln des Buches finden wir dann die gleichsam bekenntnishafte Zu-sammenfassung der Ansichten Feuchtwangers. Elead versteht sich nicht wie Ja'ala als ‚Künder' und ‚Seher'; er muss sich nicht wie Schamgar darauf be-schränken, ‚Geschehnisse' niederzuschreiben (706): Mit ihm konzipierte Feucht-wanger ein letztes Mal eine Figur, die mit dem eigenen Selbstanspruch korrespon-diert, nicht Machtmensch zu sein, sondern Betrachter, Analytiker, Geschichts-schreiber, historischer Dichter. Begründet das Auftreten dieser modernen Figur in einer Jefta-Geschichte einen Mangel an Glaubwürdigkeit? Man mag so denken. Aber hier wie auch etwa bei dem Spinoza-Motto oder bei der Szene, in der Abi-jam die ‚Zeichen Jahwes' befragt und das herausbekommt, was seinen Interessen entspricht (498ff.), handelt es sich meines Erachtens um bewusst gesetzte und zugleich verfremdend wirkende Anachronismen – um das Beharren des Autors auf einer unkonventionell und weit gefassten Konzeption künstlerischer Freiheit; mithin um einen Aspekt der spezifischen Modernität Feuchtwangers.

Als ein überlegener, skeptischer Denker der Neuzeit hat Elead Jefta die ‚verfängliche' Wahrheit, die ‚gefährliche Lehre' vermittelt, dass die jeweiligen Gottesvorstellungen nichts seien als Projektionen des Menschen, und damit Jeftas Erkenntnis vorbereitet:

> Er hatte sein bestes, eigenstes Blut für einen Gott vergossen, der nicht war. Jefta der Held, Jefta der Narr. Kein Gott hatte ihm geholfen, Efraim hatte ihm geholfen. Und dafür hatte er die Tochter erschlagen, die liebe, liebliche. Er hatte das beste, röteste Blut seines Leibes um nichts verschüttet (714).

Ein Gott, der ‚nicht war'! Deutlich wird, dass die Auseinandersetzung mit

Problemen des Judentums für Feuchtwanger keinerlei Rekurs auf biblisch-
jüdische Glaubensvorstellungen einschließt. Deshalb glaube ich auch nicht, dass
das ‚Hauptthema des Romans' in einem ‚Ringen um den Begriff von Gott und
Israel' bestehe,[13] sondern es gilt für den Autor von *Jefta und seine Tochter* dasselbe wie für Heine: die Bibel ist ihm ein großartiges historisches Dokument, ein
Buch, das wundervolle Kunstwerke enthält, ein weltgeschichtlich überaus wichtiges Buch. Aber dieses Buch betrachtet Feuchtwanger von einem durchgehend
säkularisierten Standpunkt aus. Die Bibel ist für ihn nicht ein göttlich-heiliges,
sondern ein menschlich-irdisches Buch. In diesem Zusammenhang fällt in der
Sekundärliteratur gelegentlich das Stichwort Spinoza.[14] Aber ist das Spinoza-
Motto des Jefta-Romans wirklich Ausdruck einer spinozistischen Weltsicht seines
Autors? Oder aber ein versteckt-listiger Hinweis auf eine Weltsicht, die auf jeg-
liche Gottesvorstellung verzichtet?

Jedenfalls ist *Jefta und seine Tochter* vielleicht noch mehr als die *Jüdin von
Toledo* auch das Ergebnis einer interessanten, produktiven Bibelrezeption des
Autors. Unmittelbar vor Abschluss der Arbeit an seinem letzten Roman schreibt
Feuchtwanger an den langjährigen Briefpartner Arnold Zweig, die Arbeit habe
ihm ‚große Freude gemacht und macht mir weiter Freude. Es ist sehr erfrischend,
Dinge, von denen die Bibel berichtet, ihres Weihrauchs zu entwölken'
(20.2.1957). In diesem Sinn heißt es in Feuchtwangers ‚Nachwort', der Leser solle
‚den Gott des Jefta sehen, den andern der Ja'ala, den andern des Abijam, der
Ketura, des Elead' (729). Und wirklich hat Feuchtwanger in seinem ‚biblischen
Roman' unterschiedliche Göttervorstellungen gestaltet und so tradierte Auffas-
sungen ‚entwölkt'. Jahwe ist für Abijam der Gott der Einigkeit Israels, für Jefta
hingegen ein schmeckender, ‚leckerer', ein eifersüchtiger, vor allem: ein Kriegs-
gott. Für Ja'ala fallen die Bilder des geliebten Vaters und dessen Gottes in eins
zusammen. Der ‚heidnische' Gott der Ketura hingegen ist ein Gott des wilden,
freien, nomadischen Lebens.

Das Erlebnis des Todes der Tochter und das Gespräch zwischen Elead und
Jefta sind zugleich die Ausgangspunkte für die ‚Wandlung' des Jefta, über die
Feuchtwanger sich mehrfach äußerte. Ganze vier Kapitel zerrte Jefta an den
Stricken, mit denen er selbst sich fesselte. Erst jetzt erfolgt die Befreiung, erst jetzt
verändert seine Psyche sich nachhaltig. Die Erkenntnis, dass der Gott, dem er
seine Tochter geopfert hatte, ‚nicht war', dass sein Opfer sinnlos war, lässt die Erkenntnis reifen, dass es gerade jetzt möglich sei, etwas Gutes für sein Volk zu tun:

> Nun er, Jefta, das Große, Törichte getan hatte, wollte der Priester es nützen – und hatte
> er nicht recht? Das Blut sollte nicht einfach in Erde, Holz und Feuer versickert sein, der
> Priester wollte dem großen Grauen, das aus dem Blut herausgewachsen war, Sinn geben
> – und hatte er nicht recht? (715)

Und so begnügt sich der Kämpe Jefta mit einer militärisch undankbaren Aufgabe,
lässt sich durch den Priester eines Gottes salben, der ‚nicht war', und verschafft
dem Land ein paar Jahre Ruhe und Frieden.

Mit dieser Wendung des Romans bezieht sich Feuchtwanger unmittelbar auf sein Nachwort zu dem Toledo-Roman. Der historische Dichter, meinte er, ‚schreibt nicht nur Historie, er gibt Problemen unserer Zeit Licht und Sinn.' Und was sich in der nur scheinbar ‚realen', tatsächlich aber märchenhaften Geschichtlichkeit der *Jüdin von Toledo* vollzog, vollzieht sich in der schönen Utopie des *Jefta* auf andere Weise: die Überwindung des Barbarischen, die Vereinigung von Geist und Macht. ‚Sinn'-gebung geschichtlicher Ereignisse, ja des Lebens überhaupt, erscheint in Feuchtwangers Konzeption als ein fundamentaler existenzieller Vorgang, ein im Nachhinein erfolgendes Korrektiv ursprünglicher Wünsche, Hoffnungen, Intentionen des Handelns. Diese Art Sinngebung ist ein Akt menschlichen Denkens, geknüpft an in Anspruch genommene und verantwortlich gehandhabte menschliche Vernunft und darauf gerichtet, das eigene Handeln in den Kontext des unwiderruflich Geschehenen wie des Erhofften, Erwünschten, für notwendig Erachteten zu stellen. Erst die Analyse und Deutung der ‚Geschehnisse' ermöglicht deren Sinngebung. Erst die Überwindung von Machtambitionen, erst Entideologisierung, erst die Akzeptanz der Interessen des Anderen (diese spezielle Problematik entwickelte Feuchtwanger in der Geschichte um Raquel) ermöglicht verantwortungsvolles Handeln. Der Roman *Jefta und seine Tochter*, so schmal er auch immer ist, erweist sich mithin als ein geschichtsphilosophischer Roman par excellence.

Insofern ist dieser Text zugleich Zusammenfassung und – vielleicht – Korrektur des Geschichtsverständnisses seines Autors. Jedenfalls funktioniert hier alles ganz irdisch, ganz unspekulativ: Kein Jahwe noch Milkom, keine geheime aufklärerische oder Hegelsche ‚Idee', kein unfassbar-geheimnisvoll über der Geschichte schwebender Sinn der Geschichte, kein Weltgeist, kein anonymer, sich listig durchsetzender Fortschritt wird hier tätig oder liegt als geheime treibende Ursachen hinter allem Geschehen und garantiert eine ‚Höherentwicklung' der Gesellschaft.

Sondern das Handeln der Figuren in *Jefta und seine Tochter* resultiert aus konkreten, höchst widersprüchlichen individuellen oder gruppenspezifischen Interessen, Vorstellungen, Lebenslagen, aus ihrer Psyche, ihrer Individualität. So auch resultiert Geschichte hier aus dem Zusammenstoß von Altem und Neuem, Nahem und Abgelegenem, Zufälligem und Geplantem, Erwartetem und Überraschendem; aus Materiellem und Ideellem, Individuellem und Gesellschaftlichem, Nationalem und Übernationalem. In diesem Geschichtsbild stimmen Intention und Ergebnis von Handlungen keineswegs überein. Jede Handlung hat ihre Voraussetzungen, ihre Konsequenzen wie ihren Preis (sie fordert ihre Opfer). Widersprüche erweisen sich als Ursachen aller geschichtlichen Bewegung. Nochmals: Hätte Jefta seine Tochter nicht geliebt, hätte er sie an Nachasch verkuppelt – völlig andere geschichtliche Verläufe wären das Ergebnis gewesen, nicht nur im östlichen und westlichen Israel, sondern auch in den angrenzenden Ländern. Indem der Roman jeglichen Automatismus geschichtlicher Kräfte verwirft, verwirft er alle Theologie wie Teleologie.

Der späte Feuchtwanger führt uns also sein Geschichtsbild vor, sein ‚Weltbild':[15] ein großes poetisches Gemälde, das die Komplexität geschichtlicher Aktionen ebenso abbildet wie das Funktionieren geschichtlichen Handelns. Und gerade in diesem Funktions-Modell (nicht aber in einzelnen Momenten des Romans) scheint der Dreh- und Angelpunkt des Romans zu liegen. Von hier aus wird – vielleicht – jenes ‚Gleichnis' fassbar, von dem der Autor in seinem ‚Nachwort' aus dem Jahre 1957 mehr verhüllend als erklärend spricht (728). Und von hier aus fällt nicht nur auf die damalige, sondern auch auf unsere heutige Gegenwart ein scharfes, grelles Licht. Die unterhaltende, ja spannende, über weite Strecken poetische Gestaltung eines weit zurückliegenden historischen Moments, die reiche Motivik, die (anregende) Knappheit und Kargheit des Textes wie die dichte Komposition des Ganzen, die hintergründigen Anspielungen, die Konzentration auf die Figur des Jefta: alles läuft einerseits auf eine drastische Kritik jener Handlungsstrukturen hinaus, von denen das 20. Jahrhundert weitgehend geprägt wurde und die gerade in der Zeit des Kalten Krieges bestimmend waren, und zwar in Ost und West; Handlungsstrukturen, die auch heute, fast ein halbes Jahrhundert nach dem *Jefta*, unter sehr gewandelten weltpolitischen Bedingungen mit brutaler Selbstverständlichkeit benutzt werden wie eh und je.

Andererseits aber ist da die Konzeption der Sinngebung geschichtlicher Verläufe durch verantwortliches menschliches Denken und Handeln: ein Glaubensbekenntnis. Und ich gestatte mir, hier herzusetzen, was ich an anderer Stelle mit Blick auf Feuchtwangers Roman *Erfolg* notiert habe: ‚Vielleicht benötigt der eine oder der andere von uns gerade heute gerade einen solchen Glauben. Vielleicht benötigen wir alle einen derartigen Glauben – er sei säkularisiert oder nicht –, wenn wir nicht untergehen wollen'.[16]

Anmerkungen

[1] Lion Feuchtwanger, *Das Haus der Desdemona oder Größe und Grenzen der historischen Dichtung*, Rudolstadt: Greifenverlag, 1961, S. 146.

[2] Gisela Lüttig, ‚Zu dieser Ausgabe', in: Lion Feuchtwanger, *Jefta und seine Tochter*, Berlin und Weimar: Aufbau, 1996, S. 269-77.

[3] In: Harold von Hofe, Hg., *Lion Feuchtwanger/ Arnold Zweig: Briefwechsel 1933-1958*, Berlin und Weimar: Aufbau, 1984, Bd. II, S. 381.

[4] In: Harold von Hofe und Sigrid Washburn, Hgg., *Lion Feuchtwanger: Briefwechsel mit Freunden 1933-1958*, Berlin und Weimar: Aufbau, 1991, Bd. I, S. 206.

[5] Lion Feuchtwanger, *Die Jüdin von Toledo/Jefta und seine Tochter. Zwei Romane*, Berlin und Weimar: Aufbau, 1962, S. 536ff. Auf diese Ausgabe beziehen sich die Seitenzahlen im Text.

[6] Hans Wagener, *Lion Feuchtwanger*, Berlin: Morgenbuch, 1996, S. 79. Siehe auch Volker Skierka, *Lion Feuchtwanger. Eine Biographie*, Berlin: Quadriga, 1984, S. 284f.

[7] Wulf Köpke, *Lion Feuchtwanger*, München: Beck 1983, S. 162 und Wilhelm von Sternburg, *Lion Feuchtwanger. Ein deutsches Schriftstellerleben*, Berlin und Weimar: Aufbau, 1994, S. 520.

[8] Lion Feuchtwanger, *Centum opuscula. Eine Auswahl*, zusammengestellt und herausgegeben von Wolfgang Berndt, Rudolstadt: Greifenverlag, 1956, S. 373.

[9] ‚Thraenen der Tochter Jephte', in: Christian Hofmann von Hofmannswaldau, *Gesammelte Werke*, Hg. Franz Heiduk, Hildesheim-Zürich-New York: Georg Olms, 1984, Bd. I/2, S. 18 [618].

[10] Giacomo Carissimi, ‚Jephte', in: Giacomo Carissimi. *Jephte/Jonas/Judicum Extremum*. Erato-Disques S.A. 1990. Beiheft, S. 56.

[11] In: Lord Byron, *The Complete Poetical Works*, Hg. Jerome J. McGann, Oxford: Clarendon Press, 1981, Volume III, S. 294.

[12] *Das Buch der Richter*, 4:21.

[13] Tanja Kinkel, *Naemi, Ester, Raquel und Ja´ala. Väter, Töchter, Machtmenschen und Judentum bei Lion Feuchtwanger*, Bonn: Bouvier, 1998, S. 109.

[14] Siehe etwa Kinkel, *Naemi*, S. 114; Köpke, *Lion Feuchtwanger*, S. 165.

[15] Feuchtwanger, *Centum opuscula*, S. 509.

[16] Arnold Pistiak, ‚Lion Feuchtwangers Roman „Erfolg"'. In: *Welfengarten. Jahrbuch für Essayismus*, 10 (2000), 27-44.

Pól O'Dochartaigh

The Present Sense of an Historical Novel:
Feuchtwanger's *Waffen für Amerika*[1]

Feuchtwanger's concept of the historical novel went beyond the confines of any single ideology. If there is a core belief underlying his writing, it is a belief in reason. Though ideologically-driven critiques of *Waffen für Amerika* accused the author variously of having written a novel sympathetic to 'American imperialism' and of having written an 'analogy' that was sympathetic to Stalinism, the novel is neither. Rather, Feuchtwanger in this novel offers us an historical vision, warts and all, that is against narrow chauvinisms and ideologies and in favour of European-American co-operation to promote enlightenment and reason. This vision remains relevant today.

In his 1935 essay 'Vom Sinn und Unsinn des historischen Romans' Lion Feuchtwanger confessed to a clear political agenda in his writing of historical novels. Quoting first Benedetto Croce on the contemporary relevance of history writing ('Die Gegenwärtigkeit ist der eigentliche Charakter aller lebendigen Geschichte, im Gegensatz zur bloßen Chronik'), he professes his own belief in his historical novels as instruments of reason:

> Ich für mein Teil habe mich, seitdem ich schreibe, bemüht, historische Romane für die Vernunft zu schreiben, gegen Dummheit und Gewalt, gegen das, was Marx das Versinken in die Geschichtslosigkeit nennt. Vielleicht gibt es auf dem Gebiet der Literatur Waffen, die unmittelbarer wirken: aber mir liegt, aus Gründen, die ich dar-zulegen versuchte, am besten diese Waffe, der historische Roman, und ich beab-sichtige, sie weiter zu gebrauchen.[2]

By engaging with the concept of reason, Feuchtwanger goes beyond the mere present. He is right to take the concept of 'Gegenwärtigkeit' as an essential element in the serious historical novel, but if this is the only element then historical novels may easily become dated. Feuchtwanger's *Waffen für Amerika* (1947/48), written in the shadow of the European-American alliance in World War II and the Cold War that followed it, is, in fact, not simply a commentary on the World War II alliance dressed in the historical clothes of France's support for the American revolution. Rather, it is a statement of Feuchtwanger's belief in the importance of historical (and historic) links between Europe and North America in the cause of reason and human progress. As such, the novel serves as a reminder of the significance of, and mutual benefits that have accrued from, the cultural and ideological exchanges that have taken place for more than two centuries, a reminder that remains entirely relevant in this early 21st century when powerful voices on both continents would prefer to distance themselves from, and even insult, the other side.

Right down to the 1980s *Waffen für Amerika* was subjected to ideologi-cally-driven interpretations that appeared to serve one or other side in the Cold War. The title and content of the novel aroused suspicions in the East and led to criticism there in the early phase of the Cold War. A reviewer in the Soviet

journal *Novy Mir* accused Feuchtwanger of having written 'einen Propaganda-
roman für das imperialistische Amerika'.[3] In the GDR Alfred Kantorowicz had
cause, as a result of similar criticisms, to organise a defence of Feuchtwanger by
asking Heinrich Mann and Bertolt Brecht to review the novel.[4] Representing the
USA as a progressive force, even in a 170-year-old setting, was undesirable in
the context of the political hostilities of the late 1940s. The title was changed to
Die Füchse im Weinberg for the GDR edition of 1952, thereby removing any
reference to 'imperialist' America or the supply of weapons to it, or, as Feuchtwanger put it in his correspondence with Arnold Zweig, 'um gewisse sinnlose
Vorurteile zu zerstreuen'.[5] Though he agreed to the change of title, Feucht-
wanger did not accept that the criticism was justified, pointing out as he did to
Zweig that the novel also presents the 'ersten Repräsentanten amerikanischen
Größenwahns'.[6]

   More recently, in the mid-1980s, Hans-Albert Walter drew a narrow analogy between the events portrayed in this novel and the World War II anti-Nazi
alliance and used it to attack Feuchtwanger from an anti-communist perspective.
Whereas some early Soviet commentators objected to any comparison between
the 'glorious' Soviet struggle against Nazi Germany and anything American
(even the fight against colonial, imperialist England), Walter objected to any
attempt inflate the importance of the American War of Independence in world
historical terms ('Stilisierung des amerikanischen Unabhängigkeitskrieges zum
menschheitsrettenden Befreiungskrieg'[7]) and also to what he saw as, in the end,
praise for the Soviet Union. By analogising so closely that he all but calls the
novel a *roman à clef*, Walter criticises Feuchtwanger for supposedly presenting
the Soviet Union as a 'Hort der Wahrheit und Freiheit'.[8] Walter even integrates
into his thinking the complete misinterpretation that was the title of the American translation of the novel, *Proud Destiny*,[9] and sees the novel as a kind of
hommage à Franklin and the United States and therefore, by analogy, to Stalin
and Soviet Russia. As an interpretation of the novel this is, frankly, no more
useful than early Soviet attempts to damn it as propaganda for the USA or later
GDR attempts to offer similar close analogies in an anti-American sense, such
as that offered by Joseph Pischel:

> Wenn dagegen König Louis, der die Amerikaner immer nur so weit unterstützen woll-
> te, *daß sie sich halten, aber keinen Sieg erringen können,* vom ersten Augenblick an
> nur an die Folgen dieses Sieges denkt, *daß er nämlich jetzt um die verhaßte Allianz
> schwerlich werde herumkommen,* dann ist die Parallele zur Hinhaltetaktik der West-
> mächte bei der Errichtung der zweiten Front unübersehbar.[10]

   Such interpretations are inadequate, since Feuchtwanger, despite the embarrassing one-sidedness of his *Moskau 1937*,[11] was not a committed Stalinist.
Neither did he believe in any kind of 'proud destiny' represented by American
capitalism. He did, however, firmly believe in reason, and he saw it as central to
human progress. He also, as a result of his exile first in France and then in the
USA, came to appreciate political and cultural representatives of enlightenment
in Europe and the USA as the main driving forces of reason and progress in

history, especially when they acted in conjunction with one other. Most of all he saw, and was able to portray in convincing narrative terms, the various roles, active and passive, willing and sometimes unwilling, played by individuals in the struggle for progress.

One of the two central characters in Feuchtwanger's novel is the historical figure of Benjamin Franklin, a journalist, scientist, businessman, enlightenment figure and diplomat whose range of activities and achievements mark him out as the outstanding international figure among the American revolutionary leaders. Franklin's role as American emissary in Paris caused rivalry with another American envoy, Arthur Lee, and it is in the characterisation of this conflict within the American delegation that Feuchtwanger portrays one of the key struggles for progress, namely between enlightened defence of the American cause, as represented by Franklin, and self-interest in the service of the cause, as represented by Lee. Feuchtwanger's representation of Lee seems to be a somewhat colourful paraphrasing of the words used by Franklin's entirely sympathetic biographer, Carl Van Doren, whose Pulitzer Prize-winning tome on Franklin's life was published in 1938.[12] Of Lee Van Doren writes:

> Chosen in 1770 as associate and future successor to Franklin in the Massachusetts agency, Lee could not help being eager to come into the influential position and the substantial salary. Though he admired Franklin, he was exasperated by Franklin's staying on [in London] year after year, and he became acutely suspicious.[13]

We may compare this to the passage in *Waffen für Amerika* in which the relationship between Franklin and Lee is first broached:

> Schon damals schien es dem jungen, fanatischen, grelle Worte und Gesten liebenden Arthur Lee schwer erträglich, zusammengespannt zu sein mit dem alten, ruhig wägenden Doctor honoris causa – er nannte ihn niemals anders – und er hatte sehnsüchtig darauf gewartet, daß ihm der Alte endlich Platz mache.[14]

The contrast is between on the one hand the 'Weltbürger' Franklin, who is comfortable on two continents and in three countries and who, recognising the Americans' weakness in the early days of the conflict, is prepared to make strategic compromises in both political and personal matters, and on the other hand the upstart Lee, who demands respect both for himself and the American cause as of right and who fumes when such respect is not accorded, for example by French governmental aristocrats.

Lee's hostility to Franklin is a constant feature of the novel: the manner in which this rivalry is portrayed by Feuchtwanger has been compared (by Hans-Albert Walter) to Feuchtwanger's description of the rivalry between Stalin and Trotsky.[15] This analogy may well hold water in terms of the kind of language used by the author in the two texts, but the parallel must surely end there. *Moskau 1937* was an embarrassing slip in Feuchtwanger's literary-political career, and by the mid-1940s he had certainly moved beyond such one-sided simplicity. In any case, even Feuchtwanger, despite his hostility to Trotsky in 1937, described him as 'geistreich' and noted his ability to express himself without difficulty in several languages, whereas Stalin he described as 'eher schwerfällig' and not smooth of tongue.[16] Thus the idea that Stalin could correspond politically to the 'Weltbürger' Franklin while the internationalist Trotsky is equated to a narrow chauvinist like Lee is risible. What Walter calls Feuchtwanger's 'Analogieverfahren' surely has its limits.[17]

The manner in which Lee is shown to be a character full of petty jealousies and paranoia and also an enemy of Franklin strengthens the reader's identification with the latter. The depiction of Lee rather than Franklin as the emissary with important allies in America is an example of Feuchtwanger's criticism of chauvinist aspects of the American revolutionary side, but it also highlights another point. Those whose life experience has largely been gained on the North American continent are more likely to have a narrow attitude and to miss the importance of America's need for allies in the conflict. Even those who accept the need for allies may, because of their limited horizons, be unable to engage in the kind of dialogue needed to persuade potential allies of the benefits of supporting the American cause. Lee himself had a cosmopolitan (if monoglot English) background, having been born in Virginia and educated in Eton and Edinburgh, but many of his closest allies back in America did not, and his own character failings negated much of his wide experience.

Not so Franklin, who had been born in Boston, run away to Philadelphia as a teenager and as a young man spent eighteen months working in London. His involvement with science, his work as a printer and publisher, his political activities in London on behalf of the colonies and his Fellowship of the Royal Society gave him a wider perspective on events than most and also gave him experience of the modalities of negotiation. He was a giant of the American revolutionary movement and, crucially for his appointment to Paris in 1776, his scientific achievements had earned him great respect in France and other parts of the European continent. He was no warmonger, having tried unsuccessfully to make the British colonial government see the errors of its treatment of the American colonists and only given up hope in 1775, some 18 years after he had arrived to live in London. When the war was over and peace treaties had been signed, Franklin rejoiced at both independence from and friendship with Europe: "'We are now friends with England and with all mankind," Franklin wrote to Josiah Quincy on the 11th [September 1783]. "May we never see another war! For in my opinion there never was a good war or a bad peace"'.[18]

His cosmopolitan attitudes are reflected in the novel again and again, never more forcefully, if also idealistically, than in a passage near the end when Franklin debates with another American revolutionary, John Adams, who is clearly meant to represent American chauvinism and reaction. Despite the sentiment expressed by the historical Franklin in his letter to Quincy, which in any case stands somewhat in contrast to his support for the American armed rebellion, Feuchtwanger's Franklin is no pacifist, but he is an internationalist:

> [...] Ich träume von einem Zeitalter, da Leute wie wir, wohin immer auf dem Planeten wir unsere Schritte lenken mögen, sagen dürfen: Hier bin ich zu Hause. Gesetzt den

Fall, es ließe sich ein solches Zeitalter herbeiführen, finden Sie, Mr. Adams, es wäre mit Blutvergießen zu hoch bezahlt?[19]

The historical figure of John Adams, who took part in the peace negotiations in France, was selected by congress because he was thought to be less pro-French, and it is also recorded that 'Adams never liked Franklin'.[20] Adams went on to become Vice-President of the United States under George Washington (1789-97) and 2nd President of the US (1797-1801). As President he pursued an anti-French diplomatic policy, which met with much resistance in the US and contributed to his failure to achieve a second term.[21] His nationalist and at the same time anglophile policies contained a strong element of europhobia. In characterising Adams in Paris in 1783 Feuchtwanger goes beyond these policies, however, and puts thoughts of imperialist expansion, of a coming '*amerikanisches* Imperium' in the nineteenth century into Adams' head as an unspoken reply to Franklin's internationalist dreams.[22] This is clearly intended to exemplify the negative side of the American revolution, a strain of thinking in American politics that has remained prominent up to the present day. For if the colonists fought for their own freedom from empire, they also acquired an empire of their own in much of which black people remained enslaved and in which vast lands to the west were seen as legitimate territory for expansion at the expense of the native tribes who inhabited those lands. As early as 1785 Thomas Jefferson worked out a land grid that divided up the lands to the west (in territories with characteristically straight lines), so that with few exceptions (among them Texas and California) 'every new state from Ohio to Hawaii has followed the path that he laid out'.[23] Feuchtwanger is under no illusions about the Americans, despite his somewhat one-sidedly sympathetic portrayal of the flawed master Franklin.

In the persons of Lee and Adams Feuchtwanger offers us traits and beliefs such as individual vanity and American expansionism, personal envy towards Franklin and xenophobia. Franklin himself, though by no means flawless, is nevertheless an enlightened, cosmopolitan, forward-thinking representative of bourgeois revolution against despotism. Yet it is clear that a combination of all three of these individuals, and many more besides, was necessary in order to help bring the American revolution to a successful conclusion. Far from presenting the Americans (and thus, as Walter and others would have it, the Soviet Union) as a unified positive force for progress, Feuchtwanger shows us a tense, at times narrow-minded array of individuals often given to petty-mindedness but united in a single political cause, namely, the defeat of (British) colonialism in the Americas. What he also shows us is that this group of individuals would not have achieved success on their own.

For it was to Europe that Americans had to turn for help in order to free themselves from their European colonial masters, a paradox that was not lost on Franklin, who 'would have preferred to keep America independent of the rest of Europe as well as England'.[24] Franklin was prepared to accept French aid out of necessity, but he was under no illusions that France might not have aims of its own in fighting England, though there seems to have been little fear historically that France might attempt to establish itself as the colonial master in place of England. In the end, whatever France's real aims may have been, the benefit to the Americans was likely to be the same, Franklin reasoned.[25]

The real point, highlighted most forcefully in Feuchtwanger's novel, is that France's real motivations for supporting the Americans were unclear. Though monarchists and more enlightened thinkers were generally united in their opposition to England, it was for different reasons. Feuchtwanger, again using characterisation, brings out these differences most forcefully. All the while, however, and despite the different motivations of his characters, it is clear that the author sees all of their roles as contributing, wittingly or unwittingly, willingly or unwillingly, towards progress, enlightenment and new democracy.

Charlot Lenormant perhaps best incorporates some of the contradictory emotions felt by Frenchmen whose natural sympathies were both with the existing French monarchy and with the American insurgents. A wealthy man who bears no aristocratic title, Lenormant combines mildly progressive beliefs with traditional French prejudice. On hearing the words of the American Declaration of Independence, read aloud at his birthday celebration, Lenormant is uncomfortable:

> Er war fortschrittlich, er sympathisierte mit der Sache der Insurgenten und gönnte den Engländern jede Niederlage. Doch er war ein überzeugter Anhänger der autoritären französischen Monarchie, er hielt aufgeklärten Despotismus für die beste Regierungsform, und er fürchtete, ein zu klarer Sieg der Insurgenten könnte den Geist der Rebellion und Anarchie auch im Königreich Frankreich schüren.[26]

The expression 'aufgeklärter Despotismus' appears again, when Josef, Emperor of Austria, rebukes the Marquis de Vaudreuil for his pro-Franklin attitude and, above all, for his comment that progress and change will happen, whether the aristocracy wishes it or not. Specifically, he recognises the role that is played by such as himself in supporting Franklin: 'Wir sägen an dem Ast, auf dem wir sitzen, weil wir wissen: es ist ihm bestimmt, zu fallen'.[27] Lenormant, as a supporter of enlightened despotism, would support the Americans, while Josef von Habsburg, as an enlightened despot, would oppose them. Perhaps, Feuchtwanger is suggesting, nationality is the key to this difference. Austrian despotism may not be as enlightened as the Austrian ruler would like to think. Or perhaps French despotism is 'enlightened' by the specifics of Anglo-French rivalry.

This rivalry is at the core of the political thoughts of Count Vergennes, foreign minister to Louis XVI. He wishes to help the Americans because, like Lenormant, he would not begrudge the English any defeat. Yet he is also shown to be aware of the dangers of too great an American success, for he has little or no sympathy for the ideas that underpin the American revolutionary movement. Anglo-French rivalry was centuries old, but the recent humiliation of France in the war of 1756-63 was fresh in the memory. Vergennes saw an opportunity to inflict political damage on a now dominant British Empire.

What Feuchtwanger offers us with his characterisations of the French is an effective description of political scheming. Vergennes uses Franklin's popularity in France, and the American success at Saratoga in October 1777 (achieved with the help of a large consignment of French arms), to persuade Louis to enter a war in support of a cause to which he is antipathetic. When Louis asks what his people will make of the victory at Saratoga, Vergennes replies:

> 'Ihr Volk, Sire,' antwortete unerwartet kühn Vergennes, 'freut sich, daß England eine so ungeheure Schlappe erlitten hat.' Der alte Maurepas wackelte zustimmend mit dem Kopf und Vergennes fuhr fort: 'Ihr Volk, Sire, würde es nicht verstehen, wenn man jetzt noch länger zögerte, den Pakt abzuschließen'.[28]

Ultimately, the alliance is signed, but Louis remains full of unease, for though the American Declaration of Independence was directed at one particular monarch, he sees the Americans' ultimate aim as being to remove all divine authority from this earth. Yet he is but another pawn in a great international move towards a more enlightened future, and for all his royal power, Feuchtwanger portrays him as an ultimately helpless figure.

Perhaps the most enigmatic of all the French characters, however, is the central one, Pierre Beaumarchais, whom Feuchtwanger described as 'eine überaus anziehende Figur; blitzend geistreich, mit tausend teils fruchtbaren, teils hohlen Ideen um sich werfend'.[29] A dramatist, a supporter of enlightenment, a businessman, vain, Beaumarchais is an essentially bourgeois figure whose imagination is set alight by the wonderful language of the American Declaration and the sense of adventure that attaches to actively supporting it. He has wildly romantic notions of the nature of guerrilla warfare, for which Franklin, at their first meeting, belittles him in front of Lenormant.[30] Yet he is the most active Frenchman in support of the American cause, organising shipments to the rebels and asking again and again for money from the French government to support them. Simultaneously, he manages to actively promote enlightenment ideals at home, with the first performance of his *Marriage of Figaro*, which is moved by Feuchtwanger to 1778 from the historically accurate 1784.

Together with Franklin, Beaumarchais is the key player in Feuchtwanger's novel. Though they are from broadly comparable backgrounds (Franklin's father appears to have been a shop-owning candlemaker, Beaumarchais' a watchmaker), he is the artist to Franklin's scientist, the wildly flamboyant individual to Franklin's staidness, the French romantic supporting deadly earnest Americans. Taken together, these two characters, though they do not meet more than a couple of times and develop no great love for each other, represent artistic progress combined with philosophical reason. They have neither intellectual disciplines nor nationality in common, but their combined efforts in France help ensure that the bourgeois, progressive, anti-colonialist American revolution

achieves success against a European power with the aid of European progres-
sives (as well as some reactionaries). In these two characters Feuchtwanger
epitomises what he called 'die Wechselwirkung zwischen dem fortschrittlichen
Frankreich und dem Unabhängigkeitskampf in Amerika'.[31] This interaction by
definition worked both ways, for if French support helped the Americans to get
rid of their tyrants, American success helped persuade the French that they
could do more than simply write about progress. Their own revolution began in
the same decade in which the American one ended.

Feuchtwanger's aim with *Waffen für Amerika* was far greater than his
'analogist' detractors would have us believe, even if the events of World War II
provided him with the impetus to finally write a novel the idea for which had
been in his head for twenty years. The American struggle for independence was
a struggle for progress, as most surely was the struggle against Nazism, and
Feuchtwanger says this quite clearly in the postscript to the 1952 GDR edition
of his novel:

> Als das Amerika Roosevelts in den Krieg gegen den europäischen Faschismus ein-
> griff und den Kampf der Sowjetunion gegen Hitler unterstützte, wurden mir die Ge-
> schehnisse im Frankreich des ausgehenden achtzehnten Jahrhunderts leuchtend klar,
> und sie erleuchteten mir die politischen Geschehnisse der eigenen Zeit.[32]

In his short 1954 essay on the novel Feuchtwanger makes it clear that his own
personal experience of exile in France and America made clear to him 'die
geschichtliche Verbundenheit der beiden Kontinente'.[33] Living in America also
allowed Feuchtwanger to finally get to grips with the character of Franklin,
which enabled the project to be completed. It allowed him to analyse both
historical and contemporary events on two continents first from his European
home and, subsequently, from his American place of residence.

These statements by the author are a far cry from any direct analogy
between events and characters in 1776-83 and 1939-45. He implies parallels, he
sees certain historical processes at work, and he sees a wide range of characters
and political opinions contributing to the American success. Most of all,
however, it must be remembered that in the final analysis Feuchtwanger was
writing an historical novel, not attempting to reconstruct history. When Hans-
Albert Walter raises 'die Frage nach der Berechtigung des Analogiever-
fahrens',[34] by which he means Feuchtwanger's, he is missing the point. When
he then states: 'Man formuliert nicht zu scharf, wenn man sagt, Feuchtwanger
gehe mit der Geschichte manipulierend um',[35] it is clear that it is Walter's
'Analogieverfahren' rather than Feuchtwanger's which is at fault, for it is surely
the entitlement of any writer of fiction to manipulate historical fact.

Feuchtwanger's real forte, namely 'the drawing of characters in an
historical framework',[36] is used to good effect in this novel, but none of the
characters is the real hero of the book, according to Feuchtwanger: 'Der Held
des Buches vielmehr ist der *Fortschritt*. Es handelt nicht von Franklin oder von
Beaumarchais, sondern vom Sinn des geschichtlichen Geschehens'.[37]

Most of all, however, Feuchtwanger is absolutely clear that the historical processes do not end there, whether in 1783/89 or in 1945. For Feuchtwanger, Europe and the United States were not simply linked by these specific historical events, but linked historically, period. For if progress is the real hero of this novel, then the lesson is that it can only be achieved by coalitions, sometimes of opposites, because one single-minded ideal, one single nation left to its own devices may fall on its own sword, its own narrow-mindedness, its own bigotry and chauvinism. In *Waffen für Amerika* Feuchtwanger developed a concept of human progress achieved through European-American co-operation both historically and in a contemporary context. His own biography, his experience of living in both Europe and America and his opposition to colonialism, and fascism, to reaction and exploitation, enabled him to successfully approach this theme in the form of an historical novel. The concept of European-American co-operation is one that he felt would survive despite all the chauvinists on both sides of the Atlantic. Since he believed in continuing historical processes and certainly not in an end of history, and in the rights of mankind as a whole rather than of any single nation, his novel retains a particular relevance in the global political situation of the early 21st century.

Notes

[1] I am indebted to the British Academy for the travel grant that enabled me to participate in the conference in California in April 2003 at which an earlier version of this paper was presented.

[2] Lion Feuchtwanger, 'Vom Sinn und Unsinn des historischen Romans', in L.F., *Centum Opuscula*, ed. Wolfgang Berndt, Rudolstadt: Greifenverlag, 1956, pp.508-15 (here pp.514-15).

[3] Quoted in Wilhelm von Sternburg, *Lion Feuchtwanger. Ein deutsches Schriftstellerleben*, Berlin and Weimar: Aufbau, 1994, p.481.

[4] See Frank Dietschreit, *Lion Feuchtwanger*, Stuttgart: Metzler, 1988, pp.123-24.

[5] Lion Feuchtwanger, *Die Füchse im Weinberg*, Berlin: Aufbau, 1952. See Dietschreit, op. cit., p.124.

[6] Dietschreit, op. cit., p.124.

[7] Hans-Albert Walter, 'Der falsche Franklin *oder* Ein echter Feuchtwanger. Kritische Anmerkungen zu einem Bestsellerroman der Exilliteratur', in Lion Feuchtwanger, *Waffen für Amerika*, Band II, Frankfurt am Main: Büchergilde Gutenberg, 1986, pp.355-432 (here p.387).

[8] Ibid., p.396.

[9] Lion Feuchtwanger, *Proud Destiny*, translated by Moray Firth, New York: Viking Press, 1947.

[10] Joseph Pischel, *Lion Feuchtwanger*, Leipzig: Reclam, 1983[2], p.184.

[11] Lion Feuchtwanger, *Moskau 1937*, Amsterdam: Querido, 1937.

[12] Carl Van Doren, *Benjamin Franklin*, New York: Penguin, 1991. First published 1938. Feuchtwanger specifically states that he approached Franklin's life carefully and thoroughly via Van Doren's biography and its extensive bibliography. See Lion Feuchtwanger, 'Zu meinem Roman "Waffen für Amerika"', in L.F., *Centum Opuscula*, pp.403-11 (here 408).

[13] Van Doren, *Benjamin Franklin*, p.480.

[14] Lion Feuchtwanger, *Waffen für Amerika*, Band I, Amsterdam: Querido, 1947, p.112.

[15] Walter, 'Der falsche Franklin', pp.405-10. See also Feuchtwanger, *Moskau 1937*, pp.101-16.

[16] Feuchtwanger, *Moskau 1937*, p.115.

[17] Walter, 'Der falsche Franklin', p.388.

[18] Quoted in Van Doren, *Benjamin Franklin*, p.698.

[19] Lion Feuchtwanger, *Waffen für Amerika*, Band II, Amsterdam: Querido, 1948, p.407.

[20] Van Doren, *Benjamin Franklin*, p.665 and p.600.

[21] See Peter N. Carroll and David W. Noble, *The Free and the Unfree. A New History of the United States*, Harmondsworth: Penguin, 1980, p.192.

[22] Feuchtwanger, *Waffen für Amerika II*, p.407.

[23] Edward Countryman, *The American Revolution*, 2nd edition, New York: Hill & Wang, 2003, pp.204-36 (here p.209).

[24] Van Doren, *Benjamin Franklin*, p.699.

[25] Ibid.

[26] Feuchtwanger, *Waffen für Amerika I*, p.77.

[27] Ibid., pp.208-09.

[28] Feuchtwanger, *Waffen für Amerika II*, p.9.

[29] Feuchtwanger, 'Zu meinem Roman', p.403.

[30] Feuchtwanger, *Waffen für Amerika I*, pp.144-45.

[31] Ibid., p.404.

[32] Quoted in Pischel, *Lion Feuchtwanger*, pp.183-84.

[33] Feuchtwanger, 'Zu meinem Roman', pp.409-10.

[34] Walter, 'Der falsche Franklin', p.388.

[35] Ibid.

[36] Harold von Hofe, 'Lion Feuchtwanger and America', in John M. Spalek, ed., *Lion Feuchtwanger. The Man His Ideas His Work*, Los Angeles: Hennessy & Ingalls, 1972, pp.33-50 (here 42).

[37] Feuchtwanger, 'Zu meinem Roman', p.410.

Ian Wallace

Hangmen also die. Varieties of Collaboration

Hangmen also die (1943) is generally regarded today as one of the most important anti-Nazi films to come out of Hollywood. Besides exploring the troubled collaboration between Fritz Lang and Bertolt Brecht during the making of the film, this chapter focuses on its depiction of the underground resistance in Prague following the assassination of the *Reichsprotektor*, Reinhard Heydrich. It finds here clear evidence of the struggle between the two very different conceptions of the film developed by Lang and Brecht. Particular attention is paid to the role of the quisling, Emil Czaka, and to the moral questions raised by the resistance's successful conspiracy to 'frame' him as Heydrich's assassin. The important contribution made to the film's success by Hanns Eisler's music and, at key points, by excerpts from Smetana's *Ma Vlast* is also discussed.

On 3 January 1943 Brecht wrote in his *Arbeitsjournal* in praise of a literary collaborator:

> die zusammenarbeit geht gut und ist eine erholung nach der filmarbeit [...] er hat sinn für konstruktion, versteht sprachliche feinheiten zu schätzen, hat auch poetische und dramaturgische einfälle, weiss viel von literatur, respektiert argumente und ist menschlich angenehm, ein guter freund.[1]

The collaborator in question was Lion Feuchtwanger, with whom Brecht was at the time developing their joint project on Simone Machard; the film work had been with Fritz Lang on one of Hollywood's most important, if controversial anti-fascist moves, *Hangmen also die*.[2] Although well aware of how they differed in political and aesthetic terms, Brecht clearly admired in Feuchtwanger the very qualities which, by implication, he had not found in Fritz Lang: literary and linguistic sensitivity, honest craftsmanship, openness to the arguments of others, and a human warmth which made him a pleasure to work with.

Whatever the rights and wrongs of Brecht's disaffection with Lang, working with him had been a gamble from the start. Unlike Feuchtwanger and Brecht, Lang and Brecht had not known each other well, far less been close friends in pre-1933 Germany. It is true that Lang played an important role in Hollywood's efforts, via the European Film Fund set up in 1938, to secure US visas for Brecht and his family, but this appears not to have led Brecht to feel any particular warmth or gratitude towards him. Their attitudes to Hollywood itself were poles apart. Whereas Brecht never sought to conceal a visceral disgust with what he saw as Hollywood's corrupting values (and a degree of *self*-disgust at having to serve them), Lang set out to embrace what he could not in any case change. Indeed, as David Thomson points out, it was he who, of all the European refugees, 'adapted most naturally to America'.[3] Far from being 'an almost perfect match',[4] the coming together in Hollywood of two such different partners was essentially a marriage of convenience, a pragmatic response to the political and professional demands of the day. Given the nature of the contract between them, it was not a partnership of equals but, fundamentally, one between employer (Lang) and employee (Brecht).[5] Both men needed commercial success in Hollywood, but for fundamentally different reasons. For Brecht, the film was essentially no more than a 'brotarbeit' (which is of course not the same as saying that he could under any circumstances be content to churn out inferior work) – a 'brotarbeit' which was a basically unwelcome and temporary diversion in an unfamiliar genre which he saw as a means of earning sufficient money to be able to devote time and energy to his real work (it is one of the ironies of the fraught collaboration with Lang that the film did in fact earn Brecht enough money to be able to work on *Die Gesichte der Simone Machard*, *Die Herzogin von Malfi*, and *Schweyk*). For Lang it must be recognised that the stakes were rather higher, since his entire future as a Hollywood director ultimately depended on a successful box-office. Brecht's early description of the project as 'ganz einfach Monte Carlo'[6] and his growing unease at Lang's concern to provide only what a mass public would 'buy' led before long to an overpowering sense of desperation at being involved in such an apparently tawdry enterprise: 'ein unendlich trauriges gemächte [...] was für schemen, intrigen, falschheiten!'[7] Needless to say, Lang challenged Brecht's account of events while certainly not denying the tensions in their relationship.[8]

Such tensions held out little obvious promise of success, and critical judgements on the film do diverge widely. For Comolli and Géré, for example, it enjoys the status of a masterpiece,[9] but for others it is a flawed and uneven work,[10] while for Gunning it is 'neither a great Brecht opus, nor a great Lang film'.[11] Similarly, views specifically on the importance of Brecht's contribution to the film vary considerably. For some, this is in every important sense a Fritz Lang film. The striking structural similarities to his masterpiece *M*, the characteristic fascination with the manhunt theme, the brilliant technical skills evident in (for instance) the interrogation scenes or the careful crafting of Inspector Gruber's death – all this and more betrays the hand of this master cinematographer, leading one critic to the conclusion that 'Wexley wrote the movie Lang wanted him to write, and Lang shot it the way he had intended'.[12] In other words, Brecht was essentially excised from the film. Comolli and Géré agree: '[N]othing of his [Brecht's] "collaboration" [note the sceptical inverted commas] survives in the final script'. (126) Brecht purists have tended to give sustenance to this line of argument, with the editors both of his two-volume *Texte für Filme* (published in 1969) and of the 30-volume *Werke* published in the 1990s declining to include the screenplay for *Hangmen also die* even though this was the only one of the many film projects with which he was involved in Hollywood which came to fruition and in which he is actually named in the credits. By contrast, John Winge believes that Lang emasculated the film with his many compromises to Hollywood's demands but that it is precisely Brecht's contribution which nevertheless makes the film superior to most Hollywood movies about the resistance in Europe.[13]

This playing off of Lang and Brecht against one another has been a rich source of controversy over the years. Although James K. Lyon has recently stated that there can now be no doubt about the justification for including the film in the list of Brecht's works, it seems less certain whether a definitive account of Brecht's encounter with Lang can yet be written. For one thing, there are too many areas of fundamental dispute about key aspects of their collaboration. Is it true, as Wexley claims, that Lang had promised him sole credit for the screenplay on which he worked with Brecht? Is it the case, as Hans Viertel states but Lang denies, that Lang and Brecht had completed a treatment of about 100 pages in German which was then translated into English by Viertel, or had Lang and Brecht written no more than a page of rough notes when Wexley came on the scene, as the latter claims?[14] Was it Lang alone who cut down the screenplay from the original 280 to a more workable 192 pages, or (as Lang himself says) Lang together with an assistant named Milton L. Gunzberg, or Wexley alone (as, for example, Schebera and Hamilton state)?[15] Above all, it is the disappearance Brecht's copies of scripts on which he himself worked, and in particular the continuing argument about the so-called 'ideal script' which he supposedly wrote in secret with Wexley as an alternative to the screenplay being overseen by Lang,[16] which makes it at present impossible to use an indisputable Brecht text as a yardstick against which to measure the precise nature of his contribution to the film as finally realised, particularly as changes continued to be made even as the film was being made. Without that yardstick, there is inevitably a large measure of speculation in any attempt to ascribe to him with any certainty particular aspects of the work.

This has not of course prevented the critics from speculating and nor should it, given that Brecht never disowned the film (partly no doubt because, as noted above, the money it earned him bought him by his own admission the time to complete three important works that were entirely his own) and given also that in his *Arbeitsjournal* and other sources he provided enough trenchant comments on the making of the film to justify any attempt at explication. Indeed, despite all the bitter frustrations, Brecht did express satisfaction with particular aspects of the script, specifically the opening scene, scenes showing class differences among the Czech hostages, the film's epic structure, the three distinct strands focusing on Svoboda, Mascha and Czaka respectively, and the insistence that the heroic underground makes mistakes. So great was this satisfaction that Brecht even confessed he would have included such material in his *Versuche* if he had been in a position to continue with them. There can be no doubt, then, that he felt a clear sense of ownership of the original script but that he felt betrayed when Lang shot the film with only limited respect for his wishes. No doubt partly in an attempt at self-justification, Lang claimed in 1971 that, in cutting the screenplay back to 192 pages, he had not sacrificed any scene of importance and that instances of Brecht's contributions to the final script were innumerable. He mentions in particular the scenes in which Svoboda seeks refuge in a cinema, Mascha attempts to visit the Gestapo, Professor Novotny defines the word 'no-one' for his daughter and runs through the alphabet as far as 'G stands for Gestapo', the same character dictates a final letter to his young son, and Czaka is exposed as a traitor by his tell-tale reaction to a joke in German. In arguing that 'Brecht's mark is all over *Hangmen also die*',[17] John Russell Taylor supports Lang's claim by pointing to examples of 'Brecht's savage humour', his 'teaching tone', his 'heritage of Expressionist stage-craft' (though why this should be ascribed to Brecht rather than Lang is not clear), and 'hints of the famous alienation-effect in the film's attitude to its characters'. (185) Similarly, Lyon points additionally to 'unalloyed Brecht' in the opening scene in which Heydrich confronts members of the Czech industrial and military elite, in the 'dozens of German lines spoken throughout' (67), in the original version of the 'Song of Freedom' sung by the hostages, in the hostage scenes as a whole, in the use of the names Karel Vanek (the writer who completed Jaroslav Hasek's novel *The Good Soldier Švejk* which Brecht so admired) and Gruber (which he sees as a cunning reminder of Schickelgruber), and in many other (but unspecified) aspects of the script which he says could be fruitfully mined. Ben Brewster draws attention to the 'Brechtianism' of many of the scenes, particularly the interrogation scenes,[18] while Schebera sees in the conclusion the realisation of Brecht's wish to make a *Volksfilm*, underpinned by Eisler's music. More recently, Bonnaud has unearthed a previously unknown version of the screenplay which contains 'Volksszenen' of the kind (she maintains) which Brecht mentions in his journal but which were not included in the final version of the film.[19] This may not always be Brecht at his most impressive – we can say in summary – but his fingerprints are in evidence everywhere.

I would like to suggest that the same is true of the depiction of the resistance. Here the film's anti-fascism appears to operate on two conflicting levels which are perhaps the outcome of the failed collaboration. In this sense they can be seen as reinforcing the structural dislocation caused by the collabo-rators' doomed attempts somehow to marry two very different conceptions of the film, each of them based on pure invention and almost entirely unhampered by the requirements of historical accuracy[20] – the Hollywoodesque manhunt melodrama familiar to the American audience which Lang had in mind, and the film about mass popular resistance which, with more than one eye on a post-war German audience, Brecht so clearly envisioned. On the one hand, then, the resistance as presented in the film revolves around the liberal democratic values immediately recognisable to an American audience – good versus evil, human-ism versus brutality, patriotism versus a foreign threat, freedom versus slavery, democracy versus dictatorship. Dedic and Novotny are the mouthpieces of these values, Svoboda its mainly inarticulate instrument. Mascha's description of her father as one of the 'founding fathers' of the republic both associates him at once with Thomas Masaryk and Eduard Benes and also gives him some of the authority of George Washington and Thomas Jefferson. As he is arrested he pointedly reminds his students of the American War of Independence – for a US audience a particularly pertinent example of resistance to foreign oppression. The resistance conducts its affairs in the spirit of the US Senate, taking a vote on Czaka's proposal that the assassin be surrendered to the Nazis and announcing the result as 'I think the nays have it'. All of this can be reconciled with Lang's keen nose for what the American public would – in an expression which disgusted Brecht – 'buy'. On the other hand, the fifth column in Czechoslovakia is clearly associated above all with both capitalism – the venal brewer Czaka – and with the military – the turncoat General Votruba,[21] while the spirit of patriotic resistance is best expressed in a poem written and spoken by a simple worker and subsequently sung in a courageous show of solidarity by the hostages but by what *sounds* (thanks to the soundtrack) like a mass choir. Given that Lang's own political sympathies were not notably left-wing and that he was acutely aware of what the public and the Hays Office would accept, it is surprising that these elements not only survived but played such a major part in the film. Despite what we are told by Wexley and others of Lang's determination to remove all politically sensitive references from the screenplay (e.g. we know that Brecht quite explicitly wanted the hostages to display symptoms of anti-semitism even as they were led to their deaths, and that the 'Freedom Song' was depoliticised by the replacement of the words 'comrade' (Genosse) and 'flag' (Fahne) by the less politically resonant 'friend' and 'torch'), there is also the remarkable fact that Czaka asks the resistance to convey his proposal to the Central Committee for consideration – a reminder to the knowledgeable of the leading role played in the Czech resistance by communists. Otherwise, there is no explicit reference to communism or to anti-semitism in the entire film, although Brecht had wanted to include 'a realistic depiction of Nazi anti-Semitism and anti-Communism' but this was cut, as was Heydrich's line 'Everything is contaminated with Jews and Communists'. Conscious of Hollywood's disinclination to appear philosemitic (because so many Jews enjoyed prominent positions there), Lang evidently objected to scenes showing Jews wearing the Star of David or Nazis maltreating Jewish resistance fighters. Similarly, Brecht had planned a scene at a mass grave which, in McGilligan's words, 'would have constituted the first on-screen depiction of Jewish victims of Nazi terror' but this too was cut even though it had actually been filmed *and* photographed for publicity purposes before Lang had second thoughts.[22] Even fascism is mentioned only once when a woman hostage berates Czaka as a 'fascist bloodhound'.

It can scarcely be chance – and yet hitherto it appears to have been overlooked by the critics – that the name Emil Czaka so obviously echoes that of the Czech President, Emil Hacha, who symbolised more than anyone else the humiliation of the Czech nation by its fascist occupiers. Under brutal pressure from the Nazis and, as he later said, in an attempt to save the nation by sacrificing the state, it was he who, on 15 March 1939, had signed the mendacious communiqué in which '[t]he Czechoslovak President declared that, in order to serve this object [of safeguarding calm, order and peace in the country] and to achieve ultimate pacification, he confidently placed the fate of the Czech people and country in the hands of the Führer of the German Reich'.[23] After the immediate German occupation of Czechoslovakia Hacha remained State President at the head of a collaborationist government. In a film, the main purpose of which is to call for resistance whatever the price, Hacha's name easily suggested itself for the role of the quisling. Czaka's statement of loyalty to Gruber – 'As a real Czech patriot I realise our entire future depends on unconditional collaboration with greater Germany' – encapsulates the policy identified with the Czech President.[24]

The collaborationists in Prague constantly warned the Czech population against working with the government in exile which had begun to form around former President Benes, but ordinary Czechs nevertheless offered passive resistance where they could, often in a clear manifestation of national pride. George Kennan, at that time working in the American Legation in Prague, described on 11 May 'a recent scene at the National Theater where the Prague Orchestra's rendition of Smetana's patriotic suite, *Ma Vlast* (My country), was followed by a wild ovation which lasted for a full quarter of an hour and which ended with the conductor kissing the score and holding it up before the audience'.[25] The piece was in fact subsequently banned by the Nazi occupation authorities because of its nationalist sentiments. Likewise, among the many restrictions on liberty introduced by the Nazis was a ban on booing and whistling in cinemas while German newsreels were being shown: 'Offending audiences were expelled without refunds and the cinema closed for eight days' (42). MacDonald and Kaplan include in their study a photograph of an announcement which was displayed on Prague cinema screens: 'We kindly request the audience to refrain from loud comments during the newsreel. Thank you' (42). This kind of information, in all likelihood conveyed to Brecht through the Czech government in exile which had provided the makers of the film with so much of their knowledge of events in Prague,[26] underpins the important scene where Svoboda finds temporary refuge in a Prague cinema. He joins the audience in the middle of a movie showing what the screenplay terms 'a German cultural film on the "beautiful Rhine Valley" with a German commentary and corresponding music'. What the film in fact presents is something very different, although critics appear not to have recognised this.[27] Apart from the fact that there is no German commentary, the background music which fills the Prague cinema and, by extension, the cinema in which Lang's audience sits is provided by the second symphonic poem, *The Moldau*, in Smetana's movingly patriotic cycle *My Country* (*Ma Vlast*). Given the political realities of life in Prague as noted above, the scene in the cinema can be described as unrealistic – certainly much less realistic than the later scene in which Novotny crouches over his radio listening to a broadcast of the same music at the very moment, significantly, that Heydrich's executioner seeks and finds refuge in his home, or the scene which immediately follows in which the conclusion of that same broadcast can be heard as the Novotnys eat dinner –, but in cinematographic terms it provides the perfect backdrop for the news of Heydrich's assassination as it spreads by whispers among the audience, leading to an outburst of applause and an open demonstration of the kind of patriotic enthusiasm embodied in the music. The juxtaposition of the German landscape with quintessentially Czech music sits comfortably with Hanns Eisler's conscious use of music elsewhere in *Hangmen also die* as a counterpoint to the filmic image.

Eisler's music for *Hangmen also die*, which brought him considerable recognition in Hollywood including an Oscar nomination for best film music of the year 1943,[28] was written between December 1942 and March 1943 – in other words, in the later stages of the film's making and well after the period of Brecht's most intensive involvement. These were a far cry from the ideal collaborative conditions of 'planendes Komponieren'[29] for which Eisler pleaded in his important theoretical work *Komposition für den Film*.[30] First published in 1947 in English, this was essentially written in 1942 just before he began work on the film, and it is therefore not surprising that Eisler refers explicitly to *Hangmen also die* on five occasions when providing concrete examples to illustrate his theories. Contradicting the conventional Hollywood view of film music as a matter of secondary importance, he argues for the necessity of according music a central role at *every* stage of a film's gestation: 'Der planmässige Einsatz der Musik müsste beim Drehbuch beginnen [...]'.[31] Not to do so is to risk trivialising music and reducing it to the banal and merely illustrative function familiar from any standard Hollywood production. This is, of course, not an accusation that could be levelled at Eisler's music for *Hangmen also die*, which succeeds in being 'nicht Ornament, sondern wesentlicher Träger des szenischen Sinnes'.[32] A powerful tension and even conflict between music and image is evident at important junctures. The most striking example of such musical counterpoint is the short scene lasting fourteen seconds which shows the dying Heydrich (described by Schebera as 'Höhepunkt des Films' at least as regards as the music).[33] A German fascist, Eisler notes, would have written heroic music. By contrast, Eisler chooses to associate Heydrich with the death of a rat and thus to make sure that no sense of heroism is evoked:

> Heydrich nach dem Attentat mit zerschmettertem Rückgrat im Wasserbett, Bluttransfusion. Grausige Krankenhausatmosphäre um den Sterbenden. Sichtbar wird nichts als nur das Tropfen des Blutes. Der Handlungsablauf wird gleichsam stillgestellt. Darum braucht die Szene Musik. [...] Heydrich ist der Henker, das macht die Formulierung der Musik zu einem Politikum. [...] Die Aufgabe des Komponisten bestand darin, dem Zuschauer die wahre Perspektive der Szene zu vermitteln. Die Musik muss die Bedeutungsakzente durch Roheit ersetzen. Die dramaturgische Lösung wird angezeigt durch die Assoziation: Tod einer Ratte. Brillant kreischende Sequenz, fast elegant, sehr hoch gesetzt, eine Auslegung der Redensart: auf dem letzten Loch pfeifend. Die Begleitfigur hält sich synchron an die szenische Ausgangs-

vorstellung: pizzicato in den Streichern und eine hohe Klavierfigur markieren das Tropfen des Bluts.[34]

A second example occurs at the end of the film where Daluege (the Gestapo chief) quietly reads and then signs the report on the shooting of Czaka before the last scene shows the people of Prague paying their silent respects at the mass grave of the hostages martyred by the Nazis. In stark contrast with these purely visual impressions, the orchestra and choir give full voice to 'ein Kampflied gegen die gleichförmige Szene' which expresses the indomitable will of the oppressed people; its function is 'die sinnliche Suggestion eines Unsinnlichen, der Illegalität'.[35] Schebera comments:

> Während gezeigt wird, wie die Prager Bevölkerung den erschossenen Geiseln die letzte Ehre erweist, erklingt dazu aus dem Off – und bis unter die Schlusstitel – das nun als *No surrender* camouflierte *Kominternlied* ('Brother, it is time'), das der Komponist nach Paris 1933 (in dem Film *Dans les rues*) nun auch 1943 in Hollywood 'ein-schmuggelte'.[36]

Originally written to a text by Franz Jahnke and Maxim Vallentin for the Berlin agitprop group *Das Rote Sprachrohr* which, in March 1929, had presented a programme of songs in Berlin to mark the tenth anniversary of the Communist International, this song rapidly established itself as the official *Kominternlied* even though Eisler himself was not a member of the German Communist Party. In the United States, the Comintern Song appeared in *New Masses* on 31 October 1931 as the first music to be published by the Workers' Music League, in the English translation by V. J. Jerome, one of the leading cultural function-aries of the US Communist Party. One year later the Comintern Song became the song printed on the cover of the *Red Song Book* (New York 1932). One can only speculate on how Eisler was able to 'smuggle' (Schebera's term) a song with such well-known communist associations into Lang's film – doubtless to Brecht's great satisfaction.

The dilemma produced by the murder of Heydrich – should Svoboda give himself up in order to prevent any more hostages being killed? Or should he remain undetected because he represents the will of the people and his survival is an essential expression of their victory? – is presented as divisive throughout the film and in this way reflects a conflict of opinion which, as Brecht was undoubtedly aware, did exist within the resistance both at home and in exile.[37] However, the film clearly stacks the cards against the first option. It is Jan, Mascha's fiancé, who is its first proponent. Since he is presented throughout as ineffectual and even slightly ridiculous, his belief that the assassination was a mistake because it will only lead to more Nazi terror carries little weight. This holds too for feather-brained, garrulous Aunt Ludmilla when she unsuspectingly asserts in Svoboda's presence that the assassin should give himself up 'in order to save others'. And also for Mascha, whose hysterical appeal to Svoboda's conscience almost leads her into complicity with the Gestapo, much to the displeasure of the people (as represented by the kind of threateningly ugly crowd familiar from other Lang films). The fact that it is the treacherous Czaka who argues this case to a meeting of anti-Nazi conspirators finally robs it of any validity, particularly since the other conspirators unanimously agree that in their experience no-one among the people thinks this way. This is reinforced by Dedic, the resistance leader who talks Svoboda out of his conflict of conscience after the murder by formulating the resistance's policy of 'no surrender' which is also the film's clear message.

Although the film is honest in acknowledging the conflict within the resistance,[38] Lang clearly had to find a way out of the moral dilemma which would not undermine that message. Dedic's daring plan to hand over to the Nazis not Svoboda but Czaka is therefore to be seen as a Langian stratagem whose function is 'to suppress this awkward debate, to show a people and a resistance united above and beyond, and in spite of, the split'.[39] It is a stratagem which two of the leading reviewers of the day described as 'ingenious' because of the vitality and suspense with which it infuses the final stages of the film.[40] Dedic's plan kills a number of birds with one stone: it saves Svoboda, brings the execution of hostages to an end, unifies the resistance round a common cause, and rids it at the same time of a traitor in its ranks. It is also a highly successful way of circumventing rather than resolving the divisive moral dilemma produced for the resistance by the assassination of Heydrich. However, having found its way out of one moral maze, the film avoids any exploration of the equally complex moral ambiguity involved in what is effectively Czaka's assassination. The death sentence which is passed on Czaka by the underground is simply posited – without the least sign of the kind of discussion surrounding the death of Heydrich – as just retribution for his treachery, with any unspoken suspicion that the particular means employed to engineer his arrest and cold-blooded murder might be morally unjustified seemingly being offset by the opportunity he is given to find redemption as he dies under a hail of Nazi bullets on the steps of a church. Joe Breen of the Hays Office was predictably concerned about the film's 'glorification of a lie',[41] although he did finally – and reluctantly – agree to let it pass. Nevertheless, the moral ambiguity remains and is intensified by our sharp awareness since the striking opening shots of the film that the national motto is 'Pravda vitezi' (Truth is victorious) – which is precisely what the film does *not* show. Or is it fanciful to see here an example of the invidious argument that the ends justify the means – of 'minor' lies being a necessary pre-condition for the victory of that 'greater' truth which is the cause of patriotism and anti-fascism?[42] Despite all his difficulties with Lang, it is not hard to imagine Brecht's keen interest in this dimension of the film, but, as we noted at the outset, the relief with which he subsequently turned to a new project and a more sympathetic collaborator in Feuchtwanger is no less palpable.

Notes

[1] Bertolt Brecht, *Arbeitsjournal*, Bd. 2: 1942 bis 1955, ed. Werner Hecht, Frankfurt am Main: Suhrkamp, 1974, pp.366f.

[2] In addition to their producer Arnold Pressburger, the two celebrated émigrés were joined on the film by at least 8 German émigré actors with roles of varying importance. The actors were Alexander Granach, Reinhold Schünzel, Tonio Selwart, Hans von Twardowsky, Louis Donath, Arno Frey, Felix Basch, and Poldy Dur. If Brecht had had his way, there would also have been roles for his wife, Helene Weigel, as Mrs Dvorak and for Oscar Homolka as Czaka, but Lang preferred to have his German-speaking actors playing only roles as Germans, i.e. Nazis: 'Um einem amerikanischen Publikum halbwegs klar zu machen was es fuer ein Volk bedeutet von fremdsprachigen Soldaten und Geheimpolizei beherrscht und unterdrueckt zu werden, hatte ich alle tschechischen Rollen auch die kleinste, mit amerikanischen Schauspielern besetzt, die also <u>fliessend englisch</u> sprachen. Im Gegensatz zu ihnen, im Film also im Gegensatz zum tschechoslowakischen [sic] Volk, besetzte ich alle deutschen Rollen mit deutschen Schauspielern, die wenn sie englisch – (im Film also tschechisch) – sprachen, es mit deutschem Akzent taten.' (Fritz Lang, 'Antwort zu Ihrer Frage "What was done to help Brecht to come to the United States"', Fritz Lang Collection, USC, Box 1:15). Although understandable in cinematic terms, Lang's policy was not without its own grim irony as far as the anti-fascist émigré actors who were entrusted with Nazi roles were concerned. Interestingly, much of the success of the film can be attributed to the performances of the émigrés. Even Manny Farber, who in his generally unsparing review criticised much of the acting as 'beginners' stuff', described the Nazi portraits as 'good' (Manny Farber, 'The Nazis Again', *New Republic*, 3 May 1943). Similarly, the reviewer in the *New York Times* lambasted the performance of the leading actors as 'almost uniformly inadequate' but made an explicit exception of Alexander Granach (TS, 'At the Capitol', *New York Times*, 16 April 1943). Joy Davidman went even further, noting that Granach's performance established him as 'one of the world's great actors' (Joy Davidman, 'But the people live', *New Masses*, 4 May 1943, 28f., here: 29). In his obituary to Granach, Lang paid tribute to the actor's portrayal of Inspector Gruber: '[…] Du stelltest eine Nazi-Bestie auf die Beine, die uns erschauern machte. Und wieder sagte die Industrie: "Granach as Commissar Gruber stole the show!" Und Presse und Publikum sagten es auch.' (see Fritz Lang, '[Zum Tode von Alexander Granach,] *Aufbau*, 30 March 1945). Twardowsky ('ein sensationeller Heydrich': Paul Schiller, 'Ausländer-boom in Hollywood?', *Aufbau*, 19 February 1943) and Schünzel also received well-deserved plaudits. – The idea for the film was conceived immediately after news reached Hollywood of the attempted assassination of Heydrich on 27 May 1942. Within four months a screenplay had been produced. The shooting of the film took place in November/December 1942, with the editing and other final changes occurring at the beginning of 1943. The premiere took place on 26 March 1943, almost exactly ten months after the assassination attempt on Heydrich. It is not known whether Brecht was in attendance, but it seems unlikely.

[3] David Thomson, *The New Biographical Dictionary of Film*, London: Little, Brown, 4th ed., 2002, p.491. This is not, of course, the same as saying that – despite Brecht's bitter comments in his *Arbeitsjournal* – Lang 'sold out' to Hollywood, a charge against which he vigorously defended himself.

[4] Ian Hamilton notes that their decision to collaborate in 1942 'seemed an almost perfect

match.' Cf. Ian Hamilton, *Writers in Hollywood 1915-1951*, London: Mandarin, 1991, p.246.
– The collaboration of Brecht and Lang occurred at about the same time as Heinrich Mann
was working on his novel *Lidice*. Given that the novel also deals with Heydrich's
assassination and its consequences, and that Mann's striking use of dialogue suggests he may
have been hoping to sell his work to Hollywood, it is perhaps not surprising that Willy Jasper
should speculate on Mann's possible influence on Brecht's work for *Hangmen also die* (see
Willy Jasper, 'Heinrich Mann in Hollywood', *Filmexil*, 7, December 1995, 5-8, here: 7), but
there appears to be no real evidence to support this idea.

[5] The signed agreement between Lang and Brecht, dated 14 July 1942, makes this clear. It
also shows that Brecht conceded to Lang the right to make any use he wished of the writer's
work: 'Your services shall be rendered until the completion of the story and you agree to
collaborate with me at my request and to make such changes or revisions as I may desire.
[…] I shall own and you hereby transfer and assign to me all rights of every kind in and to all
material written, prepared or suggested by you and as well to all other results and proceeds of
your services.' (Fritz Lang Collection, USC, Box 1:13).

[6] Bertolt Brecht, *Arbeitsjournal*. Band. 1: 1938 bis 1955, ed. Werner Hecht, Frankfurt am
Main: Suhrkamp, 1974, p.311 (werkausgabe edition suhrkamp). The quotation is taken from
the entry dated 5.6.42.

[7] Ibid., 328. The quotation is taken from the entry dated 27.7.42.

[8] Years later, in a letter to James K. Lyon dated 23 August 1971 (available in the Fritz Lang
Collection at USC), Lang described Brecht's account as 'very incorrect' and added: 'I
personally think that it will not be possible to write the very truth without calling Brecht
untruthful and I ask myself if the whole thing is really so important to besmirch the memory
of a fine and great writer, who maybe was carried away by his emotions.' That said, there can
be no doubt that, for example, Brecht was greatly irritated at being paid less than Wexley,
failing to secure roles for Weigel and Homolka, and not being consulted when Lang made his
final changes to the script.

[9] Jean-Louis Comolli and François Géré, 'Two Fictions concerning Hate', in: Stephen
Jenkins, ed., *Fritz Lang. The Image and the Look*, London: BFI Publishing, 1981, p.127.

[10] For example Toeplitz, cited by Jürgen Schebera, '*Henker sterben auch* oder: Vom Versuch
eines "Brechtfilms" in Hollywoods Anti-Nazi-Produktion', in: Jürgen Schebera, ed., *Henker
sterben auch (Hangmen also die). Drehbuch und Materialien zum Film*, Berlin: Henschel,
1985, p.231.

[11] Tom Gunning, *The Films of Fritz Lang. Allegories of Vision and Modernity*, London: BFI
Publishing, 2000, p.262.

[12] Bruce Cook, *Brecht in Exile*, New York: Holt, Rinehart and Winston, 1982, p.95.

[13] Cited by Patrick McGilligan, *Fritz Lang. The Nature of the Beast*, London: Faber and
Faber, 1997, p.290. – The first anti-Nazi film, Anatole Litvak's *Confessions of a Nazi Spy*,
appeared in 1939, but it was not until after the USA declared war on 7 December 1941
immediately after Pearl Harbour that Hollywood too really went to war. It has been

calculated that between 1942 and 1945 about 500 war films were made there (out of a total output of about 1700), that 300 of the 500 were specifically anti-Nazi films, and that only 30 or so of this 300 are of sufficient quality to remain of interest to film historians today. Many of the 30 were made by European émigrés with personal experience of European conditions. They included *To be or not to be, Casablanca, This Land is Mine, The Seventh Cross* as well as *Hangmen also die*.

[14] Lyon has recently argued cogently in favour of Viertel's version of events. See James K. Lyon, 'Hangmen also die', in: Jan Knopf, ed., *Brecht-Handbuch*, vol. 3: *Prosa, Filme, Drehbücher*, Stuttgart and Weimar: Metzler, 2002, pp.457-65 (here: p.458).

[15] Schebera, *Henker sterben auch*, p.226; Hamilton, *Writers in Hollywood*, p.250. Bonnaud estimates that the script comprised not 280 but about 230 pages. Cf. Irène Bonnaud, 'Neue Entdeckungen', *Dreigroschenheft. Informationen zu Bert Brecht*, 4, 1999, 15f.

[16] Once again, Lyon has argued, on the basis of a recently discovered letter from Wexley to Lang, that this script was in all probability not a secret at all but part of the evolving screenplay which was handed over to Lang at appropriate intervals. See James K. Lyon, 'Hangmen also die', 460. Lang himself has placed on record his serious doubts about whether an 'ideal script' ever existed. See Fritz Lang, 'Antwort zu Ihrer Frage "What was done to help Brecht to come to the United States"', Fritz Lang Collection, USC, 9.

[17] John Russell Taylor, *Strangers in Paradise. The Hollywood Émigrés 1933-1950*, New York: Holt, Rinehart and Winston, 1983, p.184.

[18] Ben Brewster, 'Brecht and the Film Industry', *Screen*, Winter 1975/6, 16-33, here 29.

[19] See footnote 15.

[20] For example, a crucial fact about the assassination of Heydrich was that it was the work not of the resistance in Prague but of agents trained and flown in from Britain. Less significant but another sign of the film's creative use of history is that the poet Nechval did not die as a hostage but in fact survived the war. Bernard Dick criticises the film for taking 'so many liberties with the facts' of Heydrich's assassination (see Bernard Dick, *The Star-spangled Screen. The American World War II Film*, Lexington: University Press of Kentucky, 1985, p.193), but in its defence it should be stressed that it was never the intention of the film to deliver documentary accuracy. The nearest the film comes to linking up with the historical facts of Britain's involvement in training Heydrich's assassins occurs when it is discovered that the gun found in Czaka's drawer was manufactured in England just like the one used for the assassination.

[21] Horak sees here a possible reference to General Joseph Tiso and the Slovak rump state. Jan-Christopher Horak, *Anti-Nazi-Filme der deutschsprachigen Emigration von Hollywood 1939-1945*, Münster: Maks, 2nd ed., 1985, p.333. In his review John T. McManus described Votruba as 'vengefully made up, complete with paunch and eye-patch, to resemble Jan Sirovy, the Czech militarist who formed the collaborationist government after Benes had been forced to flee his country.' Cf. John T. McManus, 'The Hangman hangs high', *PM*, 16.4.43. Joy Davidman took the same view; cf. Joy Davidman, 'But the people live', *New Masses*, 4 May 1943, 28f.

[22] The quotations are from McGilligan, *Fritz Lang*, p.296. – Among the stills which are available in the Fritz Lang Collection held by the University of Southern California is one which shows Professor Novotny in the prison camp surrounded by other prisoners, including one wearing a yellow Star of David and another dressed as a Catholic priest. Another still shows the priest about to climb on the lorry which will take a group of prisoners off to their deaths. Next to him is the Jew wearing the Star of David, followed by the worker who wrote the poem 'No surrender'. A further still shows the worker declaiming his poem before an intent Novotny, behind whom the Jew and the priest can be seen. Neither the Jew nor the Catholic priest was included in the final version of the film.

[23] Cited by Callum MacDonald and Jan Kaplan, *Prague in the Shadow of the Swastika. A History of the German Occupation 1939-1945*, London: Quartet, 1995, p.20

[24] McGilligan (*Fritz Lang*, p.298) is wrong to say that Czaka is given a thick foreign accent. Like all the other Czech characters in the film – and in line with a decision by Lang which was, as noted earlier, not to Brecht's liking because it meant Weigel could not be given the role of Mrs Dvorak – Czaka unmistakably has an American accent.

[25] Cited by MacDonald and Kaplan, *Prague in the Shadow of the Swastika*, p.41. Subsequent quotations from the same source in this paragraph are given in brackets.

[26] Brecht and Lang doubtless received much valuable information from the film's producer Arnold Pressburger, described by John T. McManus at the time (cf. footnote 21) as 'a Czech democrat who has had the full confidence and cooperation of the Benes family and their official records in preparing the production.' John Wexley reportedly received from the Czech government in exile copies of the leaflets distributed among Czech factory workers, among them the one used in the film showing a tortoise urging workers to slow down production. Brecht was clearly so delighted by this that it inspired a poem, 'Im Zeichen der Schildkröte.' See Bertolt Brecht, *Die Gedichte*, Frankfurt am Main: Suhrkamp, 1981, pp.855f.

[27] Cf. Lotte H. Eisner, *Fritz Lang*, London: Secker and Warburg, 1976, p.224. – The name of Mrs Dvorak, the maltreated but solidly anti-collaborationist grocer, is surely meant to remind us of that other patriotic composer, Anton Dvorak.

[28] The Oscar went in the event to Alfred Newman for his music for *Song of Bernadette*. The money which Eisler earned for his contribution to *Hangmen also die* allowed him to buy a house of his own in Pacific Palisades.

[29] Hanns Eisler, *Komposition für den Film*, Berlin: Henschel, 1949, pp.86f.

[30] See ibid., 102f.

[31] Ibid., 16f.

[32] Ibid., 29

[33] Jürgen Schebera, *Hanns Eisler im USA-Exil 1938-1948*, Meisenheim: Hain, 1978, p.137.

[34] Eisler, *Komposition für den Film*, pp.32f.

[35] Both quotations in this paragraph: ibid., 30

[36] Jürgen Schebera, *Eisler. Eine Biographie in Texten, Bildern und Dokumenten*, Mainz, London: Schott, 1998, p.184

[37] Benes's government in exile favoured a policy of pin-prick resistance, avoiding the kind of high-profile actions which it feared were bound to provoke Nazi terror. The attack on Heydrich's life which it planned and carried out was a break with this policy and was undertaken under pressure from the British. It led to the kind of internal divisions, notably among the resistance in Czechoslovakia, which are reflected in the film. See Callum MacDonald, *The Killing of SS Obergruppenführer Reinhard Heydrich*, London: Macmillan, 1990 (Papermac).

[38] Of course, it also reflects the conflict in US society between isolationists and those who pressed for US involvement in the antifascist war. This is echoed in Dedic's frantic appeal to a temporarily misguided Mascha as she tries to make her way to a meeting with the Gestapo: 'This is war, and you're in it!'

[39] Comolli and Géré, 'Two Fictions concerning Hate', p.133

[40] TS, 'At the Capitol', *New York Times*, 16 April 1943; Manny Farber, 'The Nazis Again', *New Republic*, 3 May 1943.

[41] Peter Bogdanovich, *Fritz Lang in America*, New York: Praeger, 1969, p.62. – The conspiracy among Prague's citizens to bring about Czaka's downfall is an inversion of the situation in Lang's *Fury* (1936) where the citizens of a small American town seek to provide themselves with alibis for the time when they were part of the mob which attempted to lynch the central character, Joe (played by Spencer Tracy), for a crime he did not commit. In this case their stories are exposed as (self-serving) lies and Joe's innocence is confirmed. In *Hangmen also die*, by contrast, the 'innocent' Czaka is found guilty and condemned to death, while the citizens' lies are in effect condoned.

[42] A similar ambiguity is apparent in the depiction of Gruber – a corrupt, dissolute, brutal, and ruthless agent of the Gestapo, whose vitality and quick intelligence in pursuit of *the truth* about Heydrich's murder paradoxically make him strangely attractive, especially set beside the characters with whom he has most to do – the mendacious and repulsive Czaka and the somewhat anaemic Svoboda, Mascha and Jan.

David Midgley

Döblin in Hollywood

Exile in Los Angeles from 1940 to 1945 was a period of isolation and privation for Alfred Döblin, following the shock of having to flee from the German invasion of France. It was also during this time that he surprised his fellow exiles by converting to Catholicism. This paper assesses the relationship between his long-term intellectual and spiritual concerns on the one hand, and his personal and cultural situation on the other, in the light of recent publications. The factors which prompted him to adopt the Catholic faith point back to what he individually, and his family collectively, had experienced in France between 1933 and 1940 rather than to their situation in California.

In the spirit of this volume I shall try here to assess the 'reality' of Alfred Döblin's life in California, both in external, practical terms, and in terms of what he was doing with his life at the time. Döblin lived in Hollywood – from October 1940 until September 1945 – and was initially employed to write film scenarios for Metro-Goldwyn-Mayer. But as Klaus Weissenberger established when he investigated Döblin's circumstances in the 1970s, the scenarios he wrote were unlikely to appeal to Hollywood film producers because, like much of his later fiction, they tended to focus on anguished relations between husbands and wives or fathers and sons, ending in a death.[1] Döblin never established a reputation in North America that came anywhere near the standing he had enjoyed in Germany before 1933. After a fee of $500 received on arriving in New York in 1940 – not for any work of fiction, but for a small anthology, *The Living Thoughts of Confucius*, which was published in New York, London and Buenos Aires during the early 1940s[2] – the only significant royalties he appears to have received during the period in question are $255 from South America, for the Spanish translation of *Land ohne Tod*. This sum was the equivalent at that stage of his life of two months' living costs; and it arrived very late in the day, in September 1944.[3] His financial situation rapidly deteriorated and his social contacts seem to have been largely restricted to the company of other German exiles and a few benefactors. Along with Heinrich Mann, Döblin clearly belonged among the most wretched of the German exiles in California.

The more intriguing question about Döblin's period in California, however, and one that is more difficult to answer, is how he was positioning himself intellectually at the time. He evidently dedicated a lot of this time to the writing of some texts which have only relatively recently become the subject of sustained critical attention, and it was also during this period that he converted to Catholicism – to the puzzlement and annoyance of some of his fellow writers. What I therefore wish to do is firstly to bring the record up to date on what we know about Döblin's circumstances during this time, and secondly to consider how best to make sense of his intellectual orientation at this stage of his career.

The recently published second volume of Döblin's letters does not radically alter the picture of his life in exile, but it does firm up the evidence on some aspects of it.[4] Döblin fled from France in the summer of 1940, as it fell to the German army, with his wife Erna and their youngest son Stefan. They left behind two other sons, Wolfgang and Klaus, who were serving in the French army. They gained entry to the USA on an Emergency Visa, as 'politically endangered' persons, and on the basis of financial guarantees from their eldest son Peter (who had trained as a printer and was working in New York) and an old friend, Arthur Rosin, the former President of the Darmstädter Bank (who had moved to New York in 1936), with MGM providing the offer of employment in the form of a one-year contract.

Döblin's first impressions of Los Angeles, which he conveyed in a letter to Arthur Rosin and his wife Elvira in October 1940, show that he had not lost his sense of humour. He described it as more of a vicinity than a city, consisting of scattered settlements with oilfields and garbage dumps in between, where pedestrians had died out and people came into the world as motorists.[5] In a second letter he added, '¼ Stunde nach rechts und links von uns beginnt die Wüste'.[6] Remarks that he makes here and elsewhere in his correspondence make it clear that this famous denizen of Berlin would have felt much more at home in New York. (An additional reason would have been the fact that it was in New York that Yolla Niclas, the young woman with whom Döblin had enjoyed a particularly profound friendship since the early 1920s, had settled after similarly fleeing before the German invasion of France.[7])

The family quickly found an apartment at Cherokee Avenue, Hollywood, in the same block where the theatre director Leopold Jessner and the actor Alexander Granach were living, which was convenient for young Stefan to attend a nearby school, but they found the rent high at $65 a month. They still had debts to repay in connection with their journey from France, and they soon found it necessary to look for accommodation in the $40 range.[8] During their first twelve months in Los Angeles they moved steadily down market, first to Genesse Avenue in West Hollywood, and then back to North Citrus Avenue, close to their first address. There was the added cost and inconvenience of hopping across the Mexican border in March 1941, which was a common way of meeting the formal requirements for acquiring a permanent immigration visa: that procedure alone cost them $750. When the contract with MGM was not renewed, Döblin drew unemployment benefit of $18 a week for the six-month period to which he was entitled,[9] and was otherwise dependent on the charitable funds that had been set up to assist writers in exile. In the course of 1942 he complains increasingly often of isolation and straitened circumstances, and by May 1943 he is writing to Hermann Kesten that only here in California is he experiencing 'waschechtes Exil', 'zehnmal präciser als in Paris'.[10] When the war came to an end, Döblin was prompt to seek an opportunity to return to France.

Ludwig Marcuse's autobiography *Mein zwanzigstes Jahrhundert*, published in 1960, has not lost its value as a source of vivid accounts of the lives that the erstwhile great literati of Weimar Germany led, stranded and unknown in the California of the early 1940s – even if the reader needs to be wary of the aspect of self-stylisation that enters into some of his descriptions. Of Döblin, whom he recalled as 'the most amusing sceptic' of the 1920s, Marcuse notes, 'Er schrieb, lachte, riß die besten Berliner Witze – und ging, hinter meinem Rücken, zu den Jesuiten'.[11] The personal note in 'hinter meinem Rücken' relates to the fact that when Marcuse had published his novel on Ignatius de Loyola in 1935, Döblin, whose sense of Jewish solidarity had led him to become involved with the League for Jewish Colonisation from 1934 to 1937, had publicly criticised Marcuse's choice of subject matter, apparently implying that for a Jew to focus his efforts on the founder of the Jesuit Order at that time amounted to a kind of betrayal. And then, at the celebration held in a small Hollywood theatre to mark his sixty-fifth birthday on 14 August 1943, Döblin had let it be known that he had acquired a new religious outlook: 'Zu seinem Fünfundsechzigsten […] sprach der Jubelgreis eigensinnig von seinem Gott, mit tausend Zungen, von denen wir nicht eine verstanden: aber Jehova war es bestimmt nicht mehr'.[12] Again, Marcuse's words have a background resonance to which I shall return. What he knew when he wrote his memoir of that occasion was that Döblin, after receiving formal instruction from Jesuit priests throughout 1941, had converted to Catholicism on 30 November of that year, just over a year after arriving in California. It is the significance of that act in Döblin's life that is my main concern in this paper.

It has been suggested that Döblin kept his conversion a secret in order to avoid offending his Jewish benefactors,[13] and there is of course some plausibility in that. Döblin states explicitly in a letter to the Rosins of 17 September 1941, 'Würde ich mit irgendwelcher christlicher Haltung und entsprechenden Worten an die Öffentlichkeit treten, und gar jetzt, so würde das ein "Verrat" sein, nämlich an dem, was ich ja auch bin, am Jüdischen'.[14] The word 'Verrat' appears here in inverted commas because Döblin was responding to the indignation the Rosins had evidently shown when Peter Döblin had made them aware of the family's new-found religious convictions, and in that context Döblin is keen to emphasise the continuity in his own concerns with spiritual and metaphysical issues: 'Es ist nichts weiter als meine (oder im Grunde die allgemeine) ewige Unterhaltung über das "Ich" und die "Natur"'.[15] In the same letter, and again in a later letter to Peter Döblin,[16] he distances himself expressly from Judaism on the grounds that it is a purely national religion. (Generally he recalled his own upbringing as having been Jewish in a merely formal sense, and as an assimilated Jew in Berlin he had been content to have his children baptised Protestant.) But there is also evidence that Döblin remained self-conscious about his decision and the impact it was likely to make on those who knew him well from former times – his fellow exiles. The manner in which Thomas Mann records the event is particularly revealing in this regard, both because his testimony is likely to be highly reliable, and because it registers an unforeseen change in Döblin's whole outlook and an apologetic note in the way he was speaking about it. On 20 August 1943 Mann wrote to Wilhelm Herzog:

> Die Dankesworte des Jubilars waren bemerkenswert. Der Relativismus sei der Ruin, sagte er. Heute gelte es, 'das Absolute' anzuerkennen. Nachher, im Gespräch mit mir, ging er weiter und erklärte: 'Die Gêne, von Gott zu sprechen, die wird einem ausge-trieben!'[17]

He was evidently conscious of documenting a significant event by quoting Döb-lin in this way, as well as of having to hide his own embarrassment, because he continues, 'So steht es. Ich habe mich noch mit meiner protestantisch-huma-nistischen Tradition zu drücken gesucht und gesagt, Katholiken und Juden hätten es leichter. Aber so steht es.' There is at least an implication here that Döblin had kept his new-found convictions to himself in order to avoid causing embarrassment to fellow exiles who he knew would be unsympathetic towards those convictions, as indeed other exiles were careful to avoid giving public voice to some of their deepest convictions.

One of these was of course Brecht, whose reservations about Commu-nism are known to us chiefly through the notes Walter Benjamin took when he visited Brecht in Denmark, and who refrained from publishing his responses to the formalism debate that raged in the pages of the Moscow-based journal *Das Wort* in the late 1930s, evidently for fear that they would be received as a breach of solidarity.[18] Brecht's extensive response to Döblin's sixty-fifth birth-day speech is interesting because it plays precisely on this note of solidarity amongst exiles and the sense of betrayal to a common cause. Brecht and his wife Helene Weigel had organised the celebration;[19] and since Döblin's ar-rangement with MGM had come to an end the previous autumn, Brecht was also among those contributing to Döblin's regular income.[20] So his personal in-volvement may have contributed to the note of irritation he strikes in his *Arbeitsjournal*, recording that formalities had concluded with Döblin speaking 'gegen moralischen relativismus und für feste maße religiöser art, womit er die irreligiösen gefühle der meisten feiernden verletzte'.[21] He continues, 'ein fatales gefühl ergriff die rationaleren zuhörer, etwas von dem verständnisvollen entset-zen über einen mitgefangenen, der den folterungen erlegen ist und nun aussagt.' Whether we allow ourselves to be reminded at this point of the famous recanta-tion scene in Brecht's *Leben des Galilei*, or of the powerful anti-clerical impulse that had been a consistent feature of Brecht's writings since the First World War, a later passage from the same note gives a very clear sense of the terms in which he had interpreted this moment as a betrayal:

> als döblin anfing zu beschreiben, wie mit vielen anderen schreibern auch er mitschuldig wurde an dem aufstieg der nazis ('sagten nicht Sie, herr thomas mann, er sei wie ein bruder, ein schlechter natürlich', fragte er nach der ersten reihe herunter) und die frage entschlossen aufwarf, warum denn, glaubte ich für minuten kindlich, er werde jetzt fortfahren: 'weil ich die verbrechen der herrschenden vertuscht, die be-drückten entmutigt, die hungernden mit gesängen abgespeist habe' usw. aber er fuhr

nur verstockt, unbußfertig, ohne reue fort: 'weil ich nicht gott suchte'.[22]

Brecht looks for extenuating circumstances in Döblin's personal situation — the loss of two sons in France, the loss of a readership for his works, and the onset of angina pectoris ('die große bekehrerin') — but the tenor of his remarks is clearly akin to what is implied in his Bavarian homeland to this day by the expression, 'Den haben sie katholisch gemacht!' The dissenter, the radical questioner, has succumbed to intimidation and swallowed his awkward questions.

Even Robert Minder, the French scholar who appears to have been as close to Döblin as anyone, both before and after his period in California, conveys the impression that he finds Döblin's conversion not quite intelligible when he speaks of him laying down his arms in the face of the superior debating skills of the Jesuit fathers:

> Entscheidend für die Konversion wurden hochgebildete Jesuitenpater in Los Angeles, unter deren Leitung Döblin Thomas von Aquin und die Kirchenväter und immer wieder das Neue Testament las. Sie sprachen deutsch und waren große Dialektiker, Florettfechter höchsten Ranges. Der geborene Polemiker staunte, focht und streckte die Waffen.[23]

Walter Muschg, the first editor of Döblin's collected works, who generally gives positive emphasis to the religious dimension of Döblin's writings, similarly speaks of Döblin's 'capitulation' before God.[24]

In his autobiographical narrative *Schicksalsreise* (1949), Döblin records with evident irritation that the news of his conversion generated a widespread preconception of him in Germany after 1945 as someone who had retreated into mysticism,[25] and the reviews of his religious writings in the late 1940s confirm the sense of a sharp divide between those who were sympathetic to his repudiation of the uncertainties of modernist agnosticism and those who were not, as well as displaying some stereotypical resentments towards the exile who had returned to Germany with the French occupying forces.[26] The question of precisely how Döblin's conversion should be interpreted in relation to his life and works has also continued to excite scholarly controversy in recent years. There is no scope here to give a comprehensive survey of the relevant secondary literature. What I shall try to do is summarise the main points of contention, drawing on what seems to me the most fruitful research on the topic,[27] before adding an observation of my own on the factors that have a bearing on Döblin's decision.

The continuity in Döblin's spiritual concerns, on which he insisted in his letter to the Rosins in 1941, is easily demonstrated – but its character is manifestly eclectic. Motifs from Taoism and Hinduism, from Expressionist utopianism and Romantic nature philosophy, can be found worked into Döblin's writings from the period before 1910 to the period after 1933; and anyone who has tried to give a serious interpretation of *Berlin Alexanderplatz* has had to wrestle with the re-working of motifs from the Old Testament that the text contains, and with the relationship in which they stand to the intimations of a mystical awareness of the natural world.[28] In *Unser Dasein* (1933) Döblin attempted an integrated discursive account of these spiritual concerns which he had dealt with sporadically in his narrative works, emphasising the senses in which human beings are products of the material world and subject to the cycles of creation and destruction that characterise the nature of competing life systems, but also insisting on the underlying connectedness of all material phenomena, of which human beings can only be dimly aware.[29] The philosophical vocabulary with which he addresses the relationship between human consciousness and the natural world is not rigorously defined, and he uses the word 'Ich' to refer both to the individual who experiences the world and to the notion of an essential 'Ursinn' inherent in material reality.[30] But the dominant purpose apparent in *Unser Dasein* might be summed up as keeping open the possibility of speculating on the ultimate design ('Ursinn') at work in the universe, while also taking full cognisance of what scientific analysis has demonstrated about its nature and functions. Döblin goes so far here as to consider how he might respond to his own observations about the nature of being *if he were* a believer,[31] but he also builds into his text the mocking voice of a 'Spottvogel' which intermittently deflates the pretension to high spiritual seriousness.[32]

Döblin's fellow exiles who remembered him from the Weimar period as a sceptic were therefore not wrong, and for a period after 1933 his treatment of spiritual themes continued to be characterised by ironic and burlesque effects. When he imagines a Babylonian god coming to earth and experiencing the destructive potential of humanity – including the persecution of the Jews of Strasbourg in the fourteenth century and the situation in Europe in the 1930s – as he does in *Babylonische Wandrung* (1934), then he incorporates into that god's encounters with humanity both theological discussions and an episode in which a satanic tempter seeks to persuade him of the inherent worthlessness of the world; but the latter episode comes across as a *parody* of the temptation of Christ within the context of a satirical narrative in the spirit of Voltaire.[33] And when he treats the fate of the Jesuit colonies of South America in his *Amazonas* trilogy, on which he worked between 1935 and 1938 (and which reflects, amongst other things, his reading of Kierkegaard in Paris), his dominant purpose appears to have been to assess the project of an ideal Christian state as an emanation of European civilisation which ultimately decays into a repressive state.[34] A significant change in Döblin's approach to such issues occurs after 1940. Thomas Isermann has noted an important indicator of this: in the later fiction – which includes the last volume of *November 1918* (1942-43) as well as *Hamlet* (1945-46) – a moment of crisis *initiates* the plot, whereas the earlier plots had tended always to *lead up to* a crisis which is often peremptorily resolved.[35] (Isermann's thesis is concerned with the manner in which Döblin, at all stages of his career, tends to resolve the intellectual aporias he encounters in his contemplation of existential issues by resorting to narration or the rhetorical devices of mystical tradition. He discreetly passes over Döblin's act of conversion as an essentially private matter.[36])

The most thorough investigation of the shifts in Döblin's attitudes to religious matters remains Helmuth Kiesel's book *Literarische Trauerarbeit. Das Exil- und Spätwerk Alfred Döblins* (1986). Kiesel acknowledges the strength of the association between Döblin's writings and prayer, from his earliest prose sketch of 1896 onwards, but in the broad sense of a communion with and celebration of nature; and he points out that, for all the interest Döblin shows in speculative nature philosophy in the 1920s, he still rejects the notion of a creator God in *Unser Dasein*.[37] While there is an increase of specifically Christian motifs in Döblin's fiction of the 1930s, particularly in the *Amazonas* trilogy, that too stops short of evidence of any doctrinal commitment.[38] Kiesel argues that the dominant trend in Döblin's writings after 1933 is the working-through of grief (*Trauerarbeit*), and that the reflections on suffering and the possibility of redemption which are central to his later Catholicism represent an intensification of that process. Döblin's attitude to the crucifixion in particular undergoes a significant change around 1940. Whereas he had previously written of it as a deeply moving symbol of human suffering (Christ the *Schmerzensmann* as he had witnessed it in Veit Stoß' carving of the crucified Christ in Cracow in 1924[39] and again in the religious shops of Paris in the 1930s[40]), in 1940, while fleeing the advancing German army, he appears to have begun to see it as embodying the hope of salvation.[41]

I say 'appears', because the passage from Döblin's *Schicksalsreise* which describes his experiences as a fugitive, separated from his wife and family, and which he wrote while he was living in Los Angeles, still bears the traces of a self-conscious scepticism. Kiesel speaks of three distinct perspectives built into the narrative of *Schicksalsreise*. One of these is that of a distraught and mentally disorientated man who is experiencing moments of apparent visionary coherence which have no rational foundation; another is that of the scientific mind trained to recognise such experiences as a pathological phenomenon; and the third is that of the writer engaged, here as elsewhere, in a search for the connectedness of all natural phenomena in quasi-mystical terms.[42] All three perspectives are particularly evident in the passage where Döblin describes his meditation on the crucifixion in the cathedral of Mende in Southern France, where he briefly stayed in a refugee camp. Döblin begins the section with reflections about the state of mind in which cumulative mishaps of a quite random nature – separation from his family, the inaccessibility of his luggage, a taxi driver who swindles him – are interpreted as if there were a systematic connection between them; he labels this 'Beziehungswahn', a mild form of paranoia. He then rehearses thoughts that are familiar from earlier writings about the sense in which individuality is rooted in the realm of nature with all its ramifications; and finally he gives us his reflections on the crucified Christ, which allude to the possibility of salvation, a doctrine familiar to him in abstract terms from the years he had spent in Paris, and which he discusses at this point only as a hypothetical possibility:

> Es heißt, wir würden so erlöst. Auf die Erde und unsere Existenz fiele durch dieses
> Bild mehr Licht als von den Sonnen aller Sternensysteme.
> Während ich sitze, fällt mir ein:
> Wenn dies stimmt, wenn dies richtig wäre – und was nutzt der bloße Glaube? Wahr-
> heit muß in der Sache liegen – wenn dies richtig wäre, so erhielte die menschliche
> Existenz überhaupt erst einen Boden.[43]

He continues with words which convey that yearning for the absolute that
Thomas Mann recalled from his speech in 1943:

> Unsere Existenz würde erst eine Wahrheit erhalten, ich meine: sie würde 'bewahrt',
> gehalten, gesichert. So ist sie nur Zufall, Fall ins Leere. [...] Eine Welt ohne dieses,
> ohne einen Inhalt dieser Art, ohne einen Jesusgedanken kann nicht von einer wahr-
> haftigen Urmacht geschaffen sein. Sie wäre nur eine Farce.[44]

In a later passage Döblin emphasises that the quest for salvation through Christ
represents the only conceivable way of looking for a principle of justice at work
in the world that would compensate for the immense suffering it contains.[45]

Clearly what he experienced in Mende remained of immense importance
to Döblin. But his published account of that experience contains a multiplicity
of perspectives determined by the various dimensions of his earlier life, as well
as by considerations of how to present it to others, be they believers or sceptics.
His account is also explicit about his own self-doubt after the event, about his
inner rebellion against his new-found conviction, and about his recurrent impulse to diagnose the experience as a nervous breakdown ('Klaps'), as well as
about how the impulses of his reflections in Mende will not subsequently let
him go: 'mein eigener Hohn bringt die Gedanken nicht zum Schweigen'.[46] The
step from the experience of Mende to his decision to adopt the Catholic faith in
Los Angeles is again not an automatic one; it involves a process of intellectual
deliberation as well as intuitive conviction.[47] Contrary to the impression left by
Robert Minder and Döblin's fellow exiles, he evidently approached the formalities of catechism in 1941, not in a spirit of submission, but in a state of advanced intellectual preparedness.[48]

In addition to his autobiographical reconstruction of his experiences and
reflections, Döblin has left us the record of his intellectual reorientation in the
form of two religious dialogues. *Der unsterbliche Mensch*, which was largely
written in 1942 and provides the most direct evidence of his adoption of Catholic precepts, was the first new text he published after the Second World War, in
1946. *Der Kampf mit dem Engel*, which testifies specifically to his assimilation
of the thinking of St. Thomas Aquinas,[49] was completed in 1951. Both texts
have the character of 'spiritual exercises', even if they also contain moments of
low irony and urbane self-deprecation characteristic of Döblin's style elsewhere, and it requires specialist knowledge and aptitude to assess the precise
nature of their relationship to Catholic orthodoxy – which is why Friedrich
Emde's study, *Alfred Döblin. Sein Weg zum Christentum* (1999), is to be welcomed, even if it tends, as its title suggests, to treat Döblin's earlier writings as

evidence of a progress towards his later Christian commitment. In *Der unsterb-liche Mensch* an older speaker defends his Christian beliefs and practices against a younger man whose anti-religious attitudes are akin to those that Döb-lin had himself displayed in earlier years. In this way, Döblin can both voice critical misgivings about Christianity and mount a defence against them: he disarms the accusation of irrationality by pointing to the unexamined assump-tions that science is also bound to make, and he counters the objection that the presence of suffering and evil in the world discredits the notion of a benevolent creator by distinguishing between the suffering that is a consequence of natural processes and the suffering that is brought about by the exercise of human choice. In these ways he develops arguments which are consistent with Catholic dogma as well as with his own earlier cosmological speculations.[50] While Döb-lin is fervent about his Christian commitment, he does not come across as dog-matically Catholic in his expression of that commitment. It even appears that the arguments Döblin favours when justifying his own position – giving promi-nence to a conception of divine 'justice', for example, rather than the principle of divine 'mercy' – belong to the medieval canon of Christian doctrine rather than the teachings of twentieth-century theologians.[51] In this perspective, Döb-lin's conversion looks much less like an appeal for spiritual support in the dis-tressing circumstances of exile, and more like a gradual assimilation of theo-logical arguments which satisfy his long-term intellectual quest for an accept-able account of the relation between the human will and the realm of nature.[52]

Emde's research shows how it was possible for Döblin to reconcile his adoption of the Catholic faith with his earlier spiritual concerns, but not, as he acknowledges, that the Catholicism automatically followed from those con-cerns.[53] The centrality of the crucifixion to Döblin's reflections since the sum-mer of 1940 clearly made it natural for him to seek affiliation with some form of Christianity rather than the Judaism in which he had been brought up, and which he would have found equally well represented in Los Angeles. But by his own account it was a further element of chance – an encounter with a German art historian from a Westphalian Catholic background – that led to his accep-tance into the Church of the Blessed Sacrament in Hollywood.[54] Of his dealings with the local priests Döblin says that he was reassured by their warmth and humanity, and by the sense of being admitted into an age-old community, but also by the knowledge that they belonged to the Jesuit order that he had researched in Paris for his *Amazonas* trilogy.[55] It is here that we begin to sense the personal and private factors which must have had a bearing, alongside the intellectual and public ones, on Döblin's decision to join the Catholic Church.

In the scholarly discussions of Döblin's conversion, which have under-standably focused primarily on his intellectual and literary writings, relatively little attention is given to the fact that when he was baptised in 1941 he was not alone. His wife Erna, who appears to have adopted the language of piety very readily in her letters, and two of their sons – Stefan, the youngest, in Los

Angeles; Peter, the eldest, in Philadelphia – converted with him. Even if the precise nature of the discussions within the family circle that led to this collective decision must remain a matter for conjecture, there is at least an indication here of the sense in which private circumstances supplied a practical and ethical dimension to the religious commitment into which the Döblins entered. The family had taken French citizenship in 1936. That carried with it an implication that the sons would serve in the French army;[56] and one of them, Wolfgang, was lost in the defence of France against the Germans in 1940, as the family learned only at the time of the liberation in 1945. (Wolfgang Döblin appears to have taken his own life rather than fall into the hands of the Germans, and the guilt that Döblin may have felt towards him is commonly taken into account in interpretations of his *Hamlet* novel.) Another son, Klaus, managed to survive in France, initially working with the Jewish underground, and the family only met up with him again in 1945. The sons who had effectively grown up in France – Wolfgang, Klaus and Stefan – adopted French names: Vincent, Claude and Etienne; and when Stefan's time came to enlist in 1945, it was in the French army that he chose to serve. Döblin himself served in the French Ministry of Information (under Jean Giraudoux) for several months during the early stages of the war, and eagerly returned to French service when the war ended. It is also apparent from his letters how much more at home Döblin had become in the French language since 1933 than he was ever to become in English.

These personal connections to France do not in themselves provide an adequate explanation for why the family converted to Catholicism in 1941, but they do surely constitute a set of circumstances which made the adoption of Catholicism a more natural step for the family to take. When I speak of an ethical dimension to their collective act of religious commitment, I am thinking of their decision not so much as a commitment to France, but as a commitment to what they had experienced as a family in France, including their separation in chaotic and highly distressing circumstances in the summer of 1940. In the context of the memories they would have shared as a family, Döblin's own new-found religious conviction would have provided a central focus for the attempt to maintain a common sense of order and purpose in their lives together in America.

The reorientation of Döblin's intellectual outlook, at which he worked while he was in Los Angeles, essentially consists in the resolution of some cosmological problems which had concerned him for some time, stimulated by his reflections on the crucifixion in Mende in 1940. But beyond this quest for intellectual coherence which provided the rationale for his religious conversion, there appears also to have been a need to achieve cohesion in his private life which prompted him, with his family, specifically to adopt the Catholic faith in 1941. Perhaps an awareness of that need is as close as we can get to the lived reality behind Döblin's post-war publications.

Notes

[1] Klaus Weissenberger, 'Alfred Döblin im Exil. Eine Entwicklung vom historischen Relativismus zum religiösen Bekenntnis', *Colloquia Germanica*, 8 (1974), 37-51 (here 46).

[2] Klaus Weissenberger, 'Alfred Döblin', in: John M. Spalek and Joseph Strelka, eds, *Deutsche Exilliteratur seit 1933* I: *Kalifornien*, Bern and Munich: Francke, 1976, pp.298-322 (here p.305). For details of Döblin's publications, see Louis Huguet, *Bibliographie Alfred Döblin*, Berlin and Weimar: Aufbau, 1972.

[3] Alfred Döblin, *Briefe II*, ed. Helmut F. Pfanner, Düsseldorf and Zurich: Walter, 2001, p.183.

[4] Ibid. Of particular interest to Feuchtwanger scholars is the rather macabre letter Döblin sent to Feuchtwanger on the occasion of the latter's 60th birthday in July 1944: p.181f.

[5] Alfred Döblin, *Briefe*, ed. Heinz Graber, Olten and Freiburg: Walter, 1970, p.242.

[6] Ibid., p.244.

[7] Cf. 'Döblin-Chronik', in: *Alfred Döblin 1878 · 1978*, Marbach: Ausstellungskatalog des Deutschen Literaturarchivs im Schiller-Nationalmuseum, 1978, pp.23, 47.

[8] Döblin, *Briefe*, p.257. According to Jochen Meyer's 'Döblin-Chronik' (loc. cit., p.44) their actual rent at 1347 North Citrus Avenue was $35 per month.

[9] Ibid., p.263.

[10] *Briefe II*, p.170.

[11] Ludwig Marcuse, *Mein zwanzigstes Jahrhundert*, Munich: Paul List, 1960, p.277f.

[12] Ibid., p.278.

[13] Cf. Helmuth Kiesel, *Literarische Trauerarbeit. Das Exil- und Spätwerk Alfred Döblins*, Tübingen: Niemeyer, 1986, p.188; Weissenberger, 'Alfred Döblin im Exil', p.47. Conversely, Anthony Riley, in his notes to Alfred Döblin, *Schicksalsreise. Bericht und Bekenntnis*, Solothurn and Düsseldorf: Walter, 1993, p.463f, has drawn attention to evidence that the Döblin family found it necessary to conceal their Jewish origins in order to avoid the effects of anti-Semitism within the Catholic community they had joined.

[14] Döblin, *Briefe*, p.258.

[15] Ibid. Döblin is alluding in particular to his earlier publications *Das Ich über der Natur* (1927) and *Unser Dasein* (1933).

[16] Ibid., p.274f.

[17] Thomas Mann, *Briefe 1937-1947*, Frankfurt am Main: S. Fischer, 1963, p.330; quoted in Kiesel, p.189.

[18] See Walter Benjamin, *Versuche über Brecht*, Frankfurt am Main: Suhrkamp, 1981, pp.165-71; cf. also David Midgley, 'Svendborg 1938: a historical sketch', in Ronald Speirs, ed., *Brecht's Poetry of Political Exile*, Cambridge: Cambridge University Press, 2000, pp.16-28 (here p.22f).

[19] Cf. James K. Lyon, *Brecht in America*, Princeton: Princeton University Press, 1980, p.256.

[20] Döblin, *Briefe*, p.284.

[21] Bertolt Brecht, *Arbeitsjournal*, Frankfurt am Main: Suhrkamp, 1974, vol.2, p.389. Brecht voiced the same sentiment in a sharply satirical poem with the title 'Peinlicher Vorfall': *Gesammelte Werke*, Frankfurt am Main: Suhrkamp, 1967, vol. X, p.861f.

[22] Ibid.; cf. Kiesel, p.188f.

[23] Robert Minder, 'Alfred Döblin zwischen Osten und Westen', in: R.M., *Dichter in der Gesellschaft*, Frankfurt am Main: Insel, 1966, pp.155-90 (here p.181).

[24] Walter Muschg, *Die Zerstörung der deutschen Literatur*, Bern: Francke, 1958, p.132.

[25] Döblin, *Schicksalsreise*, pp.348-51; cf. *Autobiographische Schriften und letzte Aufzeichnungen*, Olten and Freiburg: Walter, 1980, pp.408-11.

[26] See Ingrid Schuster and Ingrid Bode, eds, *Alfred Döblin im Spiegel der zeitgenössischen Kritik*, Bern and Munich: Francke, 1973), pp.387-98 and 417-24; also Anthony W. Riley, 'Nachwort des Herausgebers', in Döblin, *Schicksalsreise*, pp.484-91.

[27] The publications which I cite most frequently, and which provide further bibliographical references are Hellmuth Kiesel, *Literarische Trauerarbeit*; Thomas Isermann, *Der Text und das Unsagbare. Studien zu Religionssuche und Werkpoetik bei Alfred Döblin*, Idstein: Schulz-Kirchner, 1989; and Friedrich Emde, *Alfred Döblin. Sein Weg zum Christentum*, Tübingen: Gunter Narr, 1999.

[28] The fullest attempt to do justice to this dimension of *Berlin Alexanderplatz* remains Otto Keller, *Döblins Montageroman als Epos der Moderne*, Munich: Wilhelm Fink, 1980.

[29] Döblin, *Unser Dasein*, Olten and Freiburg: Walter, 1964; see esp. pp.165, 168-75.

[30] Cf. Emde, pp.172-82, where Döblin's use of the term 'Ich' is analysed with reference to his essay 'Das Ich über der Natur' of 1927.

[31] Döblin, *Unser Dasein*, p.55: 'Schrecklich und unheimlich der Satz: Es ist Sein. Unheimlich der Satz: Es ist Sein im Ich. / Wäre ich ein Frommer, ein Gläubiger, so würde ich verzweifeln und die Hände ringen: Wodurch habe ich das verdient?'

[32] Ibid., pp.17, 31.

[33] Döblin, *Babylonische Wandrung oder Hochmut kommt vor dem Fall*, Olten and Freiburg: Walter, 1962, pp.584-603.

[34] Cf. Kiesel, pp.242, 249-52.

[35] Isermann, p.228.

[36] Ibid., p.190.

[37] Kiesel, pp.148-72; cf. also Isermann, pp.29-41. For Döblin's own description of his works as 'Gebete', see *Schicksalsreise*, p.135 (*Autobiographische Schriften*, p.214).

[38] Ibid., pp.268-70.

[39] Döblin, *Reise in Polen*, Olten and Freiburg: Walter, 1968, p.239.

[40] Döblin, *Schicksalsreise*, p.105 (*Autobiographische Schriften*, p.186).

[41] Kiesel, pp.184-87.

[42] Ibid., p.215.

[43] Döblin, *Schicksalsreise*, p.105 (*Autobiographische Schriften*, p.186).

[44] Ibid., p.106 (p.186f).

[45] Ibid., p.135f (p.214f); cf. also p.168f (p.244f).

[46] Ibid., p.207 (p.281); cf. also pp.210f, 215 (pp.283f, 288).

[47] Cf. Christoph Bartscherer, *Das Ich und die Natur. Alfred Döblins literarischer Weg im Licht seiner Religionsphilosophie*, Paderborn: Igel, 1997, pp.123-30.

[48] See Anthony W. Riley, 'Christentum und Revolution. Zu Alfred Döblins Romanzyklus *November 1918*', in Wolfgang Frühwald and Wolfgang Schieder, eds, *Leben im Exil. Probleme der Integration deutscher Flüchtlinge im Ausland 1933-1945*, Hamburg: Hoffmann und Campe, 1981, pp.91-102 (here p.98).

[49] Cf. Emde, p.310.

[50] Cf. Emde, pp.276-99.

[51] Cf. Emde, pp.295-98.

[52] The notion of a 'gleitende Bekehrung', which now seems to be generally accepted in the secondary literature on Döblin, appears to have originated in Hans Jürgen Baden, *Literatur und Bekehrung*, Stuttgart: Klett, 1968, p.14.

[53] Emde, p.242.

[54] Döblin, *Schicksalsreise*, p.279 (*Autobiographische Schriften*, p.345f).

[55] Ibid., p.279f (p.346f).

[56] See 'Döblin-Chronik', p.39.

Daniel Azuélos

Lion Feuchtwanger und Franz Werfel in der jüdischen Exilzeitschrift *Aufbau* oder Schriftsteller zwischen Engagement und künstlerischer Selbstbehauptung

Very early on, *Aufbau*, the New York weekly, tried to represent the interests of German Jews exiled to the United States under Nazi Germany. And with Manfred George's appointment as editor in 1939, its attachment to Judaism and commitment to the Zionist cause were reinforced. This did not prevent it, however, from instrumentalizing writers like Lion Feuchtwanger and Franz Werfel who, although members of its advisory board, did not necessarily share its views. When associating itself with literary figures embodying the German cultural heritage it showed little concern for ideological purity.

Die New Yorker Exilzeitschrift *Aufbau* hatte schon sehr früh versucht, mit einem dezidierten jüdischen Profil an seine Leserschaft heranzutreten, obwohl die ersten Redakteure eher als laue Verteidiger der jüdischen Sache und des Zionismus gelten konnten. Das änderte sich 1939, als der Berliner Journalist Manfred George zum Chefredakteur ernannt wurde und sowohl die Leser als auch die festen Mitarbeiter auf eine straffe politische Linie glaubte einschwören zu können, die jüdisches Bewusstsein, gemäßigten Zionismus, sozial-demokratisches Gedankengut und Treue zu den amerikanischen Grundwerten zu einem neuen Selbstverständnis der deutsch-jüdischen Exilbevölkerung zusammenfassen sollte. Lion Feuchtwanger als Mitglied des *Advisory Board* der Zeitschrift gehörte mit Franz Werfel und vielen anderen zu den Intellektuellen, die nicht nur den *Aufbau* mit Artikeln und Auszügen aus ihren Werken versorgten, sondern den Anschein erweckten, als würden sie auch den politischen Diskurs der Redaktion mittragen und mitgestalten.

,Wir, für die Manfred George schreibt, denken in Deutsch, fühlen jüdisch und leben amerikanisch':[1] mit diesem 1949 geäußerten Ausspruch hatte Feuchtwanger gleichsam den Menschen aus der Seele gesprochen, die das deutsch-jüdische Bekenntnis im Sinne der *Aufbau*-Ideologen erneuern wollten. In seinen privaten Äußerungen hat er allerdings nie einen Hehl daraus gemacht, dass seine Ansichten mit denjenigen des *Aufbau* niemals ganz übereinstimmten.[2] Am Beispiel von Lion Feuchtwanger und Franz Werfel, die des öfteren ihre Feder der wohl verbreitetsten Exilzeitschrift in Amerika liehen, soll hier gezeigt werden, dass es dem *Aufbau* nicht immer gelang, die brillantesten Köpfe des deutsch-jüdischen Exils, auch wenn sie fast niemals ihre Mitarbeit verweigerten, an die Kandare zu nehmen. Das Schwanken der Zeitschrift zwischen hohen intellektuellen Ansprüchen und populistischem Gebaren, um auf eine ziemlich breit gefächerte Leserschaft Rücksicht zu nehmen, sollte jedoch manchen Autor vor den Kopf stoßen und der Indienstnahme dieser Aushängeschilder der deutsch-jüdischen Emigration abträglich sein.

Wie schon eingangs festgestellt, gehörte Feuchtwanger neben Thomas

Mann zu den exilierten Schriftstellern, die sich sehr früh mit ihren Stellungnahmen oder Erklärungen zur politischen Lage und zur Lage der Emigration einer
Zeitschrift andienten, die sie auch mit zahlreichen Essays und besonders im
Falle Feuchtwangers mit Auszügen aus seinen Werken meist unentgeltlich oder
zumindest ohne übertriebene Geldforderungen versorgten. So heißt es zum Beispiel in einem Brief an Manfred George vom 20. April 1942, in dem über einen
Teilabdruck der deutschen Fassung der *Josephus*-Trilogie verhandelt wurde:
,Nennen Sie mir bitte einen Betrag, der Ihrem Etat entspricht. Ich halte Ihr
Unternehmen für so <u>wertvoll für unsere gemeinsame Sache</u>, dass ich jedes
Entgegenkommen zeigen werde'.[3] Manfred George vertrat als Chefredakteur
des *Aufbau* eine politische Linie, der sich nicht alle exilierten Schriftsteller
unbedingt anschließen mochten. Und wenn Lion Feuchtwanger sich auf die
,gemeinsame Sache' des Exils beruft, die in der deutsch-jüdischen Zeitschrift
bestens aufgehoben wäre, so ist das bestimmt nicht so zu verstehen, als würde
er ohne wenn und aber einem Kurs zustimmen, an den alle Exilanten jüdischer
Abstammung sich laut den *statements* des *Aufbau* zu halten hatten. Sein Briefwechsel mit George in Sachen *Council for a Democratic Germany* beweist es
zur Genüge.[4] George, der spätestens seit dem Kriegseintritt der Vereinigten
Staaten der unbedingten Unterstützung Amerikas und der Amerikanisierung der
deutschen Juden vor der Bewahrung des deutschen Kulturgutes den Vorzug
gegeben hatte, war klug genug, es sich mit keiner Seite zu verderben und solche
Schriftsteller auch gelten zu lassen, die die Akzente anders setzten. Georges
gewieftes Taktieren und vorsichtig-behutsame politische Grundhaltung wurden
einmal treffend von Siegfried Marck folgendermaßen charakterisiert:

> Es ist sehr freundlich, wie Sie meine Haltung charakterisieren, oft genug war sie
> durch kompromissloses Eintreten für – den Kompromiss gekennzeichnet. Gewiss,
> man kann es auch mit Weltsch das ,Wagnis der Mitte' nennen. In dieser Generallinie
> habe ich mich Ihnen zusehends näher gefühlt, und Sie haben diese Politik auch Ihrer
> Zeitung aufgeprägt bei Freiheit der Mitarbeiter, die ich mit Interesse lese, ohne mit
> allen in allem übereinzustimmen.[5]

Als erfahrener Journalist wusste George nichtsdestoweniger, dass das
Gebot der Stunde es erforderte, heilige Kühe zu schlachten und von dem antifaschistischen Selbstverständnis der Emigration Abstand zu nehmen, das alle
Parteien in einer Volksfront bis hin zu den Kommunisten zusammenzufassen
bestrebt war, um es zugunsten einer an Amerika angelehnten Koalition der neueingebürgerten oder die amerikanische Staatsbürgerschaft anstrebenden
deutsch-jüdischen Exilanten abzulösen. So ging im *Aufbau* das Desinteresse an
den innerdeutschen Verhältnissen, solange das nicht die Außenpolitik Amerikas
tangierte, Hand in Hand mit der Ablehnung der *free movements*, die sich vorgenommen hatten nicht nur an der Befreiung Deutschlands mitzuwirken, sondern auch dessen Zukunft nach dem Krieg mitzugestalten.

Dementsprechend nahm der *Aufbau* vor allem gegenüber den kommunistisch beeinflussten *Komitees Freies Deutschland* eine sehr zurückhaltende,
wenn nicht gar abweisende Haltung ein, auch wenn er nicht als moskaufeindlich

zu bezeichnen war, zumindest solange die amerikanisch-sowjetischen Beziehungen als Grundpfeiler der Antihitlerkoalition andauerten. Außerdem war die Sowjetunion eines der ersten Länder, das den neuen Staat Israel anerkannte und ihm über tschechoslowakische Waffenlieferungen militärische Unterstützung gegen die Araber angedeihen ließ.

Erst im Laufe der Zeit sollte sich im Schatten des Kalten Krieges das Blatt wenden und der *Aufbau* entwickelte sich langsam zu einem treuen Anhänger des nordatlantischen Bündnisses. George selber, der in den fünfziger Jahren neben seiner Tätigkeit beim *Aufbau* auch in Deutschland und in der Schweiz publizistisch wirkte, konnte über Hans Habe und Hans Wallenberg, ehemalige Mitarbeiter der von Amerika subventionierten *Neuen Zeitung*, Kontakt mit Axel Cäsar Springer aufnehmen und sich dessen Unterstützung vor allem in Sachen Israel erfreuen. Eigentlich hatte George jedoch während der Exiljahre in Prag und in Paris den Kreisen, die eine Volksfrontpolitik befürworteten, nahegestanden und dem *Schutzverband deutscher Schriftsteller* angehört, der diese Politik mittrug. Allerdings war er im amerikanischen Exil davon abgerückt.

Aber George musste hier sehr vorsichtig manövrieren, denn es gab in Amerika eine gewisse Anzahl von emigrierten Intellektuellen, die mit ihrer kommunistischen Grundhaltung oder zumindest ihrem Mitläufertum nicht hinter dem Berge hielten und auf deren Mitarbeit der *Aufbau* nicht verzichten mochte. Bert Brecht, Hanns Eisler, Alfred Kantorowicz gehörten zu den überzeugten Kommunisten, Oskar Maria Graf, Heinrich Mann und eben auch Lion Feuchtwanger waren mit vielen anderen auch die bürgerlichen Garanten einer von Moskau aus ferngesteuerten stramm antifaschistischen Linie gewesen und hatten schon in Europa in kommunistischen Zeitschriften wie *Das Wort* Beiträge geliefert. George wusste, dass diese Schriftsteller zu den beliebtesten Gestalten des Exils zählten, dass seine Zeitschrift, die kein einfaches Meinungsblatt war wie die sozialdemokratische *Volkszeitung* von Gerhart Seger, an Glaubwürdigkeit verloren hätte, wenn sie diese wichtigen Stimmen der Exilliteratur mit Stillschweigen übergangen hätte. George konnte sie sowieso nicht zähmen und auf eine verbindliche politische Linie festlegen. Um sie für seine Zwecke zu vereinnahmen, musste er ihnen auf halbem Wege entgegenkommen, wohl wissend, dass sie sich keinen ideologischen Maulkorb würden anlegen lassen. Diese Leute brauchten den *Aufbau* wie der *Aufbau* sie brauchte. Und dabei hatte George, der überall seine Hände mit im Spiel hatte und über ein weitverzweigtes Netz von Bekanntschaften verfügte, den besseren Riecher für die kleinen Intrigen und Eifersüchteleien eines immerhin übersehbaren Kreises von exilierten Persönlichkeiten. Er konnte sich zum Beispiel viel erfolgreicher, als es im Pariser Exil der Fall gewesen wäre, des Versuchs einer kommunistischen Unterwanderung der *German-American Writers Association* deshalb erwehren, weil diese Organisation auf den *Aufbau* angewiesen war, um ihre Veranstaltungen anzukündigen. Dabei war er sich immer der Gefahr einer möglichen Einflussnahme von kommunistischer Seite bewusst und war bereit, ihr mit Fingerspitzengefühl zu begegnen. So schrieb er im Jahre 1941 an Bruno Frank:

> Wenn man den Verband heute explodieren lässt, so gibt man die letzte Widerstandsfront auf und eine Kampfmöglichkeit, die [...] von viel größerer Wirkung sein kann als bei einem Untertauchen und Verschwinden [...]. Vor allem ist die kampflose Aufgabe eines Frontabschnitts der Antinazilinie in diesem Augenblick durchaus nicht das, was in unserer Tendenz liegt, den Alliierten und Amerikanern bei ihrem Kampf gegen Nazis zu helfen [....]. Ich bin auch der Meinung, dass der Verband in jeder Beziehung also auch gegen eine kommunistische Infiltration hieb- und stichfest sein muss, aber sind Sie nicht mit mir einer Meinung, dass bisher von solch einer Infiltration überhaupt nichts zu merken war?[6]

Es war jedermann bekannt, dass Lion Feuchtwanger den kommunistischen Kreisen nahestand, seine Freundschaft mit Bertolt Brecht, mit dem er auch früher zusammengearbeitet hatte, war auch im amerikanischen Exil nicht abgekühlt, was nicht zuletzt die Aufmerksamkeit des FBI auf seine Person gelenkt hatte, wie Alexander Stephan nachgewiesen hat.[7] Dabei blieb Feuchtwanger über die Jahre und trotz dieser Meinungsverschiedenheiten dem *Aufbau* und seinem Chefredakteur treu, wie ein Brief vom Januar 1955 an George es dokumentiert, in dem Feuchtwanger noch einmal die Zeitschrift über den grünen Klee lobt für die Rolle, die sie zur Beschleunigung der Amerikanisierung der Exilanten und zur Bewahrung der deutschen Sprache und Kultur gespielt hat.[8] Will man aber verstehen, warum die Bindung an den *Aufbau* und an George auch die Hinwendung des letzteren zum Antikommunismus oder zumindest die Zurücknahme seiner ursprünglichen volksfrontnahen Gesinnung überdauert hat, so muss man mehrere Faktoren in Rechnung stellen. Ludwig Marcuse, der in Sanary und Los Angeles im Hause Feuchtwanger aus- und einging und auch mit George als seinem besten Freund einen steten Briefwechsel führte, hat in seinem Nachruf die Persönlichkeit Feuchtwangers treffend charakterisiert. Ein vierfacher Wall soll ihn laut Marcuse sein Leben lang geschützt haben: ein unerschütterliches Selbstbewusstsein, der Stolz auf seine Zugehörigkeit zum ältesten Kulturvolk, eine sehr stabile, unproblematische Weltanschauung, nämlich der Glaube an die eine, einzige Vernunft, der ihn an das Zeitalter der Aufklärung zurückband, und schließlich die Verbundenheit mit der Weltliteratur. Marcuse bezeichnet ihn als bürgerlichen Epikuräer.[9] Er erwähnt nur beiläufig die Glückwunschtelegramme, die der ‚Anachoret von Pacific Palisades' gelegentlich an Stalin schickte, als könnte man dem vielbeschäftigten, mit einem riesigen Œuvre überlasteten Autor diese lässliche Sünde durchgehen lassen. Marcuse, der im Winter 1936/37 mit ihm zusammen die berüchtigte Moskaureise angetreten hatte, schrieb:

> Nur gab es da eine politische Achillesferse. Viele Schriftsteller unserer Zeit konnten nicht leben, ohne ihre Sehnsucht in eine Großmacht zu investieren. John Dewey und André Gide machten dann ihre Erfahrungen – und änderten ihre Meinung. Feuchtwanger gehörte zu jenen, die hinfahren und zurückkommen – und auf der Reise keine Entdeckung gemacht haben.[10]

Dabei fügte Marcuse hinzu, dass Amerika Feuchtwangers Telegramme nach Moskau wohl überschätzt hätte. Das mag schon stimmen und es ist so gut wie sicher, dass Manfred George auch so dachte und Lion Feuchtwanger, dem er seit den frühen dreißiger Jahren verbunden war, niemals wegen Unstimmigkeiten in politischen Sachen hätte fallen lassen. Außerdem war Feuchtwanger deshalb für George so wichtig, weil er schon sehr früh Partei ergriffen hatte für die jüdische Sache und sich von Anfang an für die Errichtung eines jüdischen Staates in Palästina ausgesprochen hatte. An der zionistischen Linie, die seit der Übernahme der Redaktion durch George zum unverzichtbaren Dogma des *Aufbau* geworden war, hat Feuchtwanger bis zum Ende festgehalten, auch wenn ein Artikel vom Jahre 1955 im *Aufbau* ihn rügt, weil er der Fiktion eines jüdischen Staates in Birobidjan von Anfang an aufgesessen ist.[11] Schon 1932 bat ihn George um eine Rezension seines Buches über Theodor Herzl, wohl wissend, dass er sich an jemanden wandte, der, wie er sich ausdrückte, ,auf derselben Galeere' saß wie er.[12]

George hat dann im Juli 1936 in einem Heft der *Jüdischen Revue*, die er als Chefredakteur von Prag aus leitete, einen Artikel von Feuchtwanger[13] drucken lassen, der für eine Weltvertretung der Juden plädierte. In derselben Zeitschrift hatte allerdings Gustav Krojanker aus Jerusalem Feuchtwanger scharf attackiert, weil dieser als Mitunterzeichner eines Aufrufs zum *Thomas Mann Fonds* über die moralische Wertlosigkeit einer gegängelten Literatur in einem diktatorischen Staat (gemeint war selbstverständlich Hitler-Deutschland) hergezogen war, während er gleichzeitig in seinem Russlandbericht und in der Zeitschrift *Das Wort* eine andere Diktatur, nämlich die sowjetische, in den höchsten Tönen gepriesen hatte.[14]

Interessant ist die Anmerkung, die Manfred George alias *spectator* an den Artikel angefügt hatte. George will sich hier jeder negativen Stellungnahme gegenüber der Sowjetunion enthalten und verweist auf einen anderen Artikel,[15] den er im März 1937 geschrieben hatte und in dem er sich geweigert hatte, angesichts der sowjet-russischen Zustände einen Maßstab anzulegen, der einem kultivierten Land angemessener gewesen wäre. Im Grunde versucht er mit dieser Stellungnahme, den künftigen jungen jüdischen Staat für die Entgleisungen vorab zu entschuldigen, die die Geburtswehen einer noch im Werden begriffenen Nation nach sich ziehen müssen. Ihn stört auch nicht, dass Juden in einem sowjetischen Staat weiterhin leben könnten: ,So weit die Juden in Russland aus der sozialen Knechtschaft des Zarismus in die bürgerliche Freiheit werktätiger Menschen hinüberwechselten, hatten wir das stets zu begrüßen'.[16]

George sollte noch bis in die vierziger Jahre hinein der Meinung anhängen, dass außer Amerika und dem künftigen jüdischen Staate auch die Sowjetunion eine Bedeutung für die jüdischen Massen auf dem Wege zur Normalisierung hat.[17] Feuchtwanger sollte bis zu seinem Lebensende einer solchen Gesinnung treu bleiben. Erst mit der Entdeckung der antisemitischen Wendung der sowjetischen Politik vom Jahre 1949 an und der Hinrichtung der jiddischen Schriftsteller Itzig Feffer und Salomon Michoels, die noch 1943 eine

Goodwill-Tour durch die USA unternahmen, um die amerikanischen Juden von der Richtigkeit einer Volksfrontpolitik unter sowjetischer Obhut zu überzeugen, begann sich George von der ‚prosowjetischen Haltung' zu emanzipieren, die der *Aufbau* allerdings nur als Lippenbekenntnis und im Schutze der amerikanisch-sowjetischen Freundschaft zu beherzigen bereit war.

Im *Aufbau* sollte sich Feuchtwanger immer dann zu Worte melden, wenn es galt, die ‚große Zeit der nationalen jüdischen Wiedergeburt und des Aufbauwerks in Palästina' zu beschwören.[18] Feuchtwanger unterstützte bis zuletzt mit Rat und Tat die zionistische Sache und er schickte 1948 George ein Telegramm, das seine Enttäuschung zum Ausdruck brachte angesichts der Außenpolitik der Vereinigten Staaten, deren Vertreter vor den *United Nations* in die Palästina-teilung nicht eingewilligt hatten, weil ein solcher Entschluss angeblich ihren Ölinteressen in Saudiarabien hätte schaden können: ‚Angesichts der letzten palästinensischen Aktion der amerikanischen Regierung bleibt uns Juden in Amerika nur ein Gefühl: Trauer und Scham – Lion Feuchtwanger'.[19]

Manfred George hat sich allerdings geweigert, diesen ‚lapidaren Satz', wie er sich ausdrückt, im *Aufbau* abzudrucken: ‚Es war sicher von Ihnen sehr gut gemeint, aber ich bin überzeugt, dass die Nichtveröffentlichung dieser aphoristischen Formulierung auch in Ihrem Interesse gelegen ist'.[20] Was Manfred George hier zu sagen unterließ: Es lag in Feuchtwangers, aber vor allem in Georges Interesse, die Außenpolitik der Vereinigten Staaten immer in einem günstigen Licht darzustellen oder zumindest nicht so schroff abzuurteilen. Es muss aber hinzugefügt werden, dass Feuchtwanger niemals so scharfe Töne anwandte, als er sich in die für ihn unbequeme Lage versetzt sah, ein Urteil über die judenfeindliche Haltung der Kremlherren zu fällen. Vom israelischen Botschafter in Montevideo gedrängt, auf einen Brief eines Sowjet-Juden zu reagieren, der das volle Ausmaß der katastrophalen Lage des russischen Judentums zum Ausdruck brachte, begnügte sich Feuchtwanger mit der ausweichenden Antwort, ‚es sei nicht ganz leicht, durch die Emotion des Schreibers zu einer klaren Erkenntnis der wirklichen Lage vorzudringen'.[21]

Ansonsten wurde Feuchtwanger gelegentlich auch dann herangezogen und zu Stellungnahmen aufgefordert, wenn der *Aufbau* an Stimmen des Exils im Dienste des antifaschistischen Kampfes zu appellieren gedachte. So landete zum Beispiel die Zeitschrift im Juli 1941 einen großen publizistischen Coup mit der Veröffentlichung des ‚Offenen Briefes an einige Berliner Schauspieler'.[22] Mit diesem Artikel traf Feuchtwanger zwei Fliegen mit einer Klappe: politisch rechnete er mit den nationalsozialistischen Gegnern ab und literarisch steuerte er einen glänzenden Artikel voll bissigen Humors und hintergründigen Sarkasmus bei, der sehr vorteilhaft gegen die üblichen humanistischen Plädoyers mit dick aufgetragener Suada und larmoyantem Schwulst abstach. Aber auch sonst wird im *Aufbau* niemals negativ von der Parteinahme Feuchtwangers gegenüber den *free movements* oder sonstigen politischen Exil-Gruppen gesprochen, die sich mit Rückkehrabsichten und dem Gedanken an eine Beteiligung an der zukünftigen Gestaltung Europas trugen. Das war typisch für die Haltung des *Aufbau* der vierziger Jahre, der seine Starautoren auch dann gewähren ließ, wenn sie Meinungen vertraten, die mit denjenigen der Redaktion nicht übereinstimmten.

Feuchtwanger, dessen Alterswerke *Waffen für Amerika*, *Die Witwe Capet*, *Der Teufel von Boston* oder dessen Betrachtungen über den historischen Roman allerdings eher von einer bürgerlich-fortschrittlichen denn von einer bolschewistisch-proletarischen Geistesauffassung zeugten, ist seltsamerweise niemals, im Gegensatz zu der Mehrzahl seiner Mitexilanten, von seinen politischen Sympathien abgerückt. Das hat ihn wohl die amerikanische Staatsbürgerschaft gekostet, verbunden mit Unannehmlichkeiten seitens der Geheimdienste und des Immigration and Naturalization Service (INS) und der faktischen Unmöglichkeit, die Reise nach Europa doch noch zu wagen. Ein amerikanischer Bürger Feuchtwanger hätte wohl die Reise nach den beiden Deutschland angetreten; dass er sich aber z.B. in Berlin (ob West oder Ost bleibe dahingestellt) endgültig niedergelassen hätte, ist zu bezweifeln.

In Amerika liefen alle literarischen Fäden zusammen. Es war im Grunde viel leichter, von Amerika aus, das er übrigens trotz seiner politischen Ranküne sehr schätzte, sowohl den amerikanischen als auch den europäischen Markt mit seinen Werken zu beliefern. Ein Ost-Berliner Feuchtwanger hätte es vor allem mit Zensurstellen aufnehmen müssen, die ihn hier in Amerika verschonten, zumindest was seine literarischen Produktionen anbelangte. Er war sich wohl dessen bewusst und über die Situation in beiden Deutschland ziemlich genau informiert. Nicht selten hat er sich bei seinen ostdeutschen Verlegern über die Hindernisse beklagt, die man ihm in den Weg legte, wenn er auf die Veröffentlichung einiger seiner Werke, die man hinauszögerte, allzu sehr drängte.[23] Trotz der wiederholten Sympathiebekundungen, die Feuchtwanger anlässlich gelegentlicher Jubiläumsfeiern der Sowjetunion oder der DDR den Behörden dieser Staaten zugehen ließ, hielt der *Aufbau*, der die Hysterie des McCarthyismus nicht mitmachte, bis zuletzt zu einem seiner Lieblingsschriftsteller, auch zu einer Zeit, wo die Zeitschrift selbst längst in das antikommunistische Lager hinübergeschwenkt war.

Noch exemplarischer zeigt der Fall Werfel, inwiefern der durch die bis zum Überdruss heruntergeleierten Formel des ‚bewussten Juden' beschworene Mythos eines alle Schichten der Exilbevölkerung umfassenden, einigenden Bandes sich letzten Endes nicht unangefochten aufrechterhalten ließ. Man hat manchmal den Eindruck, als wäre die Redaktion der Zeitschrift bereit, an ihrem offiziellen Dogma Abstriche zu machen, wenn es galt, solche Persönlichkeiten wie Franz Werfel in den Parnass der großen jüdischen Dichtergestalten aufzunehmen. Außerdem gehörte Werfel, wie Thomas Mann und Lion Feuchtwanger, zu den ganz wenigen Schriftstellern, die in der amerikanischen literarischen Landschaft Fuß fassen und an ihre europäischen Erfolge teilweise anknüpfen konnten.

Der *Aufbau*, als das auflagenstärkste und über die jüdischen Einwanderer hinaus meistgelesene deutsche Blatt in den Vereinigten Staaten, brauchte wohl solche Aushängeschilder, mit denen man sich gerne schmückte. Das *Advisory Board* der Zeitschrift liest sich wie ein Gotha der Exilintelligenz und zählte zu seinen Mitarbeitern herausragende Namen wie Albert Einstein, Thomas Mann, Emil Ludwig, Lion Feuchtwanger, zeitweise auch Max Horkheimer oder eben auch Franz Werfel, der 1942 in dieses Gremium kooptiert wurde. Obwohl Friedrich S. Brodnitz[24] Werfel zum ‚großen Juden' stempelte, hat der Prager Dichter nie einen Hehl aus einer Haltung gemacht, die mit der politischen Linie der Zeitschrift bei weitem nicht übereinstimmte. In einem Interview mit dem Musikkritiker Artur Holde behauptet er 1942 noch, dass er an dem *Aufbau* gerade die Besonderheit schätze, dass er ‚die einzige deutsche Zeitung' sei, ‚die den Kampf gegen den Nazismus zugleich mit dem Geist eines lebendigen, umfassend orientierten Blattes verbinde'.[25]

Im Jahre 1942 hätte sich die Zeitschrift wohl niemals zum Sprachrohr der deutschen Emigration aufgeschwungen oder gar mit deren Zielen identifiziert, auch wenn sie ihre Spalten weiterhin den widersprüchlichsten Stimmen des Exils zur Verfügung stellte und den Kampf gegen den Nazismus zur obersten Priorität erklärte. In diesem Interview ist der jüdische Weg, den es von nun an einzuschlagen galt, nicht einmal einer Erwähnung würdig. Ja, Werfel möchte die Aufgabe des *Aufbau* nicht auf eine jüdische Politik beschränkt wissen, er solle vielmehr den Juden ‚die Pflicht der Bewahrung des deutschen Kulturgutes'[26] ans Herz legen und ‚auch für die politischen Flüchtlinge und für die Menschen aus anderen Religionsgemeinschaften eintreten'.[27] Bruno Frank, der 1940 dieselben Prioritäten wie Werfel setzte und die deutschen Juden ermahnte, der Aufsaugung des jüdischen Elementes zuzustimmen und der deutschen Sprache auch im amerikanischen Exil die Treue zu halten,[28] wurde seinerzeit von der Redaktion ziemlich schroff in seine Schranken gewiesen. Sie fand aber 1942 für die Skurrilitäten Werfels, als welche seine Äußerungen, gemessen an der offiziellen *Aufbau*-Doktrin, allen Lesern erscheinen mochten, kein Wort des Missfallens oder gar der Verurteilung. Denn indem Werfel sich die Freiheit herausnahm, den *Aufbau* in den Kampf für die deutsche Kultur einzubinden und einem möglichen Regenerierungsprozess Deutschlands nach dem Krieg das Wort zu reden, machte er den *Aufbau*-Ideologen, die einem solchen Ansinnen nicht sonderlich gewogen waren, einen Strich durch die Rechnung. Werfel stellte sich in dieser Hinsicht quer zu den Grundvoraussetzungen des jüdischen Selbstverständnisses der Zeitschrift, die nunmehr von einer jüdisch-amerikanischen Warte aus auf die deutsche Vergangenheit herabzublicken gesonnen war, ja er trat sie geradezu mit Füßen. So äußerte er sich im Gespräch mit Holde: ‚Der *Aufbau* muss ganz international werden. Denn die kulturellen Kräfte, die sich in ihm sammeln, werden gerade nach dem Zusammenbruch des Nazismus von größter Bedeutung werden'.[29]

Das war ausgerechnet die Art Gesinnung, von der Abstand zu nehmen die jüdische Exilbevölkerung aufgefordert wurde. Werfel sprang also ziemlich leichtfertig mit den auf der Impressumseite prangenden Statuten und Satzungen einer Zeitschrift um, über die zu wachen er sich als Mitglied des *Advisory Board* hätte verpflichten müssen. Es war aber vielen Mitarbeitern des *Aufbau* nicht entgangen, dass Werfels Synkretismus in religiösen Sachen, ganz zu schweigen von seinem an seiner Frau Alma Mahler-Werfel geschulten reaktionären Gehabe, mit den Forderungen der Zeit nicht Schritt halten konnten. Ludwig Marcuse, der kein Blatt vor den Mund zu nehmen gewohnt war, sah allerdings einen Widerspruch in der Haltung eines Mannes, der einerseits die Neigung ‚primitiver Menschen' anprangerte, nur an die ‚Befriedigung materieller Wünsche zu denken',[30] während andererseits er selbst und seine Frau dank der Tantiemen, die die Aufführungen der Werke Gustav Mahlers abwarfen, es sich in Hollywood wohl leben ließen.[31] In Sachen Werfel wurde anscheinend immer mit zweierlei Maß gemessen. Am ‚großen Juden', dem ehrwürdigen Repräsentanten der österreichischen Literatur im Exil, dem neben Thomas Mann lebendigen Symbol der deutschen Kultur schlechthin, war nichts auszusetzen, während dessen Haltung dem Judentum und der Tagespolitik gegenüber manchmal nicht so gut wegkam.

Manfred George, der in der Zeitschrift diesen Kult um die Ausnahmepersönlichkeiten des Exils nicht ohne Emphase in Szene zu setzen wusste, hatte des öfteren seine liebe Not damit, Werfel vor den Kritikern innerhalb seiner Redaktion in Schutz zu nehmen. Als Beispiel sei die Kontroverse um das umstrittene Stück *Jacobowsky und der Oberst* genannt. Manfred George hatte als erster Werfels Stück rezensiert, einen langen Auszug daraus zitiert und es bei einem nichtssagenden Kommentar belassen, der sich nicht wirklich mit der Problematik des Stückes auseinandersetzte. Er hatte lediglich den einen Titelhelden, den vor den Hitlerhorden flüchtenden Juden Jacobowsky, auf eine Stufe gestellt mit dem braven Soldaten Schwejk des gleichnamigen Romans von Jaroslav Hasek.[32] Die Beziehung Jacobowsky/Oberst Stjerbinsky, die unter den jüdischen Exilanten Anlass zu negativen Stellungnahmen gegeben hatte, hatte er nicht problematisiert. Einer der engsten Mitarbeiter Georges, der Soziologe und Judentumexperte Josef Maier, hatte bemerkt, dass Werfel in diesem Stück mit den abgedroschensten Klischeevorstellungen operierte, die dem Wohlmeinenden auch manchmal entschlüpften, wenn er die jüdische Seele oder den jüdischen Geist charakterisieren wollten, um diese von der nichtjüdischen Umgebung abzugrenzen.

Der Donquichotte des Stückes, der polnische Oberst Tadeusz Boleslaw Stjerbinsky, ist ein Haudegen edlen Geblüts, der einen ‚Geist nationaler Wehrhaftigkeit'[33] verströmt und mit allen ‚ritterlichen Tugenden'[34] gesegnet ist, während sein Widerpart Jacobowsky als der intelligent-durchtriebene, mit allen Wassern gewaschene kleine Jude erscheint, wie er holzschnittartig in den antisemitischen Karikaturen abgebildet wird. Man wollte im *Aufbau* dem traditionellen Bild des intellektuellen, mit Witz und zersetzendem Geist ausgestatteten Juden die neue Gestalt des ‚starken Juden' entgegensetzen, der sich von bramarbasierenden Möchtegernhelden à la Stjerbinsky nicht mehr demütigen lässt und in Kriegszeiten genauso seinen Mann steht wie sein christlicher Mitkämpfer. Maier fragt sich: ‚Sind Juden wirklich primär ‚intelligent' und Polen (oder andere Völker) primär wehrhaft und den Begriffen der Ehre verhaftet?'[35] Ein paar Jahre später verstieg sich der Kritiker Kurt Hellmer, der von einer Aufführung des Stückes in Berlin berichtete, zu der Behauptung, es zieme sich nicht, dieses Stück einem deutschen Publikum zuzumuten:

> Es ist ein Wagnis, dies einem Publikum vorzuführen, das eben erst aus jener Zwangserziehungsanstalt befreit worden ist, in der es gelehrt wurde, dass die Eigenschaften des Juden der Inbegriff alles Schlechten seien – und genau diese so charakterisierten Eigenschaften führt Jacobowsky den Zuschauern vor Augen.[36]

Manfred George, der sonst nicht gerade zimperlich war, wenn es die orthodoxe Linie der Zeitschrift zu verteidigen galt, zeigte wieder einmal im Falle Werfel, dass er Kratzer am Image einer jüdisch durchgeistigten Weltanschauung dulden konnte, wenn die Sache der großen Literatur auf dem Spiel stand. Es ist erstaunlich festzustellen, dass im Nachruf[37] Franz Werfels die Tatsache seiner jüdischen Zugehörigkeit und tiefen Religiosität erwähnt wurde, während die Erklärung Pater Moenius', der bei der Beerdigung zugegen gewesen war, Werfel hätte knapp vor seinem Tod den Gedanken an eine Bekehrung zum Katholizismus erwogen, mit keinem Wort angedeutet wurde.[38] Es muss aber der Wahrheit gemäß hinzugefügt werden, dass andere Kritiker, die wie Marcuse auf Werfel nicht immer gut zu sprechen waren, aus dieser Tatsache einer möglichen Konversion keinen Hehl machten.

Niemand wollte in der Redaktion diese Gerüchte zerstreuen. Erst nachdem Alma Mahler-Werfel in unzähligen Briefen an George auf eine Richtigstellung gedrängt hatte, sah sich der *Aufbau* gezwungen, diesen Gerüchten über eine heimliche Taufe Werfels ein Ende zu machen. Die Witwe Werfels hatte an George geschrieben:

> Professor Moenius hat mit den besten Worten darauf hingewiesen, dass er nur als Freund und nicht als Geistlicher rede. – Er hatte sich selber angeboten. Kein Rabbiner hatte diese Idee – ich hätte es ihm sehr gedankt! – Franz Werfel war nicht getauft! Ich wollte Ihnen nur der Wahrheit gemäß diese kleine Berichtigung schicken![39]

Man sieht wohl, dass die Kriterien, an denen man Werfels Schriften und Erklärungen misst, sich nicht immer mit den hehren Prinzipien decken, auf die sich die Redaktion beruft. Man kann es an der Behandlung eines anderen Schriftstellers ablesen, der genauso wie Werfel zwischen Judentum und Christusverehrung hin- und herpendelte, aber aus der Sicht der selbsternannten Zensoren der Zeitschrift mit keinen mildernden Umständen zu rechnen hatte. Der Synkretismus des jiddischen Schriftstellers Schalom Asch, der bei gleichzeitigem Einfühlungsvermögen der ostjüdischen Welt einen moralinfreien und unvoreingenommenen Spiegel vorgehalten hatte, stieß bei den meisten jüdischen Journalisten auf Ablehnung. Er hatte außerdem in seinem Buch *Man fun Nazareth* Jesus Christus ein Denkmal setzen wollen, was ihm seine Religionsgenossen sehr übel nahmen. Das Buch in jiddischer Sprache fand keinen Verleger, der *Jewish Daily Forward* lehnte eine Publikation in Folgen ab. Michael Wurmbrands Fazit kommt einer scharfen Verurteilung des jiddischen Autors gleich:

> Was jedoch Asch als schwere nationale Sünde angerechnet wird, ist, dass er, indem er christliche Legende und Lehre künstlerisch zu gestalten versucht, die antijüdischen Vorurteile, ja ablehnenden Urteile, die in dieser Lehre und Legende mit enthalten sind, übernimmt und seine Feder in den Dienst dieser Konzeption stellt.[40]

Wenn Michael Wurmbrand in einem anderen Artikel Werfel und Asch in einen Topf wirft und beiden vorwirft, sie hätten trotz ihrer positiven Einstellung dem jüdischen Volkstum gegenüber nichtsdestoweniger ,der Sache ihres Volkes' ,Abbruch'[41] getan, so kommt bei aller Kritik alles in allem der österreichische Dichter besser weg als der jiddische Schriftsteller. Hätten die exilierten deutsch-jüdischen Journalisten ihren Vorzeigejuden Werfel fallengelassen, so hätten sie auch andere deutsch-jüdische Schriftsteller wie Joseph Roth, Alfred Döblin, Arnold Zweig, Hermann Broch, Arthur Schnitzler oder gar Jakob Wassermann, die genauso wenig wie Werfel in den jüdischen Kanon passten, kritisieren müssen. Sie wären in Widerspruch geraten zu ihrer Leserschaft, die nicht bereit war, sich ihre heile literarische Welt von moralisierenden Tugendwächtern madig machen zu lassen. Man war in den *Aufbau*-Kreisen nicht gewillt, sich von einer Intelligenzschicht zu lösen, die einer orientierungslos dahintreibenden Exilgemeinschaft so viel bedeutete und ihren Zusammenhalt in stürmischen Zeiten gewährleistete.

Dagegen war es ein Leichtes, über einen Schriftsteller den Stab zu brechen, der einem anderen Kulturkreis angehörte und seinen jiddischsprechenden Religionsgenossen ein Dorn im Auge war. Indem der *Aufbau* Schalom Asch als Renegat abstempelte, glaubte er den Ostjuden gegenüber, deren Beziehungen zu den Westjuden seit jeher auf gespanntem Fuß standen, Abbuße zu tun und sich einer wohlorganisierten Gemeinschaft anzunähern, die zu übergehen es unter den amerikanischen Verhältnissen nicht ratsam schien.

Und tatsächlich: nachdem ein Redakteur des *Jewish Daily Forward*, Jizchak Warschawsky, in einer Artikelserie[42] die deutschen Juden als ,Juden ohne Judentum' angeprangert hatte und die Kluft zwischen Ostjuden und Westjuden als unüberbrückbar bezeichnet hatte, besann sich die Redaktion des populärsten jiddischen Blattes eines Besseren und machte ihre Anschuldigungen rückgängig.[43] Ob bei diesem Schritt die Affäre Schalom Asch ins Gewicht fiel, ist schwer zu ermitteln. Damit wurde aber unter diese leidige Episode innerjüdischer Zerwürfnisse der Schlusspunkt gesetzt. Man sieht, dass der *Aufbau* die ideologische Messlatte nicht so hoch hängte, wenn Schriftsteller aus dem eigenen Kulturkreis sich zu den Verteidigern und Bewahrern des deutschen Kulturgutes aufschwangen.

Anmerkungen

[1] ,Aufbau-Abend an der Westküste', *Aufbau*, 25. November 1949, S. 5.

[2] Brief vom 7. 04.1947 an Maria Meixner: ,Glaube aber, bitte, um Gottes willen nicht, dass, was im „Aufbau" steht, etwa meine Ansichten seien', in: University of Southern California, Feuchtwanger Memorial Library: General Correspondence, C6-a.

[3] Brief von Lion Feuchtwanger an Manfred George vom 20. April 1942, in: Schiller-Nationalmuseum/Deutsches Literaturarchiv (DLA) /Marbach am Neckar/A: George, Eingangsnummer: 75.2531/1-2.

[4] Brief vom 13. Mai 1944 von Manfred George an Lion Feuchtwanger, Brief vom 16. Mai 1944 von Lion Feuchtwanger an Manfred George, Brief vom 16. Juni 1944 von Manfred George an Lion Feuchtwanger, in: U.S.C, Feuchtwanger Memorial Library, General Correspondence, C4-c.

[5] Brief von Siegfried Marck an Manfred George vom 5. März 1949, in: DLA/Marbach am Neckar/ A: George, Nr. 75.3339/1.

[6] Brief von Manfred George an Bruno Frank vom 7. Juni 1940, in: DLA/Marbach am Neckar/A: George, Nr. 75. 4641.

[7] Alexander Stephan, *Im Visier des FBI. Deutsche Exilschriftsteller in den Akten amerikanischer Geheimdienste*, Stuttgart: J.B. Metzler, 1995, S. 232-64. Siehe auch den Beitrag in diesem Band.

[8] Brief von Lion Feuchtwanger an Manfred George vom Januar 1955, in: DLA/Marbach am Neckar/A: George, Nr. 75.2531/9.

[9] Nachruf Ludwig Marcuses auf Lion Feuchtwanger, in: DLA/Marbach am Neckar/A: George, Nr. 75.3399/4.

[10] Ibid.

[11] Gershon Swet, ,Nachmittag bei Lion Feuchtwanger', *Aufbau* (Die Westküste), 19. August 1955, S. 25.

[12] Brief von Manfred Georg an Lion Feuchtwanger (Berlin, 15.2.1932), in: DLA/Marbach am Neckar/A: George, Nr. 75. 5664.

[13] Lion Feuchtwanger, ,Der Weg zur Weltvertretung', *Jüdische Revue*, Juli-Heft 1936, S. 15-16.

[14] Gustav Krojanker, ,Der Fall Lion Feuchtwanger', *Jüdische Revue*, Juni-Heft 1937, S. 365-68.

[15] Spectator, ,Gide, Celine und wir', *Jüdische Revue*, März-Heft 1937, S. 145-47.

[16] Ibid.

[17] Daniel Azuélos, ,Vom *Pariser Tageblatt* und der *Pariser Tageszeitung* zum *Aufbau* – vom liberalen Selbstverständnis zum wieder entdeckten Judentum', in: Hélène Roussel und Lutz Winckler, Hgg., *Rechts und Links der Seine – Pariser Tageblatt und Pariser Tageszeitung – 1933-1940*, Tübingen: Niemeyer, 2002, S. 351-62.

[18] ,Feuchtwanger über Palästina', *Aufbau*, 25. Oktober 1940, S. 10.

[19] Telegramm der Western Union von Lion Feuchtwanger-Santa Monica an Manfred George Care Aufbau – 209 West 48 ST NYK – 1948 Mar 23, in: DLA/Marbach am Neckar/A: George, Nr. 75.2531/5.

[20] Brief vom 26. März 1948 von Manfred George an Lion Feuchtwanger, in: U.S.C. Feuchtwanger Memorial Library: Correspondence with other writers, C1-c.

[21] Brief vom 14. Mai 1958 von Lion Feuchtwanger an Uri Raanan, Israelischen Botschafter in Uruguay, in: U.S.C. Feuchtwanger Memorial Library: General Correspondence, C6-b.

[22] Lion Feuchtwanger, ,Offener Brief an einige Berliner Schauspieler', *Aufbau*, 4. Juli 1941, S. 11.

[23] Brief vom 15. Januar 1951 von Lion Feuchtwanger an den Aufbauverlag, in: U.S.C, Feuchtwanger Memorial Library, Correspondence with German publishers Greifenverlag – Aufbau Verlag, C12.

[24] ,Wer soll uns führen?', *Aufbau*, 3. Januar 1941, S. 16.

[25] Artur Holde, ,Gespräch mit Franz Werfel', *Aufbau*, 30. Januar 1942, S. 13.

[26] Ibid.

[27] Ibid.

[28] Bruno Frank, ,Juden müssen die deutsche Sprache bewahren', *Aufbau*, 27. Dezember 1940, S. 9.

[29] Artur Holde, ,Gespräch mit Franz Werfel', *Aufbau*, 30. Januar 1942, S. 13.

[30] Ibid.

[31] Ludwig Marcuse, ,In theologischen Schleiern', *Aufbau*, 9. März 1945, S. 8.

[32] *Aufbau,* 24. März 1944, S.9, S. 12.

[33] *Aufbau*, 7. Juli 1944, S. 17.

[34] Ibid.

[35] Ibid.

[36] Kurt Hellmer, *Aufbau*, 18. Juli 1947, S. 11.

[37] Heinrich Eduard Jacob, ‚In memoriam. Eine Sonne ist untergegangen', *Aufbau*, 31. August 1945, S. 7.

[38] Peter Stephan Jungk, *Franz Werfel, eine Lebensgeschichte*, Frankfurt am Main: Fischer, 1987, S. 338.

[39] Brief Alma Mahler-Werfels an Manfred George vom 25. Februar 1946, in: DLA/Marbach am Neckar/ A: George, Nr. 75.3280/2.

[40] Michael Wurmbrand, ‚Krise des Judentums', *Aufbau*, 25. Februar 1944, S. 15.

[41] Michael Wurmbrand, ‚Werfel und Asch. Zwischen Christentum und Judentum', *Aufbau*, 13. April 1945, S. 17.

[42] Michael Wurmbrand, ‚Ein Angriff auf die deutschsprachigen Juden', *Aufbau*, 9. August 1946, S. 21-22. Michael Wurmbrand, ‚Ostjuden und Westjuden', *Aufbau*, 6. September 1946, S. 17.

[43] *Aufbau*, 29. November 1946, S. 26.

Alexander Stephan

Neues vom FBI zu Lion Feuchtwanger

The scholarly community has known for quite some time of the rather sizable file which the FBI Headquarters in Washington and the Immigration and Naturalization Service had compiled after 1941 on Lion Feuchtwanger, although biographers paid surprisingly little attention to these materials. Recently, I was able to obtain from the Los Angeles Field Office of the Federal Bureau of Investigation a new release of over 1300 documents which put the Feuchtwanger dossier in quality and importance on the same level with the files generated by the FBI from the surveillance of Bertolt Brecht in Los Angeles and Anna Seghers in Mexico.

There are two reasons why the new materials on Feuchtwanger are important. First, they document in great detail the methods and scope of the surveillance of the writer, his wife, employees and friends, and include, for the first time, the hand-written notes made by special agents while following Feuchtwanger through Los Angeles and while watching his residence in Pacific Palisades. Second, the L.A. file on Feuchtwanger confirms that the FBI does not see a need to distinguish between the public and political activities of a 'subject' and his private life.

Mehr als 40 Jahre ist es her, daß Marta Feuchtwanger vom Immigration and Naturalization Service (INS) jenes Aktenbündel erhielt, in dem der fehlgeschlagene Versuch ihres Mannes dokumentiert ist, Amerikaner zu werden. Weitere 20 Jahre mußten vergehen, bevor das Feuchtwanger Institute for Exile Studies Einsicht in die Unterlagen erhielt, die das Federal Bureau of Investigation (FBI) zu Lion Feuchtwanger angefertigt und gesammelt hatte. Das gleiche Material, nämlich 496 von 926 vorhandenen FBI-Dokumenten und 398 Blättern aus der INS Service File A07510026, wurde dann noch einmal 1986 an mich ausgeliefert, versehen mit der Bemerkung „previously processed materials' und nach Maßgabe von Subsection of Title 5, United States Code, Section 553 mehr oder weniger schwer durch Ausschwärzungen verstümmelt.

Meine Auswertung dieses Materials für das Buch *Im Visier des FBI* beginnt mit der Bemerkung: ,Um es gleich vorweg zuzugeben: Die FBI-Akte von Lion Feuchtwanger hat für den Literaturwissenschaftler im engeren Sinne relativ wenig Nachrichtenwert'.[1] Kaum etwas erfahre man über Feuchtwangers literarische Tätigkeit. Enthüllungen aus dem Privatleben etwa zu Alkoholexzessen, homosexuellen Ausschweifungen oder Selbstmordversuchen, wie sie in den Dossiers von Heinrich und Klaus Mann zu finden sind, fehlen. Wenig kümmert sich Amerikas Geheimdienst um die Verbindungen des Autors zur Bewegung Freies Deutschland in Mexiko bzw. Moskau und dem Council for a Democratic Germany, die bei der Überwachung anderer Exilanten aus Deutschland, etwa Feuchtwangers Freund Bertolt Brecht, wichtig waren. Und auch die Pläne des Exilanten für den politischen und kulturellen Wiederaufbau von Deutschland nach Ende des Zweiten Weltkriegs spielen, abgesehen von einem bei der CIA archivierten Interview, kaum eine Rolle in dem immerhin knapp 1000 Blätter umfassenden Aktenberg.

Interessant waren jene erst an Marta Feuchtwanger bzw. Harold von Hofe und dann noch einmal an mich freigegebene Behördenunterlagen nur aus einem Grund: den zum Teil ungewöhnlich ausführlichen Protokollen von vier Verhören der Eheleute Feuchtwanger, die vom INS und FBI zwischen 1942 und November 1958 durchgeführt worden waren. Was sonst FBI-Akten zu einer spannenden Lektüre werden ließ, war nur begrenzt wichtig: Die immerhin 43 Reports, die aus Los Angeles, New York und anderen Field Offices des FBI an das Hauptquartier nach Washington gingen, hatten die Zensoren unserer Tage durch Ausschwärzungen und das Aussortieren von fast 50% des Materials so stark verstümmelt, daß sich der Umfang der Überwachung von Feuchtwanger kaum mehr erahnen läßt. Und auch die Dokumente von der Post- und Telefonzensur waren – anders als etwa bei Anna Seghers und, wie wir seit kurzem wissen, bei Bertolt Brecht[2] – kaum ergiebig.

All das hat sich jetzt mit der Freigabe von 1317 bislang unbekannten Dokumenten zum Fall Feuchtwanger aus dem Archiv des für Los Angeles zuständigen Field Office des FBI grundlegend geändert. Mehrere hundert unbekannte Akten, die die lokale Zweigstelle des FBI in Los Angeles angefertigt hatten, geben Einblick in die Breite und Dauer der Überwachung von Feuchtwanger und seinem Umfeld. Viele Dokumente, die bei der ersten Freigabe des Materials zu Feuchtwanger zurückgehalten wurden, können jetzt vollständig eingesehen werden. Und in einer überraschend großen Zahl von Fällen schwärzen die FBI-Zensoren unserer Tage, die die Durchschläge der Berichte des Los Angeles Field Office vor der Freigabe bearbeiten, andere und meist kürzere Passagen aus, als es ihre Kollegen vor Jahren mit den im FBI-Hauptquartier archivierten Originalen getan hatten. Kurz: Das jetzt zum ersten Mal freigegebene Material aus den Beständen des FBI-Büros von Los Angeles macht Feuchtwanger zu dem neben Brecht, Anna Seghers und den Geschwistern Klaus und Erika Mann spannendsten Fall der Bespitzelung von deutschen Exilintellektuellen durch Amerikas Geheimdienste.

Zwei Leitmotive stehen dabei im Zentrum der zuletzt an mich ausgelieferten Feuchtwanger-Akte: Zum einen überrascht die Intensität der von 1940 bis 1958 andauernden Beschattung von Feuchtwanger und, eng damit verbunden, die Vielfalt der eingesetzten Überwachungsmittel, die hier zum ersten Mal in den weit über 15.000 Aktenstücken des FBI, die mir vorliegen, durch die handschriftlichen Notizen der vor Ort bei der Villa Aurora, in Pacific Palisades und Santa Monica diensthabenden Special Agents belegt wird. Zum anderen fällt der ungewöhnlich nahtlose Übergang von politischen Verdächtigungen in das Ausspionieren des Privatlebens der Zielperson auf. Treffen mit Diplomaten erhalten so den gleichen Stellenwert wie harmlose, aber in einer Fremdsprache geführte Telefongespräche. Die Information, daß Feuchtwangers Sekretärin Hilde Waldo auf der Fahrt zur Arbeit in die Villa Aurora mehrfach am Sunset Boulevard anhält (‚for five minutes on the first date and eight minutes on the latter'[3]), um, wie sich schließlich nach mühsamer Kleinarbeit herausstellt, ein

Sandwich zu essen oder im Postamt von Pacific Palisades beim Aufgeben von Feuchtwangers Geschäftspost ein paar Worte mit einem Mann wechselt, steht kommentarlos neben der Denunziation, daß Feuchtwanger ein Spion Stalins ist. Und wie andere Geheimdienste, die Schriftsteller im Visier haben, beobachtet das FBI mißtrauisch Feuchtwangers Umgang mit Büchern – den selbst geschriebenen ebenso wie den für seine Bibliothek gesammelten.

Von besonderer Bedeutung sind in dem vom Los Angeles Field Office des FBI freigegebenen Dossier über Lion Feuchtwanger zweifellos jene Dokumente, in denen es um die Überwachung von Hilde Waldo geht, die seit 1940 die Schreibarbeiten für Feuchtwanger erledigt. Und das nicht, weil hier neue Details etwa über die privaten und beruflichen Beziehungen zwischen Feuchtwanger und Waldo zutage kämen. Interessant ist das knapp 100 Blätter umfassende Material vor allem, weil es zum ersten mal in allen mir bekannten Dossiers nicht nur Zusammenfassungen der Überwachungsaktionen enthält, sondern auch die von den Special Agents vor Ort angefertigten handschriftlichen Aufzeichnungen.

Angefangen hatte das Interesse des FBI an Hilde Waldo kurz nachdem Feuchtwanger die aus Berlin stammende Exilantin angestellt hatte, nämlich im November 1942. Ein Bericht der Los Angeles Field Division nach Washington hält hier unter der Rubrik ‚Undeveloped Leads' fest: ‚At Pacific Palisades, California, will attempt to develop further background information on Hilde Waldo, such as ascertaining her true name and whether or not she lives with the Subject and his wife'.[4] Zwei Jahre später – das Ergebnis der Untersuchung von 1942 war es nicht wert, aufgezeichnet zu werden, oder ist verloren gegangen – fängt das FBI ein Geburtstagstelegramm von Arnold Zweig an Feuchtwanger ab, das folgende Botschaft enthält: ‚Many happy returns in time and one in space. Letter 24 May was happy prelude. Cordially' – und erhält von Hilde Waldo offensichtlich bereitwillig folgende Auslegung des Textes: ‚Hilde Waldo secretary of adse [addressee] explained subject msg [message] for addressee as follows: July 7 was addressee's 60th birthday. „In time and one in space" means that eventually they will meet again. Addressee's letter to sender dated 24 May advised sender that Swedish publishers are already printing his book in the German language for liberated Germany quote Beil of Wandsbeck unquote'.[5]

Ob Feuchtwanger von dem Kontakt seiner Sekretärin mit dem FBI und von ihrer Interpretation des Telegramms von Zweig gewußt hat, ist in den Akten nicht überliefert. Wohl aber geht aus einem anderen Bericht des FBI hervor, daß Waldo noch bei zumindest einer anderen Gelegenheit mit den Behörden ihres Gastlandes kooperiert, nämlich Ende 1945, als sie auf Einladung des State Departments nach Washington fährt, um dort Dokumente zu übersetzen, die als ‚very confidential'[6] beschrieben werden. Und immer wieder tauschen der Immigration and Naturalization Service, bei dem Hilde Waldos Antrag auf Einbürgerung in die USA vorliegt, und das FBI Informationen aus, die ähnlich unergiebig sind wie die folgenden: ‚No info about her except she is secry [secretary] to Feuchtwanger',[7] oder „Hilde Waldo was not a Communist'.[8]

In den Mittelpunkt einer umfangreichen Überwachungskampagne gerät Hilde Waldo erst, als sie in die schon länger andauernde Beobachtung der finanziellen Transaktionen von Feuchtwanger verwickelt wird. Die mit erheblichem Aufwand durchgeführte Beschattung ihrer Bewegungen in Santa Monica und Pacific Palisades fördert nämlich zutage, daß sie neben ihrem relativ kleinen Gehalt mehrfach und bei verschiedenen Banken Schecks von Feuchtwanger über damals nicht unerhebliche Summen von $200 oder $250 deponiert bzw. als Bargeld auszahlen läßt (‚Agent Ladd observed her cash a check... The money was rolled up and placed in her purse'.[9]), um sie dann gleich wieder auf einem anderen Konto einzuzahlen. Aufgeklärt werden Waldos in der Tat etwas auffälligen Aktionen in den vorliegenden Akten nicht, obwohl sich das FBI von der Bank of America in Westwood Village, der Security First National Bank in Pacific Palisades und der Chase National Bank in New York Kontoauszüge, Kopien zahlreicher Schecks und ein Formular mit der Unterschrift des Kontoinhabers besorgt und beim Internal Revenue Service, also dem Finanzamt, Einsicht in Feuchtwangers Steuererklärung nimmt.

Was bleibt ist, wie so oft bei den Unternehmungen des FBI, ein Haufen Informationsmüll, mit dem am Ende selbst J. Edgar Hoovers Profischnüffler nichts anzufangen wissen: So habe sich Brecht, wie dem Geheimdienst von verschiedenen Banken bestätigt wird, für die ‚screen rights to his story „Simone"' von Feuchtwanger ‚approximately $30,000' auszahlen lassen, $10.000 am 1. April, ‚$5079.00 and $5000.00 on July 28, 1944; $400.00 on August 31, 1944; $3655.00 on April 28, 1945 and $5034.96 on May 19, 1945'.[10] Nahrungsmittel, die Waldo in ‚grocery stores at which spot surveillances indicated [ausgeschwärzt] traded' einkaufte, ‚were generally taken', wie ein Special Agent aufmerksam beobachtet, ‚to the Feuchtwanger residence rather than the residence of [ausgeschwärzt]'.[11] Und als Feuchtwanger, ‚55-60 – 5'3' – Grey hair, Roman nose – sharp Jewish features, wore rimless glasses',[12] am 24. Februar 1948 mit seiner Sekretärin zu La Rue's Restaurant am Sunset Boulevard essen geht, warten FBI-Männer geduldig in ihrer Limousine von 19:35 bis 21:12 Uhr vor der Tür und beobachten dann wie Waldo ihren Arbeitgeber um 21:50 Uhr zu Hause absetzt und um 22:15 Uhr bei ihrer eigenen Wohnung ankommt.

Doch das FBI beläßt es nicht bei der Überwachung von Feuchtwangers Bankkonten, es beschattet über Monate hinweg oft um die Uhr auch alle anderen Bewegungen von Hilde Waldo. In den Berichten, die von Los Angeles nach Washington gingen, tauchen zwischen September 1947 und Oktober 1948 dementsprechend mit zunehmender Häufigkeit Zusammenfassungen der ‚physical surveillance' auf wie die folgenden: ‚On February 5th, another surveillance was inaugurated with negative results until February 16, 1948, on which date, at 10:30 a.m., [ausgeschwärzt] cashed a $250 check issued by the subject at the 14th and Wilshire Branch and then proceeded to the Bank of America at Third and Santa Monica Boulevard, Santa Monica, California, where she deposited

another $250 check to her own account'.[13] Oder: ‚On February 17th, [ausge-
schwärzt] left her home at 10:45 a.m. and proceeded to the Feuchtwanger
residence at 520 Paseo Miramar, Pacific Palisades, California, after stopping to
pick up cleaning and mail at the Pacific Palisades Post Office. She remained at
the Feuchtwanger residence until 2:45 p.m., at which time she was observed by
Special Agents [ausgeschwärzt] … to depart in DeSoto Sedan, California 1947
license No. [ausgeschwärzt]…'.[14]

Nun finden sich Berichte dieser Art in den Akten von vielen Zielobjekten
des FBI. Neu ist in dem Material des Los Angeles Field Office zu Feuchtwanger, daß diesmal auch ein knappes halbes hundert jener viel detaillierteren
und lebensnäheren, weil spontan am Ort des Geschehens verfaßten Notizen der
Special Agents zugänglich gemacht werden, die den ‚Reports' zugrunde liegen.
Hunderte von Trivialitäten wie ‚went to Baer Market, 17th & Montana',[15] „out
in Olds to S.M. Canyon Cleaners'[16] und ‚enters her apartment after considerable
difficulty getting car in garage'[17] stehen dabei neben Hinweisen, die andeuten,
daß die Agenten Hoovers gewillt waren, tief in die Privatsphäre der beobachteten Personen einzudringen: ‚Lights on… in kitchen & front room (observed
from alley) until 9:50p – light on in back room until 10:05p – Surv. dropped at
10:15p.'.[18] Im Stil schlechter B-Filme aus Hollywood übergibt ‚Car 24' die
Überwachung mal an ‚Car 16'[19], mal an ‚Car No. 25… On duty 3:00 PM –
11:00 PM.'.[20] Einmal, als Waldo bis zu dem Haus von Hanns Eisler (a ‚little fat
musician'[21]) in Malibu verfolgt wird, geschieht es, daß die G-Men Feuchtwangers ‚Olds' an der Kreuzung ‚Sunset & Pac. C. Hyw. [Pacific Coast Highway]'
verlieren.[22] Ein anderes mal kommen die kriminalistischen Fähigkeiten von
Hoovers Männern zum Einsatz: ‚Believed Mrs. F. returned as car lights did not
pass house and lights went on in garage area. (Observed from across the
canyon.)'.[23] Und immer wieder müssen neue FBI-Agenten auf die Sekretärin
des exilierten Schriftstellers angesetzt worden sein, denn nur wer offen und
direkt neben der Zielperson stand, vermochte zu beobachten, daß Hilde Waldo
bei der Post ein Paket für genau $1.02[24] aufgibt oder in einem Drug Store die
Saturday Evening Post[25] und nicht die *Los Angeles Times* kauft – was immer
der Wert solcher Erkenntnisse für das FBI und die Sicherheit der Vereinigten
Staaten von Amerika gewesen sein mag.

Doch nicht genug damit. Wie elektrisiert reagieren die für die Bekämp-
fung von Schwerverbrechern ausgebildeten Agenten, als Waldo auf ihrer mor-
gendlichen Fahrt zu Feuchtwanger am Straßenrand Halt macht und von einem
Mann, ‚dressed in red plad [!] shirt',[26] angesprochen wird, der ihr einen unbekannten Gegenstand übergibt, ‚resembling a white sheet of paper'.[27] Ein anderer
Mann, ‚about 37-40 yrs. – about 6.' tall – 170-175 lbs. – medium built, dark
hair',[28] wird, weil er mit Waldo in der Post ‚for two or three minutes'
gesprochen hat, verfolgt, gestellt und nach seiner Beziehung zu Waldo befragt:
‚[ausgeschwärzt]… advised that he… aided her by fixing her automobile which
broke down regularly'.[29] Und als kleiner Höhepunkt der Beschattung von

Feuchtwanger und seinem Umfeld mag der ‚trash cover' bei einem Bewohner des Hauses ‚20840 Pac Coast Hyw.' in Malibu dienen, in dessen Hausmüll mehrere Seiten aus einem Stenoblock sichergestellt werden, die nach einigen Mühen (‚stenographers in this office who use the Pitman method recognize the notes as such but are unable to transcribe them'[30]) von einem Spezialisten auf 25 Blättern transkribiert werden und den Entwurf zu einem Roman oder einer Erzählung enthalten, der aber wohl nicht aus der Feder von Feuchtwanger stammt.[31]

Die Beschattung von Hilde Waldo bricht, ebenso wie die Überwachung von Feuchtwangers Bankkonten, Telephon und Postverkehr um die Jahreswende 1948/49 plötzlich und ohne konkrete Ergebnisse erbracht zu haben ab. Ein paar Mal korrespondiert das FBI-Büro in Los Angeles in den kommenden Jahren mit dem INS wegen des Einbürgerungsantrags des Exilantenpaars und wiederholt dabei mehrfach die Aussage von Informanten, daß Mrs. Feuchtwanger die USA nicht mag (‚Americans are quite dumb'[32]) und ihr Mann die gegenwärtige Politik des Landes mit ‚gestapo methods'[33] vergleicht, Kalifornien aber als ‚a comfortable place to live'[34] ansehe – ganz abgesehen davon, daß in der *New York Times* für jedermann zu lesen stand, ‚Feuchtwanger translated his name into J. L. Wetcheek and contributed to the „Berliner Tageblatt", a series of more or less general satires on Americanism... directed against the American scene although Feuchtwanger had never been here'.[35]

Als Feuchtwanger im September 1952 nicht ohne Stolz[36] einer dieser Informantinnen jenen bereits aus seiner Stammakte bekannten Brief von Senator Richard M. Nixon zeigt, in dem es um die Unterstützung seiner Bewerbung um die amerikanische Staatsbürgerschaft geht, hakt ein Special Agent nach und findet ein weiteres Schreiben Nixons, in dem der inzwischen zum Vizepräsidenten der USA aufgestiegene Volksvertreter dem Romancier mitteilt, ‚how much he enjoyed his last book' – worauf jemand handschriftlich auf dem Office Memorandum vermerkt: ‚Do we have anything on Feuchtwanger? What is the purpose of this memo? Is it for info or to advise the Bureau?'[37] In Section 3 von Sub file 100-6133A hat sich die Kopie eines undatierten Telegramms erhalten, das umgehend an das ‚FBI Laboratory... for a cryptanalytic examination'[38] weitergeleitet wird, weil es Kürzeln enthält wie ‚732 Lucian... 896 Philostratus 932 Porphyrius... 1070 Jesus... 1123A Talmudica'[39] – die Katalognummern und Namen der Autoren von Büchern, die der passionierte Sammler bei irgendeinem Antiquariat bestellt. Eher unaufgeregt registriert man beim FBI dagegen, daß Feuchtwanger 1950 Stalin zum Geburtstag gratuliert und wenig später den Nationalpreis der DDR erhält und daß laut Bericht eines Gastes, der am 5. Dezember 1953 zusammen mit ‚30 or 40 German speaking people' in der Villa Aurora war, Feuchtwangers ‚former secretary, who lives in Europe, brought out part of the $25,000 he was awarded for being the outstanding author of Eastern Germany, by purchasing an expensive fur coat and wearing the coat when she left the Eastern Zone. Dr. Feuchtwanger suggested to the informant that she should do the same thing'.[40]

Wohl mehr aus politischem als literarischem Interesse notiert ein FBI-Agent in New York die Aussage eines Informanten, daß der Roman „„The Jew Suess"… was written so vividly and with so much realism and imagination that Hitler's propaganda ministry transformed it to a script for a film which then became the most formidable propaganda vehicle against the Jewish race'.[41] Eine Meldung aus Washington, daß Feuchtwanger und andere ‚have been subpoened [!] for appearance before coming HUAC public session, Hollywood, Calif.'[42] wird in Los Angeles nicht weiterverfolgt, obwohl sich das FBI sonst genau über die Tätigkeit anderer Behörden informiert – allen voran das lokale Un-American Activities Committee des kalifornischen Senators Jack B. Tenney, das Ende der vierziger Jahre in regelmäßigen Abständen mit umfangreichen Namenslisten von fellow travellers an die Öffentlichkeit geht, und das Office of Strategic Services, das Ende 1944 mit Feuchtwanger und anderen Exilanten eine Reihe von Interviews zur Zukunft von Deutschland durchführt,[43] bzw. Carl Zuckmayer 1943 nach Washington einlud, um mit ihm über Deutschland und seine Mitexilanten zu sprechen.[44] Und mehrere Versuche des Los Angeles Field Office, den Fall Feuchtwanger wegen Mangel an Aktivitäten zu schließen, fallen beim Hauptquartier des Bureau in Washington auf taube Ohren. Vielmehr erwartet der ‚Director, FBI', als jemand der Zweigstelle des Bureau in New York bei einem Interview erzählt, ‚that Leon Feuchtwanger is one of the individuals he has known or heard of who he thinks might still be an active Soviet agent' und eine andere Quelle behauptet, ‚Feuchtwanger… was on his pay roll as a Soviet agent', daß die Akte offen bleibt, der sogenannte ‚character of case' von ‚Security Matter – C' zu ‚Internal Security – R'[45] geändert wird und die Angaben auf Feuchtwangers Security Index Card regelmäßig durch ‚pretext phone calls' oder ‚pretext visits' überprüft werden.

Lebhaft wird es um den inzwischen 71jährigen Exilanten erst wieder Ende 1955, als eine Gruppe sowjetischer Journalisten Los Angeles besucht und das FBI bei der Überwachung von Martha Dodd und Alfred K. Stern auf den Namen des Schriftstellers stößt. Bei der Tour der russischen Delegation gerät Feuchtwanger vor allem deshalb ins Visier des FBI, weil er sich bereit erklärt hatte, einen Empfang für die Gruppe in seinem Haus auszurichten. Doch der Besuch der Sowjets schien schon früh außer Kontrolle zu geraten. Von Anfang an war die Reise der Sowjets durch die USA nach FBI-Berichten von Demonstrationen begleitet (‚12 men and 6 women dressed in Slavic European costumes were carrying placards stating „Soviet Liars Go Home"'[46]), die bisweilen gewalttätig wurden.[47] Ähnlich wie Nikita Chruschtschow ein paar Jahre später scheinen die Sowjetrussen mehr an Vergnügungen als an Politik interessiert gewesen zu sein (‚the Soviets were like a bunch of children at Disneyland; … they went on every ride and he thought he would never be able to get them to leave there';[48] ‚they…desired to be entertained at the homes of motion picture stars'.[49]). Und über den Empfang bei Feuchtwanger, der offensichtlich unter keinem guten Stern stand (‚if [ausgeschwärzt] did not let Soviets go to Feucht-wanger's home, they would cancel tour and immediately return to Russia'[50]), berichtet das FBI, ‚that Metro-Goldwyn-Mayer had put so much pressure on Feuchtwanger (fearing unfavorable publicity) that he refused to have his photo-graph taken with the Soviets and refused to allow photographers in his home'.[51]

Weniger öffentlich als der Besuch der sowjetischen Journalisten verliefen die vom FBI genau beobachteten Kontakte zwischen Feuchtwanger und Martha Dodd Stern. Stern war in den dreißiger Jahren als Tochter des amerikanischen Botschafters in Berlin aufgefallen, weil sie gleichzeitig oder nacheinander Affären hatte mit einem deutschen Jagdflieger aus dem Ersten Weltkrieg, einem preußischen Prinzen, einem prominenten amerikanischen Schriftsteller, dem Chef der Gestapo und einem sowjetischen Diplomaten, der sie und ihre ameri-kanische Freundin Mildred Fish Harnack, die später zusammen mit ihrem Mann Arvid als Mitglied der Roten Kapelle von den Nazis hingerichtet wird, für das NKWD anwarb (‚A real internationalist!'[52], wie der russische Geheimdienst trocken anmerkte).[53] So ähnlich jedenfalls läßt es sich das FBI in einem ausführ-lichen Interview von einem ehemaligen Mitarbeiter und engen Vertrauten des ex-Botschafters William E. Dodd erzählen. Jetzt, zwanzig Jahre später, wird Martha Dodd Stern zusammen mit ihrem Mann Alfred Kaufman Stern, erst verdächtigt und schließlich von einem amerikanischen Gericht verurteilt, den Spionagering um Boris Morros und seine Music Company unterstützt zu haben.

Entsprechend ernst nimmt das FBI die Beziehungen zwischen Feucht-wanger und Stern. Wann, wo und warum sich die beiden getroffen haben, will man wissen – 1937 in Paris, 1943 bei einem Empfang in Sterns Haus in Los Angeles und Mitte der fünfziger Jahre, diesmal bei Feuchtwanger. FBI-Agenten stoßen beim Durchsuchen von Sterns Zimmer im Beverly Wilshire Hotel auf ein Adreßbuch, in dem auch der Name von Feuchtwanger steht. Ein Taxifahrer, der die verdächtige Schriftstellerin zur Villa Aurora fährt, wird ausgefragt und erzählt, daß die beiden ‚old, old friends' seien, die sich seit Jahren nicht mehr gesehen haben. Und irgend jemand berichtet dem FBI, daß die Sterns sich nicht nur Gedanken darüber machen, ob sie vom FBI verfolgt werden, sondern auch, daß die Agenten bei dieser Arbeit ‚awfully bored'[54] sein müssen.

Doch dem FBI reichen die üblichen Überwachungsmethoden diesmal offensichtlich nicht. Da die Beobachtung von Feuchtwanger und seiner Villa keine handfesten Ergebnisse bringt, entschließt man sich, den Exilanten am 28. Oktober 1957 persönlich zum Fall Stern zu vernehmen – ziemlich genau einen Monat nachdem man das Paar, das bereits im Exil in Mexiko lebte, wegen Spionage angeklagt hatte. Höflich (‚cordial enough') listet Feuchtwanger dabei alle Kontakte mit der verdächtigen Person auf, an die er sich erinnern kann. Geduldig verneint er, daß je ‚an exchange of secrets or clandestine information or material between himself and either of the Sterns'[55] stattgefunden hat. Und da ‚Martha Stern ... a true American' sei, ‚he was unable to understand how she could possibly be accused of espionage'.[56]

Als die verhörenden FBI-Agenten nicht aufgeben weiterzubohren, geht Feuchtwanger schließlich, ähnlich wie bei den endlosen Interviews mit dem INS zu seiner eigenen Person,[57] die Geduld aus. ‚A real writer' wie Stern und er selbst, belehrt er die Special Agents, ‚would not consider membership in the CP for the discipline of the Party would be such as to thwart a true writer's natural feelings and thoughts'.[58] Geheimnisse habe er mit Stern, der Verfasserin eines Schlüsselromans über die Kontroverse um die ‚loyalty oaths' an der University of California mit dem Titel *The Searching Light*, nur gehabt, fügt er ironisch hinzu, ‚when he... had told Martha that the secret of good writing was to have ideas and themes developed by actions and speech of the characters, rather than by the author'. Und als er gefragt wird, warum die Sterns im Ausland leben, stellen die G-Men angesichts seiner Antwort enttäuscht fest, daß Feuchtwangers Amerikanisierung nach fast 20 Jahren in den USA keine Fortschritte gemacht hat: ‚He… liberally sprinkled his conversation with allusions to police states, McCarthyism, etc. It was quite obvious he has not in any manner changed his thinking during his years of residence in the US'.[59]

Die Überwachung von Lion und Marta Feuchtwanger, ‚physical surveillance' von Hilde Waldo und der Fall Martha Dodd Stern machen deutlich, daß sich derartig engmaschige Netze nur dann über die Bewohner und Besucher der Villa Aurora werfen ließen, wenn Hoovers Männer mehr taten als in schwarzen Limousinen hinter den verdächtigen Personen durch West Los Angeles herzufahren. Neue Informationsquellen mußten entwickelt und besser getarnte Beobachtungsposten ausfindig gemacht werden. Zu ihnen zählen, mehr als wir bislang aus der Stammakte im FBI-Hauptquartier wußten, die Überwachung von Feuchtwangers Telephon, aussagewillige Vermieter, Nachbarn und Besucher.

Verschiedene umfangreiche Listen mit den Namen von Gesprächspartnern und ‚numbers called' belegen, daß Feuchtwangers Telephon mehrfach und über längere Zeiträume hinweg überwacht wurde. Doch so interessant oder trivial manche dieser Aufstellungen von Kontakten mit dem Konsulat der UdSSR, dem Jewish Temple, Brentano's Bookstore oder den Sunset Garden Supplies (‚this number was called frequently'[60]) auch sein mögen, sie geben ähnlich wie bei anderen FBI-Akten kaum mehr her als trockenes statistisches Material, das sich heute kaum mehr nachverfolgen läßt. Spannender ist es deshalb, einen kurzen Blick in die ebenfalls gerade erst an mich freigegebene Akte des FBI-Büros in Los Angeles zu Bertolt Brecht zu werfen, weil sich hier zumindest für ein wichtiges Jahr, 1945, auch hunderte von Mitschnitten und Zusammenfassungen von Gesprächen erhalten haben, darunter – wie zu erwarten – eine nicht unerhebliche Zahl mit Lion Feuchtwanger. So geht es zwischen den beiden Freunden mal um die Verhandlungen der Alliierten in Potsdam (‚... very bad news. Germany will be broken up'[61]); mal um eine ‚matter which interests both of us',[62] über die Brecht aber nicht am Telephon sprechen möchte; und noch ein anderes mal darum, daß Helene Weigel sich wünscht, daß Feuchtwanger und ihr Mann als Berichterstatter zu den Kriegsverbrecherprozessen in Nürnberg fahren ('My personal interest in this matter is that you take Brecht along as your secretary'.[63]). Als sie im Juli 1945 Feuchtwangers Geburtstag vergißt, erklärt die Weigel einer Gesprächspartnerin schnippisch, 'I don't care, I am not going to congratulate him'[64] – zögert gleichzeitig aber nicht, sich bei dem 'Doctor' genannten Nachbarn über die Affäre ihres Mannes mit Ruth Berlau zu beschweren: 'He may not be in New York at all, but somewhere up country in the forest with (Ruth) Berlau'.[65]

Soviel zur 'technical surveillance', also der Überwachung von Feuchtwangers Telephon. Andere Informationen kommen aus der Nachbarschaft und dem Umfeld des Schriftstellers. Hilfsbereit übergibt da zum Beispiel der Besitzer des Hauses im Manderville Canyon, dessen Mietstreit mit Feuchtwanger im September 1943 durch die lokale Presse ging, nach dem Auszug des unangenehmen Ausländers dem FBI einen Stoß Druckmaterial, das seinem Mieter offensichtlich nicht mehr wichtig war, darunter Informationsschriften der Sowjetbotschaft und des Unitarian Service Committee, drei Ausgaben von *New Masses* sowie eine Broschüre mit der Überschrift 'Rommel Can be Stopped by Jewish Army of Stateless and Palestinian Jews'.[66] Eine Nachbarin, deren Kinder ständig von Feuchtwangers 'guard'[67] verjagt werden, berichtet 'that there is a tremendous amount of books throughout the entire house'.[68] Eine andere Bewohnerin des dünnbesiedelten Paseo Miramar fährt besorgt den langen Weg bis zum Strand hinunter, um ein Licht zu beobachten, das wie ein Leuchtturm vom Dach der Feuchtwanger Residenz scheint – gut drei Jahre nach Ende des Krieges mit Japan und Deutschland. Wieder andere Anwohner notieren freiwillig oder nach Aufforderung des FBI die Nummernschilder von Autos, die vor der Villa Aurora parken. Und als ein Special Agent eine sogenannte 'neighborhood source of information' aufzumachen versucht, um Hilde Waldo und ihren Arbeitgeber ungestörter beobachten zu können als von seinem Dienstwagen aus, bieten ihm Nachbarn ('Mrs. F. has been in [ausgeschwärzt] home only once to use the phone...') ohne Umstände ihr Haus an: 'Both stated would be pleased to help in any way. Their unlisted telephone number is [ausgeschwärzt] it would be well to mention the writer's name if they are called'.[69]

Ähnlich hilfsbereit und aussagewillig, wenn auch in den Dokumenten schwerer als Quelle zu identifizieren, waren manche von Feuchtwangers Mitexilanten und Gäste. Bereitwillig und zum Teil öffentlich lassen sich die Ex-Kommunisten Hilde Eisler und wohl auch Paul und Hede Massing vom FBI verhören. Ein INS-'Inspector' ist, wie Feuchtwanger und andere Männer, von Eva Herrmann beeindruckt ('very intelligent and apparently serious in her statements about Feuchtwanger'), die ihm erklärt, daß der Schriftsteller kein Kommunist sei, auch wenn er 'for more control of economy than exists in this country' plädiert.[70] Ein anonymer Denunziant, der sich als potentieller Übersetzer von Feuchtwanger vorstellt, läßt das FBI handschriftlich wissen, daß Franz Werfel und Emil Ludwig am besten über den Autor und seine Aktivitäten informiert seien – beide eher keine guten Adressen für ein objektives Urteil über einen potentiellen fellow traveller der Kommunisten. Marta Feuchtwanger wird von ‚source [ausgeschwärzt] as a sort of Bedouin' bechrieben, ‚a shrill Yiddish type, who shrieks and shrills when the surface is scratched'.[71] Andere Quellen ‚knew definitely that the Subject and his wife have had negro help at least part of the time';[72] stoßen sich daran, daß ‚Feuchtwanger and his wife associated with every celebrity in Hollywood',[73] daß ‚a group of Jews' den Nazi-Flüchtling in die USA gebracht habe und daß er jetzt ‚in a pretentious house' lebt;[74] ‚heartily dislike the subject because of his arrogant, supercilious manner';[75] oder bezeichnen Marta als Kommunistin, weil sie ‚government ownership of utilities' befürwortet.[76] Hier und da erhalten Informanten für derartige Aussagen vom FBI einen Obolus von $50.[77] Andere bieten ihre Dienste aus ‚patriotic duty... without mentioning financial reward' an,[78] darunter eine ‚she', die nicht nur bei Feuchtwanger zum Abendessen war und ‚‚the Greek", who is a notorious Los Angles gambler'[79] sowie den Bruder von Al Capone kennt, sondern auch mit einem sehr reichen Mann zu tun hat, ‚who... keeps several lesbians and asks some of the young actresses over... and... has these Lesbians perform and requests that these young actresses observe them'.[80]

Doch genug der lesbischen Schauspielerinnen, willigen Informanten, neidischen Nachbarn und eifrigen G-Men. Was die jetzt aus dem Archiv des Los Angeles Field Office des FBI an mich freigegebenen gut 1300 Blätter zu Lion Feuchtwanger, seiner Arbeit, seiner finanziellen Situation und seinem Umfeld mitteilen, verlangt nicht, daß die Biographien des Autors neu geschrieben werden müssen. Wohl aber läßt dieses Material die Feuchtwanger-Akte nach Breite und Tiefe zu einem Kernstück der Dossiers über die deutschen Exilanten in den USA werden. Zwar fehlen auch jetzt noch jene Mitschriften von Telephongesprächen, die das FBI-Dossier aus Los Angeles über Bertolt Brecht zu einer so spannenden Lektüre machen. Andererseits gibt es, bislang zumindest, keine Akte, die einen auch nur annähernd ähnlich tiefen Einblick in die tägliche Arbeit der FBI-Agenten vor Ort erlaubt. Und wie bei Brecht, wo in den letzten Monaten eines menschenverachtenden Weltkriegs gut ausgebildete, durchtrainierte junge Männer und ein kleines Heer von Büropersonal und Übersetzern hunderte von Stunden mit dem Abhören und Transkribieren von alltäglichen Telephongesprächen verschwenden, so vermittelt auch das neu freigegebene Material zu Feuchtwanger ein tiefes Gefühl von der Absurdität moderner Bürokratien, der paranoiden Angst von mächtigen Staaten vor der subversiven Kraft einer kleinen, exilierten und marginalisierten Gruppe von Intellektuellen und der hoffnungslosen Machtlosigkeit des Einzelnen gegenüber der Gier von Geheimdiensten nach Informationen aller Art.

Anmerkungen

[1]   Alexander Stephan, *Im Visier des FBI. Deutsche Exilschriftsteller in den Akten amerikanischer Geheimdienste*, Stuttgart: Metzler, 1995, S. 232.

[2] Alexander Stephan, 'Neues vom FBI. CNDI LA-BB-1: Die Überwachung von Bertolt Brechts Telefon in Los Angeles'. In *neue deutsche literatur*, 51 (2003), Nr. 549, 123-44.

[3] FBI-Report, Los Angeles, v. 27. 4. 1948, S. 10. Alle Angaben zu FBI-Akten, die nicht anders gekennzeichnet sind, stammen aus dem Dossier, das das Los Angeles Field Office des FBI in den vierziger und fünfziger Jahren angelegt und vor kurzem an mich ausgeliefert hat.

[4] FBI-Report, Los Angeles, v. 18. 11. 1942, S. 24.

[5] Cable Censorship o. D. (ca. Juli 1944).

[6] FBI-Report, Los Angeles, v. 4. 4. 1946, S. 6.

[7] Immigration and Naturalization Service, Request for Search of Records v. 10. 1. 1946.

[8] FBI-Report, Los Angeles, v. 4.. 4. 1946, S. 5.

[9] Physical surveillance log v. 14. 1. 1947.

[10] FBI-Report, Los Angeles, v. 3. 8. 1945, S. 7-8.

[11] FBI-Report, Los Angeles, v. 29. 11. 1948, S. 2.

[12] Physical surveillance log v. 24. 2. 1948.

[13] Los Angeles Field Office, Brief an Director, FBI, v. 13. 3. 1948.

[14] A. a. O.

[15] Physical surveillance log v. 5. 2. 1948.

[16] Physical surveillance log v. 13. 2. 1948.

[17] Physical surveillance log v. 26. 2. 1948.

[18] A. a. O.

[19] Physical surveillance log v. 19. 2. 1948.

[20] Physical surveillance log v. 21. 2. 1948.

[21] SA [ausgeschwärzt], Memorandum an SAC, Los Angeles, v. 13. 4. 1956, s. 4.

[22] Physical surveillance log v. 12. 2. [1948].

[23] Physical surveillance log v. 26. 2. 1948.

[24] Physical surveillance log v. 14. 1. 1947.

[25] Physical surveillance log v. 14. 1. 1947.

[26] Physical surveillance log v. [unleserlich], ca. 17. oder 18. 2. 1948.

[27] FBI-Report, Los Angeles, v. 27. 4. 1948, S. 11.

[28] Physical surveillance log v. 18. 2. 1948.

[29] FBI-Report, Los Angeles, v. 29. 11. 1948, S. 8.

[30] SAC, Los Angeles, Memorandum an Director, FBI, v. 16. 3. 1948.

[31] In diesem Manuskript verwandelt ein David, gegen den Widerstand von Dr. Richardson, eine Stadt, deren Einwohner perfekte Zähne haben, nach dem Vorbild von Saratoga Springs und Baden-Baden in einen Kurort, weil er einer Quelle besondere Heilkraft zuspricht.

[32] FBI-Report, Los Angeles, v. 18. 11. 1942, S. 18.

[33] SA [ausgeschwärzt], Memorandum an SAC v. 27. 10. 1952.

[34] SAC, Los Angeles, Memorandum an Director, FBI, v. 25. 9. 1952, S. 2.

[35] FBI-Report, Los Angeles, v. 22. 1. 1948, S. 3-4. Bei den Satiren handelt es sich um *Pep, J. L. Wetcheeks amerikanisches Liederbuch*, das Dorothy Thompson 1929 ins Englische übersetzt hatte.

[36] „... while talking to Feuchtwanger, Senator Richard M. Nixon's name was mentioned. At this time Feuchtwanger told [ausgeschwärzt] that he wished to show her something. [Ausgeschwärzt] accompanied Feuchtwanger to the second floor of his home where his study is located. He went to his desk, unlocked a drawer and took from it what appeared to be his personal files. He showed [ausgeschwärzt] two letters... One letter was address [!] to Feuchtwanger and was signed by Senator Richard M. Nixon. According to [ausgeschwärzt] the letter was typed and appeared to be on official stationary. She said that in effect the letter stated that Senator Nixon had contacted the State Department in Washington in regards to obtaining a visa for Feuchtwanger and his wife, Martha, and that his efforts had been unsuccessful' (SAC, Los Angeles, Memorandum an Director, FBI, v. 25. 9. 1952, S. 1).

[37] SA [ausgeschwärzt], Memorandum an SAC v. 30. 7. 1953.

[38] FBI-Report, Los Angeles, v. 29. 11. 1948, S. 5.

[39] Kopie eines Telegramms, o. D. (ca. April 1948).

[40] SA [ausgeschwärzt], Memorandum an SAC v. 6. 1. 1954.

[41] SAC, New York, Memorandum an Director, FBI, v. 28. 1. 1952.

[42] Director, Telegramm an FBI, Los Angeles, v. 8. 9. 1951.

[43] Vgl. die von mir mitgestalteten Fernsehfeatures 'Exilanten und der CIA,' Zweites Deutsches Fernsehen ('aspekte'), 11. Januar 2002 bzw. ZDF, 12. Januar und 3Sat, 18. Januar 2002, sowie 'Thomas Mann und der CIA,' Zweites Deutsches Fernsehen ('aspekte'), 8. März und 9.März 2002.

[44] FBI-Report, Albany, New York, v. 8. 3. 1945, S. 2. Vgl dazu Carl Zuckmayer, *Geheimreport*, herausgegeben von Gunther Nickel und Johanna Schrön, Göttingen: Wallstein 2002.

[45] Director, FBI, Memorandum an SAC, Los Angeles, v. 9. 6. 1953. 'C' steht hier für 'Communist', 'R' für 'Radical' oder „Russian'.

[46] Director, FBI, Memorandum an FBI, Los Angeles, v. 3. 11. 1955, S. 2.

[47] A. a. O., S. 1.

[48] SA [ausgeschwärzt], Memorandum an SAC, Los Angeles, v. 15. 11. 1955, S. 2.

[49] Director, FBI, Memorandum an FBI, Los Angeles v. 1. 11. 1955, S. 1.

[50] Director, FBI, Telegramm an FBI, Los Angeles v. 4. 11. 1955, S. 2-3.

[51] FBI-Report, Los Angeles, v. 23. 1. 1956, S. 6. Vgl. auch SA [ausgeschwärzt], Memorandum an SAC, Los Angeles, v. 15. 11. 1955, S. 2.

[52] Allen Weinstein u. Alexander Vassiliev, *The Haunted Wood. Soviet Espionage in America – the Stalin Era*, New York: The Modern Library, 2000, S. 64.

[53] John F. Fox, *'In Passion and in Hope': The Pilgrimage of an American Radical, Martha Dodd Stern and Family, 1933-1990*, Phil. Diss., University of New Hampshire, 2001.

[54] SAC, Los Angeles, Memorandum an Director, FBI, v. 23. 1. 1956, S. 2.

[55] SA James H. Hoose, Jr., Memorandum an SAC v. 14. 3. 1958.

[56] FBI-Report, Los Angeles, v. 3. 12. 1957, S. 8.

[57] Stephan, *Im Visier des FBI*, S. 251-64,

[58] A. a. O.

[59] SA James H. Hoose, Jr., Memorandum an SAC v. 14. 3. 1958.

[60] FBI-Report, Los Angeles, v. 3. 7. 1947, S. 14.

[61] Bertolt Brecht, Dossier des FBI Field Office in Los Angeles, Transkript eines Telephongesprächs v. 2. 8. 1945, 16:35 Uhr.

[62] A. a. O., Transkript eines Telephongesprächs v. 23. 7. 1945, 11:56 Uhr.

[63] A. a. O., Transkript eines Telephongesprächs v. 3. 10. 1945, 11:50 Uhr.

[64] A. a. O., Transkript eines Telephongesprächs v. 8. 7. 1945, 11:55 Uhr.

[65] A. a. O., Transkript eines Telephongesprächs v. 7. 7. 1945, 12:59 Uhr. Auf eine Reihe der hier erwähnten telephonischen Kontakte zwischen Feuchtwanger und Brecht gehe ich näher ein in dem Aufsatz „Neues vom FBI. CNDI LA-BB-1: Die Überwachung von Bertolt Brechts Telefon in Los Angeles'. Siehe Notiz 2 oben.

[66] FBI-Report, Los Angeles, v. 18. 11. 1942, S. 21.

[67] SA [ausgeschwärzt], Memorandum an SAC v. 10. 11. 1948, S. 1.

[68] A. a. O., S. 2.

[69] SA [ausgeschwärzt], Memorandum an SAC v. 28. 3. 1957.

[70] FBI-Report, Los Angeles, v. 4. 4. 1946, S. 5.

[71] FBI-Report, Los Angeles, v. 18. 11. 1942, S. 18.

[72] A. a. O., S. 20.

[73] FBI-Report, Milwaukee, v. 8. 1. 1948, S. 2.

[74] Anonyme Denunziation, o. D.

[75] FBI-Report, New York, v. 10. 11. 1947, S. 12.

[76] FBI-Report, Milwaukee, v. 8. 1. 1948, S. 1.

[77] SAC, Los Angeles, Memorandum an Director, FBI, v. 4. 11. 1955, S. 4.

[78] SAC, Los Angeles, Memorandum an Director, FBI, v. 10. 9. 1952, S. 3.

[79] A. a. O., S. 4.

[80] A. a. O., S. 5.

Marje Schuetze-Coburn

Feuchtwanger's Relocation to Southern California: Frustrations & Successes

This paper explores the emotional, political, and economic challenges that Lion and Marta Feuchtwanger encountered during their emigration in the early 1940s from war-torn Europe to Southern California. During their first three years in Los Angeles, the Feuchtwangers' resources dwindled while Lion Feuchtwanger struggled as a foreigner to find literary topics relevant to Americans. The trials and successes of this tumultuous period ultimately paved the way to financial stability and great public acclaim during Lion Feuchtwanger's final years.

Introduction

Before Lion and Marta Feuchtwanger abandoned Europe for America, they experienced tremendous anxiety, frustration, and physical suffering at the hands of the French government. Their flight from France and Portugal removed the imminent danger of deportation they faced, but leaving Europe did not relieve them of emotional and financial hardship. This paper will review and explore the Feuchtwangers' economic and personal difficulties, as well as their small triumphs, during this transitional period. Lion Feuchtwanger's personal papers and correspondence in the Feuchtwanger Memorial Library, much of which remains unpublished, provide rich insights to his experiences and impressions of life in the U.S. during his first few years in Southern California.

Lion Feuchtwanger arrived in New York on 5 October 1940 aboard the American Export liner *SS Excalibur*. His arrival and dramatic escape from France made news in the *New York Times* edition of 6 October with the headline: 'Flight described by Feuchtwanger.' In this article Feuchtwanger gratefully acknowledged the support he had received throughout his harrowing escape from various American 'friends', whose identity he kept closely guarded so as not to endanger further rescue work in France.[1] Despite this, the news report mentioned that Waitstill Sharp, a Unitarian from Boston, accompanied Feuchtwanger across the Atlantic; according to the reporter, Sharp played some unspecified role in saving Feuchtwanger.

The following week, the *New York Times* covered the arrival of additional German refugees on the Greek liner *Nea Hellas*, focusing on Franz Werfel, and Golo and Heinrich Mann. This ship also carried Hermann Budzislawski, Alfred Polgar, and Marta Feuchtwanger to safety. The *Times* article of 14 October 1940 reported that Dr. Frank Kingdon, chairman of the Emergency Rescue Committee, greeted these writers upon their arrival, mentioning the role played by the ERC in the rescue operation.[2] Neither of these two *Times* articles provided specific details, although Feuchtwanger had described his 'kidnapping' from the bathing hole of the internment camp and his hike over the Pyrenees. Nonetheless, a month later, on 11 November 1940, *Time* magazine critically attacked Feuchtwanger for his careless comments to the press, which the reporter claimed had seriously impacted rescue efforts.[3] The *Time* article continued that the Emergency Rescue Committee resented Feuchtwanger's press briefing and alluded to a bidding war between the ERC and the Exiled Writers Committee over the cost of their fundraiser dinners, trivializing the grave danger and expenses required to save those still trapped in Nazi-occupied Europe. In Feuchtwanger's defense, Franklin Folsom, National Executive Secretary for the League of American Writers, berated the *Time* Literary Editor for the politicized and sarcastic tone of the article.[4]

Many scholars have puzzled as to why Lion Feuchtwanger provided any details outlining his rescue to reporters upon his arrival. In a letter Feuchtwanger wrote to Frank Kingdon on 26 November 1940 he explained that he had understood the Emergency Rescue Committee to be a delegation of the Unitarian Church, not a separate entity. Feuchtwanger continued that he 'gave statements to the press which the Unitarians judged to be useful' because he had incorrectly believed the Unitarians were solely responsible for his escape. He expressed his surprise and concern that his statements might have been considered harmful.[5] Another letter to his close friend, Eva Herrmann, dated 24 November, provides a more intimate perspective on Feuchtwanger's feelings about the affair. He explained to her that he had been 'großartig gerechtfertigt' since many Unitarians in separate interviews had provided the same information that he had. He continued that the Secretary of the Kingdon Committee had apologized to him personally. Nonetheless, he was disturbed about the *Time* article, which he described as an 'ungewöhnlich gemeiner Artikel gegen mich'; and he worried that the 'underground-Attacken gegen mich weitergehen'.[6] Feuchtwanger's private comments to Herrmann underscore his frustration at the public misperception of his interview and the continued recycling of false accusations against him.

Between 1941 and 1944, numerous issues plagued Feuchtwanger's attempts to establish himself and resume a productive career. In addition to the controversy surrounding his first public statement, he experienced anxiety about friends still in Europe, financial instability, a fickle American reading public, a lack of adequate translators, and the impact of the war and restrictions imposed on enemy aliens.

Friends still in Europe

As soon as he left Europe, Feuchtwanger began writing letters to support the rescue of friends still in danger. Over the years he gave thousands of dollars to further this cause and to help those without sufficient resources. Feuchtwanger long hoped that his former secretary, Lola Sernau, would be granted permission to come to the United States. He worked diligently to prepare the necessary paperwork and continued to send her money, but, unfortunately, his multi-year efforts to secure her entry to the U.S. ultimately failed. Separation from his closest friends was also a source of great concern. In December 1940 Feucht-wanger wrote Heinrich Mann that he felt 'bis jetzt nicht sehr wohl' in part because of the obstacles he faced trying to bring his friends, including Bertolt Brecht, to America.[7]

Financial difficulties

Feuchtwanger faced many levels of frustrations during the first year in the U.S., with his financial difficulties numbering among the most severe. In his letters to friends and colleagues, he worried about his blocked bank accounts and ex-pressed concern that he was cut off from his financial resources. However, his letter of 18 March 1941 to Benjamin Huebsch, his editor at Viking Press, is sur-prisingly positive as he comments on his financial woes. He indicates that his daily life was developing a sense of routine: 'Unsere Dinge hier konsolidieren sich jetzt ein wenig mehr' [...] and he continues 'wir haben jetzt einen Wagen, ohne den man hier nicht auskommen kann'.[8]

Feuchtwanger embraced this more predictable pattern of life that enabled him to resume his highly focused, and time-consuming writing schedule. He wrote his close friend Arnold Zweig on 21 March 1941 expressing his relief at finally having time to himself:

> In New York habe ich unzählige Menschen gesprochen, wirklich Fluchten von Men-schen, Deutsche, Franzosen und Amerikaner, und ich bin jetzt der Menschen etwas müde. Auch hier sitzen natürlich ein paar Freunde und sehr viele bekannte herum, doch die riesigen Entfernungen geben einem einen guten Vorwand, nicht allzu viele zu sehen.[9]

While 1941 saw his writing situation improve, as the year drew on, his struggles with finances continued. On 9 July Feuchtwanger again wrote Zweig, lamenting that his small bank account was frozen because the Americans con-sidered him French. Ironically, his bank account was simultaneously blocked due to his German origins and the fact that he had immigrated to the U.S. after 14 June 1940. Feuchtwanger bemoaned the amount of burocratic red tape that surrounded his efforts but agreed that: 'Geld habe ich nicht viel, doch kann ich halbwegs anständig leben. Aussichten habe ich viele und gute [...]'.[10]

Naturally financial problems distressed most of the émigrés, as Feucht-wanger explained to Zweig in his letter of 21 January 1942. Feuchtwanger could identify only four German writers who were well off: Hermann Rausch-ning, Jan Valtin (Richard Krebs), Erich Maria Remarque, and Franz Werfel. Considered much less successful were Emil Ludwig, Stefan Zweig, and Thomas Mann. And Feuchtwanger went on to elaborate that all other German writers' financial situations could be described as 'ausnahmslos nicht gut, schlecht oder erbärmlich.' Both Heinrich Mann and Alfred Döblin belonged to his final category of 'wretched.' Feuchtwanger reserved for himself a separate status; he belonged to the group who was merely 'not doing well' ('es nicht gut geht').[11]

The American reading public / The war

Feuchtwanger and his fellow exiled writers struggled to identify subject matter that would appeal to an American audience. World events unpredictably impacted the interest and sales of books written by Feuchtwanger and his German colleagues. *The Devil in France* (*Der Teufel in Frankreich*), Feuchtwanger's autobiographical account of his internment at Les Milles, provides a brilliant example. German antifascist works like this had been quite popular until the U.S. declared war on 8 December 1941. Unfortunately, Feuchtwanger's memoir was published in November just a month before Pearl Harbor. Although reviews of *The Devil in France* were favorable, the book's release, coinciding as it did with the American entry into WWII, proved disastrous, as the public understandably focused their full attention on the American war effort.

Feuchtwanger's success with a German version of this work met with equally frustrating obstacles. The German émigré publishing firm in Mexico, *El Libro Libre*, published the work in 1942 shortly before Mexico declared war. Feuchtwanger described the situation to Huebsch in May 1942:

> Das äußere Schicksal des Buches scheint weiterhin nicht sehr günstig. [...] Jetzt durch die Kriegserklärung Mexikos ist alles wieder in Frage gestellt. Vermutlich werden dort die deutschen Antifaschisten so ähnlich behandelt wie hier in California und können keine Bücher drucken.[12]

Finding an audience for his works was not his only professional concern. For Feuchtwanger, writing historical novels required ready access to research materials. In July 1941 he expressed frustration to Benjamin Huebsch that his 8,000-volume library from Sanary remained captive on the docks of Lisbon. Without his research collection, Feuchtwanger could not write the novels he wished, including one set during the French Revolution. As a compromise, he selected a contemporary topic loosely based on the clairvoyant Erik Jan Hanussen, who for a time worked closely with Hitler. Feuchtwanger decided upon this topic as he explained to Huebsch: 'weil ich dafür so gut wie kein Material brauche'.[13]

The selection of this topic, however, resulted in difficulties for him of another variety. In the fall of 1941 Feuchtwanger wrote *Die Zauberer* as a play which Leo Mittler translated as *The Wizards* (and also titled *The Brothers Ericksen*). Feuchtwanger shared without success both the German script and the rough English translation with various film and theater producers and the actor Paul Muni. According to Harold Clurman, a producer at Columbia Pictures, the play was a 'pleasure to read,' but Clurman felt that the play 'would strike an American audience, unfamiliar with the emotional, social and psychological background of the period, too schematic to be credible'.[14] When writing to producer and screenwriter Edward Chodorov on 24 January 1942 Feuchtwanger explained:

> I believe that the play is now in a phase where a European author would easily run the risk to confuse the whole thing still more for the American public's mind. Therefore Mittler and I would like to have your opinion whether you think it advisable to ask an

American playwright for an adaptation [...].[15]

American film and theater directors evidently viewed Feuchtwanger's topic as problematic and, ultimately, Feuchtwanger's efforts to secure a suitable American adapter for his play failed. However, he completed the novel *Double, Double, Toil and Trouble* (*Die Brüder Lautensack*) in 1942 and its March and April 1943 serialization in *Collier* provided the Feuchtwangers with, as Marta Feuchtwanger put it, 'salvation from financial disaster'.[16]

Translation issues

The translation of *Double, Double, Toil and Trouble* proved less difficult than other works, with Feuchtwanger mostly satisfied with Caroline Oram's English interpretation. Nevertheless, the language of the novel required special attention, as Feuchtwanger outlined in his letter to Oram on 13 June 1942. He described to her his attempts to capture Hitler's idiosyncratic diction and syntax, which Feuchtwanger criticized as a 'seltsame Mischung von Beamtendeutsch und abstract geschwollenem Geschwafel'.[17] He politely requested that the translator search for an English solution to Hitler's rhetoric.

As Feuchtwanger articulated in his paper presented at the October 1943 Writers' Congress held at UCLA:

> For even the best translation remains somehow foreign. We have perhaps wrestled with a sentence, with a word, and after a long search we have found the sentence, the word, the happy phrase which is completely molded to our thought and feeling. And then we see the translated word, the translated sentence. It is quite correct in all details, but the aroma is gone, the life is gone.[18]

The war and restrictions on enemy aliens

As an 'enemy alien', Feuchtwanger found it quite difficult to accomplish many of his personal goals. On 1 July 1941 the U.S. government enacted new restrictions for European refugees. This and other legislation drastically impacted on Feuchtwanger's efforts to secure visas for his friends and to become naturalized. Already in May 1941 Feuchtwanger filed the paperwork declaring his intention to become an American citizen. Following Pearl Harbor seven months later, Feuchtwanger expressed his worries about government regulations. Huebsch wrote on 16 December 1941 to reassure him:

> I am confident that the declaration of war will not have any unpleasant results for persons like yourself who have established themselves here with the intention of becoming citizens. From what I know it seems far from likely that there will be any regulation that will hamper you; the Attorney General is a high-minded liberal and the FBI is under intelligent direction. If there should be any trouble, it is more likely to come from busybodies than from the Government. [...][19]

Of course, the war and new restrictions on 'enemy aliens' did impact the lives of German émigrés. In a June 1942 letter to Alfred Kantorowicz, Feuchtwanger wrote: 'Dazu kommt, daß die sehr lästigen Fremdenvorschriften hier, curfew und Fünf-Meilen-Zone, den meisten das Leben und die Wirtschaft peinlich erschweren'.[20] In addition, gasoline rationing was particularly burdensome to the Feuchtwangers, who lived far outside the city limits.

Burdened under the strain of worries of family and colleagues left behind
in Europe, the stress of living in a foreign country with limited financial
resources took its emotional toll on the émigrés in Southern California. This
played out in petty gossip and infighting. Feuchtwanger expressed his exas-
peration about this to Kantorowicz in January 1942: 'Läppischer Klatsch und
kleine Verdrießlichkeiten hören nicht auf. Das Ganze ist wie ein gigantisches
Sanary'.[21]

Turning point

The year 1944 marked a turning point for the Feuchtwangers. While they
suffered future periods of financial instability, Feuchtwanger's first big success
in the U.S. occurred during this period. Although Feuchtwanger and Brecht
collaboratively wrote the play *Simone* in late 1942 and early 1943, Feuchtwanger reworked and completed his novel with the same title six months later
in September. Initially, Feuchtwanger considered the play to have few possi-
bilities. He wrote to Huebsch in November 1942: 'Vorläufig schreibe ich
zusammen mit Brecht ein kleines Stück, das zeimlich experimentell ist und
wahrscheinlich wenig Aussicht auf Erfolg hat. Aber es macht uns beiden große
Freude'.[22] However, in February 1944 MGM optioned the novel *Simone* after
previously rejecting the play. Feuchtwanger split the lucrative contract with
Brecht, leaving both writers with $20,000. After this point Feuchtwanger's
financial troubles lessened significantly. Unlike many of the other émigrés he'd
finally found his footing in the New World and, in some sense, his relocation
was now complete.

Conclusion

The Feuchtwangers encountered obstructive wartime bureaucracy and experienced periods of economic crisis during their first few years in Southern California. Lion Feuchtwanger's ability to write during this tumultuous period
remained constant, but success sometimes eluded him due to the war, his
inexperience with American readers and unlucky circumstances. Nonetheless,
the 1940s provided him great stimulation that led to the creation of some of his
most appreciated novels, including *Simone*, *Die Brüder Lautensack* and *Waffen
für Amerika*.

Notes

[1] 'Flight described by Feuchtwanger,' *New York Times*, 6 October 1940, p.38.

[2] 'Authors who fled from Nazis arrive,' *New York Times*, 14 October 1940, p.16.

[3] 'Exiles,' *Time*, 11 November 1940.

[4] Folsom, Franklin, Unpublished letter to *Times* Literary Editor, 13 November 1940, Feuchtwanger Archive, University of Southern California.

[5] Feuchtwanger, Lion, Unpublished letter to Frank Kingdon, 26 November 1940, Feuchtwanger Archive, University of Southern California.

[6] Feuchtwanger, Lion, Unpublished letter to Eva Herrmann, 24 November 1940, Feuchtwanger Archive, University of Southern California.

[7] Feuchtwanger, Lion, Unpublished letter to Heinrich Mann, 19 December 1940, Feuchtwanger Archive, University of Southern California.

[8] Feuchtwanger, Lion, Unpublished letter to Benjamin Huebsch, 18 March 1941, Feuchtwanger Archive, University of Southern California.

[9] Feuchtwanger, Lion., in: Harold von Hofe, ed., *Lion Feuchtwanger and Arnold Zweig. Briefwechsel 1933-1958*, Berlin: Aufbau, 1984, vol. 1, p.225.

[10] Feuchtwanger, Lion, *Briefwechsel*, p.231.

[11] Feuchtwanger, Lion, *Briefwechsel*, p.248.

[12] Feuchtwanger, Lion, Unpublished letter to Benjamin Huebsch, 23 May 1942, Feuchtwanger Archive, University of Southern California.

[13] Feuchtwanger, Lion, Unpublished letter to Benjamin Huebsch, 20 July 1941, Feuchtwanger Archive, University of Southern California.

[14] Clurman, Harold, Unpublished letter to Lion Feuchtwanger, 3 December 1941, Feuchtwanger Archive, University of Southern California.

[15] Feuchtwanger, Lion, Unpublished letter to Edward Chodorov, 24 January 1942, Feuchtwanger Archive, University of Southern California.

[16] Feuchtwanger, Marta, Annotation on unpublished bibliography of Lion Feuchtwanger's novels, undated, Feuchtwanger Archive, University of Southern California.

[17] Feuchtwanger, Lion, Unpublished letter to Caroline Oram, 13 June 1942, Feuchtwanger Archive, University of Southern California.

[18] Feuchtwanger, Lion, 'The Working Problems of the Writer in Exile,' in: *Writer's Congress; the Proceedings of the Conference held in October 1943 under the Sponsorship of the Hollywood Writers' Mobilization and the University of California*, Berkeley, Los Angeles: University of California Press, 1944, p.347.

[19] Huebsch, Benjamin, Unpublished letter to Lion Feuchtwanger, 16 December 1941, Feuchtwanger Archive, University of Southern California.

[20] Feuchtwanger, Lion, Unpublished letter to Alfred Kantorowicz, 18 June 1942, Feuchtwanger Archive, University of Southern California.

[21] Feuchtwanger, Lion, Unpublished letter to Alfred Kantorowicz, 6 January 1942, Feuchtwanger Archive, University of Southern California.

[22] Feuchtwanger, Lion, Unpublished letter to Benjamin Huebsch, 10 November 1942, Feuchtwanger Archive, University of Southern California.

Jeffrey B. Berlin

[...] permit me to say that you are an ideal publisher.[1]
Ben W. Huebsch of the Viking Press (New York) –
Unpublished Correspondence with European Authors in Exile,
With special attention to Lion Feuchtwanger[2]

*Dedicated to John M. Spalek, Wulf Koepke,
Edith Weiß-Gerlach, and Donald A. Prater –
friends and special colleagues*

The aim of this paper is twofold: first, it endeavors to enhance our knowledge about the remarkable American publishing entrepreneur Ben W. Huebsch (1876-1964) who forged a brilliant reputation on his own before merging with the newly formed Viking Press in 1925; and, second, it aims to delineate the nature of the personal and professional relationship between Huebsch and the internationally acclaimed German literary writer Lion Feuchtwanger. To accomplish our goal, we explicate and annotate selections from the several hundred newly discovered and still unknown and unpublished Ben Huebsch/Lion Feuchtwanger epistolary exchanges which only recently have been located.

Wilhelm von Sternburg's comprehensive biographical tribute to Feuchtwanger, using comparative analysis, brilliant conjecture, scholarly intuition and intertextual study, has acknowledged properly that the missives between Huebsch and Feuchtwanger remain a source of valuable and unique information. As von Sternburg claims, these documents should elucidate a multitude of topics, such as the genesis of Feuchtwanger's creative works, self-criticism, publisher interactions, translation issues, political viewpoints or Feuchtwanger's concept of the 'Umwelt' and 'Zeitgeist'.[3] However, von Sternburg's intent was not to pursue these topics further, and therefore at best his major study only could suggest their importance.

Similarly, exemplary investigations by András Sándor and especially Wulf Koepke also have advanced our knowledge about Huebsch's interactions with Feuchtwanger and the other exiles.[4] Illustrative of Huebsch's relationships, too, is Marta Feuchtwanger's response of 28 December 1958 to Huebsch, who had conveyed his condolences on the passing of her husband Lion, seven days earlier: 'From all the words and all the letters [I received] yours were the most precious ones. [...] and I also remembered that without you Lion couldn't have escaped from Hitler. But the best of all was your friendship and understanding for the man and his work. Thank you.' With attention momentarily directed to Lion's wife Marta (neé Löffler), whom he met in 1909 and married in 1912, it is worth recalling some of the many excellent traits she brought to their bond of happy, loving, and respectful marriage, enumerated so perceptively by Wulf Koepke as follows:

> In der Rolle der Vermittlerin hat Marta nicht nur dem Andenken Lion Feuchtwangers gedient, sie hat, im Gegensatz zu vielen anderen Witwen, eigenes Profil gewonnen.

Sie ist als Persönlichkeit eindeutig aus dem Schatten ihres Mannes herausgetreten.[5]

As Marta once observed: '[...] mein Leben beginnt mit dem Tag, an dem ich Lion das erste Mal traf. Das stimmt immer noch'.[6]

To be sure, Ben Huebsch was an extraordinary individual, who 'was from the outset interested in bringing out works of merit regardless of their marketability – assuming somehow that a good book will pay its way.' 'I enjoy an author's first book,' claimed Huebsch, 'more than publishing those subsequent ones whose results can be calculated.' Huebsch's philosophy explains the reason he sometimes was referred to as 'a maverick publisher'.[7] Huebsch was most attracted to writers who strove for freshness in art and ideas. 'I was always more likely to succumb to the persuasion of authors,' he said, 'who wanted to make the world over than to those who celebrated the world as it is'.[8] Undeniably, his name has remained well known and respected throughout the great publishing centers of Europe and America.[9]

Ben Huebsch was not only respected and emulated by colleagues in his own profession. He also gained equal admiration from individuals in other disciplines. Indeed, Huebsch's interests crossed paths with numerous other people, many of whom represented an array of different specialties. Above all, Huebsch also always was acknowledged to be an original and profound thinker whose daily, honest activities demonstrated a true phenomenon in virtually every business dealing with which he was associated. In a 2 July 1938 article entitled 'A Culture in Exile,' for example, Huebsch expressed with ample rage and justification: that '[the exiled writers] are banned from Herr Hitler's new, made-to-order encyclopedias; their books may not be sold, and anybody in Germany who even possesses them is subject to inhuman penalties'.[10] While such vulgarity sickened him, nevertheless he still approached this topic with remarkable calmness. But Huebsch had much to say about this subject, and his inquiring mind focused, as he said, on a truly 'serious question.' Thus, Huebsch declared:

> What is to become of German letters? Can there be a spontaneous flowering of literary talent when men are not free to express their thoughts and ideas openly? Such of the exiles as are famous enough to be translated into other languages will continue to write, but where will their successors come from? I am skeptical of the survival of German literature without German soil. [...] Truly, we are present at the death of a culture in so far as culture is perpetuated in letters.[11]

And about the issue of exile Huebsch always remained focused and direct:

> What is the fate of these men whom millions have read, whose works, in the last few decades, gave such a glamor to Germany as she had not yet had since Gerhart Hauptmann [1862-1946] burst on the world, forty-five years ago, with his drama of rebellion, *The Weavers.*

Huebsch's concerns present much that is provocative. Elsewhere in this same article, Huebsch introduced another matter which in consideration about *Literaturwissenschaft* does not smack us with the same wallop it symbolically might have landed sixty-six years ago. Yet, if but partially, it seems to still smart due to the publisher's direct and progressive thinking. He writes:

> One of the ironies of the present German madness is their unawareness that with

every blow that they strike they injure no one so much as themselves. That is especially true in the field of culture: when they expel a good painter, or composer or author, not only do they lose him, but they lower their standard by putting inferior men in the vacant places.

We cannot enumerate statements from every lecture Huebsch ever prepared, but an exceptionally fine presentation, delivered only three months later, in October 1938, in *The English Journal,* then under the prestigious editorship of W. Wilbur Hatfield, captures the essence of our current investigation. Hence, it is befitting to cite at least some of its quality lines such as the following: 'In five short years,' says Huebsch, 'the picture of German letters has changed utterly; a literature that lived more actively in its little day than that of any other nation, that inspired lively experimentation and healthy controversy, died a sudden and violent death'.[12] To be sure, Huebsch's survey of German literature in exile and thus the contemporary literature scene succeeds admirably and, even today, years after it has been published, continues to offer innovative, insightful, thought-provoking, and, no less so, commanding and sophisticated thought.

What is remarkable is that Huebsch was self-educated. Although his older brother, Daniel, earned a doctoral degree, Ben Huebsch was required to find employment. With guidance given by an uncle, Huebsch learned the printing trade. Huebsch's father, Rabbi Dr. Adolph Huebsch (1830-1884), was a towering, positive figure whose spiritual strength and command were immense. An immigrant from Germany, he earned the respect and admiration of Europeans and Americans by devoting himself to the cause of American Judaism and the advancement of its principles. His death in 1884, at age 54 – at this time Ben was only eight years old –, was a significant loss for young Ben.[13]

In regard to the above, 'Feuchtwanger deserves to be called a *homo judaicus* […] [because] Feuchtwanger accentuate[s] the seemingly interminable suffering of the Jewish people'.[14] Yet we must wonder, in fact, about the extent to which Huebsch might willingly have discussed his father's rabbinical profession with Feuchtwanger's own orthodox upbringing. On the other hand, Huebsch achieved in his own profession the precise respect, admiration, and recognition that his own father also had earned. And what impressions must have been imparted to young Ben Huebsch? Again, Ben Huebsch was but eight years old when his father no longer was there to care for him or guide him in the ways of life, and especially in the ways of a Jewish orthodox family. Even Huebsch's six-hundred page oral testimony in the Columbia University oral history collection provides us with few direct answers. Huebsch says much; that is quite evident. But, like Thomas Mann holding a press conference, Huebsch directed his interviewers. Like Thomas Mann, Huebsch spoke about only what he wanted to reveal – nothing more was articulated.

In 1964, the critic and columnist Maurice Dolbier had the pleasure and honor of bestowing upon Ben Huebsch the newly established Irita Van Doren

Literary Award. Dolbier expressed the following:

> [To Ben W. Huebsch] for more than half a century of tireless devotion to literature, both American and European; for exemplifying in the highest degree the best qualities of responsible editing and publishing standards that he has consistently maintained and that have served as an inspiring example for countless others.[15]

Dolbier's words evoke the essence of the man and publisher Ben W. Huebsch.

In a similar sense, Roberto Gilodi, once a reader with Feltrinelli and currently editorial director with Einaudi, viewed the overall situation from another perspective. As Gilodi has suggested, when speaking of Siegfried Unseld of the Suhrkamp Verlag, publishers have certain distinguishing qualities we can apply to Ben W. Huebsch:

> Die wesentliche Eigenschaft des 'großen' Verlegers [...] sei ein hoher Sinn für die Form seiner Arbeit. [...] Von den großen Verlegern sagt man, sie seien intuitive Geister: ihre Gabe bestehe in der Fähigkeit, die unsichtbaren Fäden wahrzunehmen, die scheinbar ganz verschiedene und thematisch weit voneinander entfernt liegende Bücher miteinander verbinden. [...] [D]ie Tüchtigkeit eines Verlegers besteht in dem Vermögen, eine Beziehung zwischen unterschiedlichen kulturellen Antworten herzustellen. Dieses alchimistische Vermögen, die Einsicht in die unterirdischen Zusammenhänge, erlaubt es, die Konturen dessen zu erkennen, was mit einem etwas verbrauchten Ausdruck ein 'kulturelles Projekt' genannt wird. Die Kataloge der kultur- und geistesgeschichtlich bedeutenden Verlage mit ihren vielen tausend Büchern enthalten diese unsichtbaren Fäden und die daraus resultierende eigentümliche Kohärenz. Es ist bekannt, daß die fruchtbaren und bleibenden Kulturunternehmen nicht aus gezielter Planung, sondern spontan geboren wurden. Ihre innere Kohärenz tritt erst dann zutage, wenn sie sich voll entfaltet haben. In diesem alchimistischen Wissen, in diesem Ahnungsvermögen der Wahlverwandtschaften, die sich unter der bunten Oberfläche von Wissenschaft und Literatur verbergen, ist [Ben W. Huebsch] ein großer Meister.[16]

Huebsch openly claimed three favorite authors: Feuchtwanger, Stefan Zweig, and Franz Werfel. In especially the Huebsch/Zweig and the Huebsch/Werfel correspondences, which I have edited elsewhere,[17] we learn much about Huebsch's attitude toward his profession, including his likes and dislikes, manner of association with various authors, and his literary imagination and skills in his multiple role as publisher, editor, critic, and friend.[18] Nevertheless, a portrait of Ben Huebsch as a publisher remains incomplete without the revealing Huebsch/Feuchtwanger component.[19] To be sure, the Huebsch/Feuchtwanger correspondence defines an image of each individual that until now has remained undisclosed.[20]

Lion Feuchtwanger was not as famous as 1929 Nobel Prize laureate Thomas Mann.[21] On the other hand, Feuchtwanger was substantially more well-known and successful in America than, for example, Heinrich Eduard Jacob, the prolific and profound culture historian, biographer of great musicians, novelist, dramatist, essayist, translator and, from 1927 until 1933, foreign correspondent in Vienna for the prestigious, democratic *Berliner Tageblatt*. Aside from Feuchtwanger's 'best seller' literary works, his involvement with British and American leaders in the fight against Nazi practices was held in awe by Jacob as both Frau Lili Kahler of Princeton and Frau Lucy Tal of the famous Viennese Tal Verlag explained to me in numerous (tape-recorded) interviews.[22]

Despite courageous and diligent efforts, H. E. Jacob's success in Europe could not be repeated as an émigré in the United States.[23] Simply stated, Jacob's serious and grand efforts would not release him from his background European culture that did not match with the likings of Americans. H. E. Jacob was inmate number 8279 of block IV, Stube 2 (later Stube 3) in Dachau and block X A (and later X B) of Buchenwald. Often he could only reflect that, at the beginning of imprisonment in KZ Dachau, in April 1938, individuals were in a veritable Kafkaesque world. Everything became indefinite and uncertain. Here human values were destroyed; individuals were dehumanized. Prisoners were reduced to nobodies. Outside suddenly the refugee was without a home shelter. Desperately, the alienated sought a sense of stability. For 'the house of civilization proved no shelter,' as George Steiner has claimed.[24]

Unlike Jacob who struggled financially, Feuchtwanger lived well in Los Angeles, at the Villa Aurora – a majestic mansion located at 520 Paseo Miramar. His income permitted such luxury, and his Spanish-style palatial home had over twenty rooms. Frequently some rooms functioned as a meeting place for those who had been expelled from Germany and Austria.

In fact, as early as 1926, Feuchtwanger reaped the benefits from his writings in translation when British publisher Martin Secker published Feuchtwanger's *Jud Süß* in English translation under the title *Power*. Since Secker's 'expectation of sales were minimal, the first edition consisted of [only] 750 copies imported from the Viking Press, New York'.[25] However, after the critic Arnold Bennett's favorable review of *Power* in the British *Evening Standard,* Secker promptly reprinted the work that was in great demand. '[M]any thousands of copies'[26] were sold, and it even reached the 'best-seller' list. Furthermore, the astonishing success stimulated interest for the work in the United States. This was Feuchtwanger's initiation into publishing in English translation. Certainly, by its own merit Feuchtwanger's work deserved such recognition, but neither he nor his publisher ever imagined such a favorable reception for *Power*.

If we more carefully compare H. E. Jacob's successes and failures with those of Lion Feuchtwanger or Stefan Zweig, for example, we recognize that the primary difference in terms of success took effect because of, above all else, the endless support given by the publisher – in this case, Ben Huebsch.

In his capacity as publisher and friend, Huebsch boosted Feuchtwanger's career – just as he enhanced Werfel's and Zweig's USA and world opportunities – to heights he otherwise might not have attained. In all such instances Huebsch's typical stance of sincerity and willing agreement[27] motivated his actions.

The Huebsch/Feuchtwanger exchange of letters chronicles the *Zeitgeist,* bringing a tremendous immediacy to Huebsch's and Feuchtwanger's life and the tumultous happenings of the era. By presenting their thoughts in an unreserved and open manner, the correspondence functions as a diary. They speak about totalitarianism and expulsion, freedom and flight, fear and apprehension. They document relief organizations, conflicts with and adjustment to American culture and linguistic issues. We are witness to a spirited conversation, which we are privileged to overhear. Of course, this is not to suggest that these epistolary documents replace Feuchtwanger's creative writings. As a literary artist Feuchtwanger, as other writers, might well have felt the vacillating hands of permission and restriction being balanced on the censorship scale. As Joseph Pischel's still valuable study about Feuchtwanger reminds us,

> Feuchtwanger hat in einem Vorwort zur Erstausgabe [*Exil*] aber sehr nachdrücklich auf den Unterschied zwischen diesen zeitgeschichtlichen Fakten und Vorbildern und seinen künstlerischen Abbildern hingewiesen, nicht nur aus Rücksicht auf die *Überempfindlichkeit* mancher deutscher Flüchtlinge [...]. Gerade für das Sujet *Exil* verbot sich das Stehenbleiben bei der Beschreibung von Oberflächenerscheinungen. Sie hätte notwendig in resignierende Elendsmalerei münden müssen, und jeder Versuch einer Perspektivgestaltung wäre in willkürliches Sich-Erheben über die realen geschichtlichen Chancen umgeschlagen. [...] Auch Klaus Mann führt seine Helden [in *Der Vulkan*] schließlich in die politische Bewährungssituation, nämlich die des Spanienkriegs, auch er formuliert am Schluß des Romans den Glauben an kommende Generationen.[28]

These missives recreate the environment, revealing the cognitive, physical, and emotional ways in which the majority of the displaced responded to exile. After all, as the distinguished critic Harry Levin once proferred:

> Writers in exile have been among the most impressive witnesses to human experience. Though the testimony of their writings or their biographies is uniquely individual in each case, history has lately been accumulating so much of it that it speaks with the voice of our time.

And elsewhere in this same chapter – simply entitled 'Literature and Exile' – Levin presents the interesting statement:

> Exile has been regarded as an occupational hazard for poets in particular ever since Plato denied them rights of citizenship in his republic. His attitude, prompted by the belief that they could exercise a demoralizing influence over other citizens, might have been invoked by Augustus in banishing Ovid.[29]

Another topic these writers dealt with was how books are marketed, including notes about their distribution and sales of foreign, newspaper, and film rights. Werfel, more so than Zweig or Feuchtwanger, was keenly interested in every aspect of the handling of his books and was quite willing to complain whenever he thought his best interests were not being properly served. On the other hand, the only problems which Feuchtwanger raised concerned the poor quality of translations, which will later be discussed in more detail. Finally, Zweig had no complaints, and he and Huebsch interacted on a personal and professional basis remarkably well for sixteen years, i.e., from 1926 to 1942.

Of course, the statement that Zweig registered no complaints refers specifically to possible book problems. About the *Zeitgeist* Stefan Zweig had much to say, and his letters and other documents forecast a bleak future for

Europe. To elaborate on this critical statement, consider the following from Zweig's posthumously published autobiography *Die Welt von Gestern*: '[…] die Zeit gibt die Bilder,' said Zweig, 'ich spreche nur die Worte dazu […].' In addition, elsewhere in the preface to this intellectual autobiography Zweig claimed:

> […] zwischen unserem Heute, unserem Gestern und Vorgestern sind alle Brücken abgebrochen. […] Dies unser gespanntes, dramatisch überraschungsreiches Leben zu bezeugen, scheint mir Pflicht, denn […] jeder war Zeuge dieser ungeheuren Ver-wandlungen, jeder war genötigt Zeuge zu sein. […] [W]enn wir mit mit unserem Zeugnis auch nur einen Splitter Wahrheit aus ihrem zerfallenen Gefüge der nächsten Generation übermitteln, so haben wir nicht ganz vergebens gewirkt.[30]

Although many of Zweig's epistolary documents with Ben Huebsch merely were a form of playful communication between them, a majority of the letters, particularly the letters written after 1933, served as the components which form the symbolic bridge of which Zweig had spoken. Thus, Zweig's communications, sincere, responsive, and respectful for Huebsch, also assumed a second function: most probably unconsciously – but sometimes consciously, too – Zweig elaborated about the *Zeitgeist* not merely to explain to Huebsch what had been happening to and around him. On the contrary, Zweig wanted to leave to humanity a detailed documentation about the *Zeitgeist,* and he chose letters as a means to best articulate many of his thoughts and views.

Overall, Feuchtwanger, Werfel and Zweig all communicated with Huebsch, but careful study of the context of their letters reveals strikingly different methodologies, and each perfectly matched the personality of the writer. In our situation, these correspondences provide us with a perspective on the exile experience, and about Feuchtwanger, Zweig, and Werfel as writers, that have not been discussed in the secondary literature. Incidentally, Huebsch had formulated for himself a specific, unusual conception of letters. In one missive (to Morris R. Cohen of Washington, D.C., 8 April 1943) Huebsch explained: '[…] letters, unless by an artist in the craft, are meagre ersatz for a handclasp.'

These documents reveal that Feuchtwanger, Zweig, and Werfel's interests in their respective books did not end with the completion of their writing, but that, to a certain extent, each followed the success of their writings in the marketplace. Of course, as Wulf Koepke explained in another of his studies on this period, Feuchtwanger was not necessarily always content with what had been presented by critics. However, as Koepke also advises us, certain perspectives in Feuchtwanger's writings – which critics effortlessly could have faulted – were virtually ignored, and possibly because of Feuchtwanger's distinguished renown and universal consequence. To support his argument, for example, Koepke cites a 27 April 1940 review by Orville Prescott that had appeared in the *New York Times*. Quoting Prescott, Koepke stated: '[…] *Paris Gazette* is too long, too crowded, and […] overburdened with plot. Feucht-wanger, a German, believes in the method of exhaustiveness.' Nevertheless, with keen insight Koepke re-examines Prescott's position. In so doing, Koepke concludes – and most justifiably, too – 'Wenn Feuchtwanger Amerikaner und nicht so berühmt gewesen wäre, so hätten die Verlagslektoren gewiß oft gestrichen und verändert – was die Kritik auch vorschlug'.[31]

In still another sense, these Huebsch/Feuchtwanger exchanges strictly could be regarded as a business correspondence, yet each set is culturally, ideologically, and sociologically informative, in that they document the writer's success against the average exiled writer, illustrated here by consideration of H. E. Jacob. The same results will be found if we substitute Werfel for Feuchtwanger. In fact, few other writers, not to say exiled authors, have ever come close to matching the extraordinary sales of *The Song of Bernadette,* which also became a Book-of-the-Month Club selection, and generated additional revenue through this lucrative market.

Interestingly enough, as Terry Reisch observed in an outstandingly well-documented analysis, neither Huebsch nor Werfel ever expected *Bernadette* to amount to any work of great interest, value, or even success. During the writing stages, Werfel did not consider that he was creating a classic work.[32] Nevertheless, although Werfel's sales revenue in the United States frequently exceeded Zweig's or Feuchtwanger's, the latter two authors still achieved remarkable public recognition. In short, the correspondences present us with an integral part of the literary history of their day.

The above situations introduce numerous thoughts, and one perspective is related to the symbolic implications found in the first powerful and provocative sentence of Thomas Mann's *Joseph* novels, which stated: 'Tief ist der Brunnen der Vergangenheit. Sollte man ihn nicht,' said Mann, 'unergründlich nennen?' After all, the Huebsch/Feuchtwanger friendship neither knew nor practiced any bounds or limitations. Accordingly, just as we found for Werfel and Zweig, so, too, may we acknowledge that Feuchtwanger and Huebsch's interaction was not fenced in by any visible (i.e., conscious) or invisible (i.e., unconscious) parameters.

The Huebsch/Feuchtwanger correspondence spans a thirty-two year period, from 1926 to the year of Feuchtwanger's death, in 1958. It consists of several hundred letters, postcards, and telegrams in addition to an untold number of pages about corrections to translations of his works. Significant amounts of Feuchtwanger's letters are handwritten, although the majority are typewritten. As Huebsch once explained, his ability to communicate with so many people at the same time necessitated that he dictate his commentary and most of his letters are in fact typewritten and often extant since he kept carbon copies of virtually all of his correspondence.[33] Important, too, are the extant unpublished epistolary exchanges between Huebsch and Marta Feuchtwanger that, unfortunately, are only fifteen in number.

At the time of the first Huebsch/Feuchtwanger exchange, on 14 May 1926, Feuchtwanger was forty-two years old, Huebsch was fifty. Obviously several of the earliest pre-World War II letters are unavailable because, while the first extant Feuchtwanger letter to Huebsch stems from 1926, the first extant Huebsch document to Feuchtwanger was written in November 1938.

The previous lack of scholarly attention directed to such an interesting relationship as that between Huebsch and Feuchtwanger remains somewhat puzzling, particularly because a wealth of remarkably informative epistolary documents is available for inspection and editing. Early in the correspondence we find statements that easily may assume the nature of a leitmotif. A typical example is seen in the following Feuchtwanger statement to Huebsch: 'It has been a truly pleasant event and the book has given me extraordinary pleasure' (13 August 1929). While these remarks seem to lack any major significance, it actually is the beginning of the period when the confidence of their relationship became permanently bonded.

Even if a minor, incidental quibble took place, they weathered it, and their resolute friendship always proved itself victorious. Accordingly, their friendship assumed an even higher level of security and trust; together with a distinctive attitude of flourishing confidence in one another – regardless of the nature of any single concern –, genuine respect for the other individual's position was always maintained. And, in fact, from this time onwards their unbreakable bond of mutual respect for one another was forged, never to be dismantled. As Feuchtwanger declared in English to Huebsch on 24 March 1930: '[…] *permit me to say that you are an ideal publisher*' (emphasis added). Feuchtwanger was not, of course, the only individual to speak about Huebsch's many admirable characteristics. Huebsch's integrity, coupled with his affable, unique disposition was the hallmark that, for each of these individuals (and others, too) – although in different ways –, ordained them as worthy recipients for authentic praise and genuine success.

The chief traits that define Ben W. Huebsch are frequently found in these remarkable historical communications with Feuchtwanger, Werfel, and Stefan Zweig. None were ostentatious, flamboyant or extravagant. On the contrary, they upheld the principles of truth, candor, and directness. As Charles Madison related in his tome *Book Publishing in America*, Huebsch 'achieved his eminence not by the size of his house or his ingenious enterprise but by fidelity to ideals and his keen appreciation of good writing. From the beginning of his career he welcomed new talent and his keen appreciation of good writing.' Not surprisingly, Huebsch was 'a publisher long universally admired and esteemed'.[34] Hence, it is not difficult to understand still another statement of Charles Madison, namely, that the list of Ben Huebsch admirers took into account a wide range of individuals, with both similar and different convictions and varying occupations.

It is fortunate that Feuchtwanger's attitude to California, even if at times cryptically expressed, has survived. In one evaluation, which Feuchtwanger had articulated just twelve days before Hitler took office as Reich Chancellor, he expressed to Huebsch:

> California was very tiring but it was really interesting. [A friend] showed me the
> Universal studio. I had a very good and interesting evening with Mr. [Alfred]
> Einstein, and I had two very attractive luncheons with Charlie Chaplin. Chaplin is
> [very] much interested in playing Hitler, as I make him in *Success*. He was so thrilled
> at this idea that he wanted to interrupt his production and accompany me to Europe;
> but I doubt [...] whether this sudden resolution will be realized. [...] All in all,
> California has improved my health very much, so that I now have really recovered.

While this single 19 January 1933 statement cannot be assumed to represent an individual's overall viewpoint or delineate his/her *Weltanschauung*, we
can learn much from Feuchtwanger's observations which focused on his U.S.A.
lecture tour. Feuchtwanger could be jovial, positive and of good spirit, but his
mood most certainly would change when his lectures became less effective and
unappreciated. James P. Pond, who had arranged the tour, wrote to Feuchtwanger on 21 January 1933 that the Los Angeles presentation, like some of his
other presentations on this same tour, was 'a great failure' and so much so that
he was asked to 'cancel the balance of the tour so far as we can.' As Pond
expressed it,

> [...] people have demanded money back for every lecture except Albuquerque, and I
> don't know what happened there. I had a most scathing letter from Athens. Atlanta
> people now have the matter in the hands of their lawyer. Newark is being patient. Los
> Angeles has refused to pay and is demanding their deposit back. San Francisco has
> paid but is demanding a refund. [...] You know that I have a very great regard for you
> personally, and it is because of this great regard that I am keenly unhappy over the
> things that have gone wrong and I think for your sake, we should try to eliminate as
> much trouble in the future as possible.

Interestingly enough, Feuchtwanger did not mention this problem in any letters
to Huebsch.

On a brighter note, just as Huebsch's personal and professional interaction with Stefan Zweig or Werfel matured over the years, so did the special
dynamics between Huebsch and Feuchtwanger. In a number of ways Huebsch
always looked out for Feuchtwanger's best interests. As we mentioned earlier in
a different context, the letters speak about the support and advice which
Huebsch provided to his writer-friend. The assistance assumed a variety of
forms but Huebsch's exceptional support to Feuchtwanger is especially evi-
denced in matters about American tax laws, the investment of money, communication with (other) publishers, and the acquisition of film rights for his
novels. Of course, the most decisive means by which Huebsch facilitated
Feuchtwanger relates to Huebsch's assistance concerning the writer's 1940
captivity in the Les Milles concentration camp in France.

On a different matter, in a letter of 22 January 1943 Huebsch told
Feuchtwanger about his activity with *Double, Double, Toil and Trouble (=Die
Brüder Lautensack)*:

> [...] working actively to place the motion picture rights to *Double, Double, Toil and
> Trouble* for the best possible price. There is interest in several quarters, and one

studio, through a certain connection of mine, has asked us what price we want. This studio is 20th-Century Fox. Otto Preminger is a producer there and he is the one who would like to have the novel for production. I quoted the figure of $75,000.00. Now the important thing in negotiations with Hollywood, in my experience, is to stand firm. […] We have a splendid story and, though it may take a little longer, if we are patient we shall get the maximum for it.

With the above-noted sale of Feuchtwanger's work to Hollywood, Huebsch acted as Feuchtwanger's friend, not as if Feuchtwanger was a mere business client.

Concern about satisfactory translations was an issue that haunted not only Feuchtwanger but, with few exceptions, almost all émigré writers whose livelihood depended upon the success of their works in another language and culture. Lothar Kahn even regarded translations as 'a vital aspect of the problems of an author in exile'.[35] As H. E. Jacob contended – though not everyone agreed with him –, in Europe his original writings, i.e. those published in his native German tongue, were on equal footing with those of Feuchtwanger, Zweig, and Werfel.

However, in exile Jacob found himself separated from his language, culture, publishers, readers, critics, and friends. It is almost as if Feuchtwanger had Jacob in mind when, in his lecture 'The Working Problems of the Writer in Exile,' delivered at a session of the Writers' Congress, held on the campus of the University of California at Los Angeles on 1-3 October 1943, he stated:

> The author who has lost the reading public of his own land frequently loses at the same time the core of his economic existence. Very many writers of the highest talent, whose products were in great demand in their own countries, find no markets in foreign lands, either because their chief merit lies in the stylistic qualities of their language, and these qualities cannot be translated, or because their choice of subjects does not interest the foreign reader. […] The economic difficulties and the enervating struggle with endless trivialities characterize life in exile. Many writers have been crushed by this life.[36]

Feuchtwanger also said in this talk:

> suffering makes the weak weaker, but the strong stronger. Banishment has constricted some of us, but to the stronger, the more able, it gave breadth and elasticity, it opened their eyes more fully to the great and essential things, and taught them not to cling to nonessentials.

Even though every aspect of the topic of Lion Feuchtwanger and matters of translation cannot be addressed within the scope of this paper, some observations can be articulated which clarify the difficulty that the exiled writer frequently experienced.[37] We need only consider Feuchtwanger's letter of 7 September 1941 to Huebsch. In it Feuchtwanger related that he had just telegraphed Huebsch as follows: 'TRANSLATION DEVIL IN FRANCE TURNS WORSE AND WORSE SOME PAGES CONTAIN DOZENS BAD MISUNDERSTANDINGS SEVERAL PAGES IMPOSSIBLE TO CORRECT STOP DOING OUR BEST.'

This telegram betrays Feuchtwanger's heightened sense of rage and disappointment. And Feuchtwanger's 7 September letter spoke in equally critical language and is no less demonstrative of his uneasiness and apprehension:

> Leider ist die gesamte stilistische Haltung der Übersetzerin recht unglücklich. Sie hat die Tendenz, das Buch zu einer Art Zeitungsreportage zu machen. Sie banalisiert, sie wendet Slangworte an, wo ich mit Absicht besonders ruhig und episch zu berichten trachtete. Sie streut Superlative überall hin. Ich habe sehr vieles stehen lassen, was mir nicht gefiel, da man sonst überhaupt kein Ende gefunden hätte. Das Schlimme ist, daß sie nicht nur vieles einfach nicht verstanden hat, sondern daß sie das ganze banalisiert, im Niveau herunterdrückt.

The 7 September 1941 letter to Huebsch continued:

> Um so glücklicher finde ich von meinem Autorstandpunkt aus die Übersetzung von *Demonic and Divine*. Ich maße mir natürlich kein Urteil an über das Englische von Miss Neilson, aber wo immer ich nachprüfte, war mein Text mit größter Treue wiedergegeben, es war kein Wort weggelassen und keines zugefügt. Bitte überlegen Sie sich, was wir mit dem *Devil in France* machen. Wir haben – Miss Waldo und ich –, was wir erhalten haben, nach bestem Wissen und Gewissen korrigiert und das Manuskript mit den Korrekturen lege ich bei. Erhalten haben wir […] die größere Hälfte. Die rein berichtenden Partien sind natürlich besser als die kontemplativen, aber offenbar versteht die Übersetzerin doch zu wenig Deutsch, um zu erkennen, worauf es in den kontemplativen Partien des Buches ankommt. Es sind vor allem noch zwei Kapitel, vor denen ich Angst habe. Das Beste wäre, wenn die Dame jene Kapitel, die mehr Reflexion erhalten als Bericht, zusammen mit einem Deutschen durchginge, der halbwegs Englisch kann. Es dürfte sich in dem ganzen Buch um etwa fünfzig Seiten handeln.[38]

The next day Feuchtwanger expressed to Huebsch in an even more irritating and depressing manner that the translation affair was still alarming him:

> Die Übersetzung des *Devil in France* wird leider immer schlimmer. Nicht nur weicht die Übersetzerin meinen Stil ungeheuerlich auf und braucht viel mehr Worte, als ich brauche, nicht nur klingt sehr vieles, was bei mir hart und sachlich klingt, in ihrer Übersetzung sentimental; sie läßt auch eine Reihe von Sätzen einfach fort, die mir überaus wesentlich erscheinen, sie übt auf altjüngferliche gouvernantenhafte Art Zensur und streicht alles fort, was mit der Verdauung zusammenhängt, so daß zum Beispiel der Zug, jene Episode, die ich seinerzeit in 'Friday' [a section deleted from the final manuscript] beschrieben habe, streckenweise einfach unverständlich wird. Ich lege Ihnen einen Absatz bei, damit Sie selber sehen, was ich meine. Davon abgesehen, ist die ganze Atmosphäre des Buches weg. Alles klingt gemütlich. Kurz: im ganzen ist es nicht mehr mein Buch.

Feuchtwanger formally concluded the letter with an apologetic thought: 'Entschuldigen Sie, lieber Herr Huebsch, wenn ich mir Luft mache, aber ich weiß, daß ich da gerade bei Ihnen Verständnis finde.' But after these remarks Feuchtwanger added two final statements: 'PS Veranlassen Sie doch bitte die Übersetzerin, sich zumindest mit jemand zusammenzusetzen, der Deutsch kann, und verhindern Sie sie, Zensur an mir zu üben.' The second remark was equally graphic: 'PPS Ich sandte Ihnen heute das folgende Telegramm: PRINTING [Elizabeth] ABBOTTS TRANSLATION IN THIS FORM IMPOSSIBLE ENDLESS GRAVE MISTAKES SOME PARAGRAPHS ABSOLUTELY SENSELESS BY TRANSLATORS CENSORSHIP STOP PLEASE WIRE YOUR ADDRESS FOR SENDING MANUSCRIPT AND CORRECTIONS[.]'

The art of translation was an issue for Lion Feuchtwanger. Kahn articulated an interesting observation that 'in Europe it would not have occurred to Feuchtwanger to read any of his translations'.[39] Aside from acknowledging the nature of the problem, at issue for Feuchtwanger and Huebsch was how to remedy the situation. After all, the process of translation involved more than the establishment of the proper tense and the correlation of words. Quality and tone, for example, are of critical importance and must be perfect. Anything that eludes 'the greatness of the original' should not be accepted.[40] As George Steiner posited in *After Babel* 'every translation is an interpretation'.[41]

Huebsch's article entitled 'Cross-Fertilization in Letters,' which appeared in the summer 1942 issue of *The American Scholar,* presents the following:

> [...] the current influx of Europeans has a significance and a portentousness quite different from the more numerous immigration of the past. [...] The cream of its intellectual leadership is a gift for which we never can be sufficiently grateful. This admixture to our scholarship comes most opportunely; we are ripe for it, the past years in our cultural development seem almost like a deliberate preparation to absorb men whom destiny has brought to us. [...] The exiles and refugees of this day who eagerly strive to attain citizenship are our own kind; they supplement our learning; they revive the meaning of those whose ideals which tend to be forgotten in the constant repetition of the words that describe them, and they supply us with living symbols of the pioneer spirit that instead of becoming a standard for daily emulation is chiefly perpetuated in history textbooks. One cannot stand still under the shock of this sudden enrichment, this copious administration of vitamins of the spirit. It will restore the currents that have given Americans continuing youth, curiosity and audacity; it will renew our awareness of the animating value of heterogeneous elements and of the absurdities of the race theories that serve dictators as a red herring.

Huebsch's words are profound and replete with several implications.[42] Yet, despite the veracity of the remarks, his position is not the viewpoint that the majority initially would consider. In one sense, the thought implied within Huebsch's message reminds us of Martin Gumpert's 1941 book *First Papers*.[43] Gumpert's intent was 'to show the painful and blissful process of adaptation' during the 'preparatory years,' and, as Thomas Mann indicated in his preface to it, Gumpert succeeded admirably.

On another issue, there are noticeable differences between the Huebsch/Zweig and the Huebsch/Feuchtwanger friendships. Feuchtwanger's letter of 1 October 1938 is revealing: 'I would be indebted to you,' he wrote, 'if you could let me know your impression of that portion of the manuscript which you already have and, also, if the contract will be as we discussed it in that last conversation together.'

Feuchtwanger's statement reveals his eagerness to learn about about the acceptance status of his current literary submission. Moreover, even though he regards his *Paris Gazette* to be superior in terms of quality, he remains uncertain if, ultimately, Huebsch will give the 'green light' for *Paris Gazette* to go to press. Feuchtwanger attempts to mask his anxiety, but his remarks are too blatant not to be noticed and, in all probability, Huebsch properly understood him.

It appears Huebsch accepted Werfel's and Stefan Zweig's works sight unseen. Yet, the young Feuchtwanger was not the recipient of such a practice. Indeed, Feuchtwanger knew that his writings were subject to acceptance, and that nothing was a given. In fact, the Huebsch/Feuchtwanger correspondence began in 1926 on a note that could have severed any future interaction between them. In one of the earliest extant epistolary documents, we even find Feuchtwanger apologizing to Huebsch, declaring that he (Feuchtwanger) understood why his work might be ineffective with an American audience. The 'American audience' factor often became the chief criteria that Huebsch applied in accepting or rejecting a work, as H. E. Jacob, for one, knew so well.

The response anticipated by Werfel and Zweig related to some form of constructive criticism, e.g., editorial suggestions, either from Huebsch or from an outside reader of Huebsch's choice. Thus, we most frequently observe Zweig and Werfel thanking Huebsch for his splendid assistance. Unlike Jacob and, in the early years, Feuchtwanger, Werfel and Stefan Zweig unquestionably assumed that their respective works would be published by the Viking Press. Nevertheless, this seems to have changed by the 1950s when Feuchtwanger's works were accepted sight unseen.

By the mid-1950s an ever closer relationship between Huebsch and Feuchtwanger had been formed, and this is seen particularly well in Huebsch's letter of 13 April 1953. In this document Feuchtwanger expressed to his publisher and friend: 'I am continually pleased when it is pointed out to me that B. W. Huebsch published it, and this occurs quite often. I know of few men who affected me so much as you, B. W. Huebsch, in your unassuming, reflective, and lasting manner.' Hence, the questioning by Feuchtwanger about the acceptability of his writings no longer was a concern. In fact, in various letters written around 1955 Huebsch acknowledged that Feuchtwanger's classic-like writing style epitomized brilliance and beauty, grace and originality, profundity and universality. Huebsch's statements in his perceptive letters of 6 October 1955 and 2 December 1955 to Feuchtwanger serve as good examples. In the October 1955 exchange Huebsch showed remarkable insight, exclaiming:

> [...] you know better than I do of the awakening of the interest of the new European generation in your books; although I think it equally likely that it is your contemporaries who are glad of the restoration of those authors who symbolize the culture of their best days.

Two months later, in December 1955, in an equally cogent and profound epistolary document, Huebsch told Feuchtwanger that his *Spanische Ballade* (=*Raquel, the Jewess of Toledo*):

> [...] demands consideration as a whole. I congratulate you on this achievement, a work that moves smoothly and almost logically step by step, with alternations of mood and tempo that creates tension and relief, that entertains as a novel should, and that presents and elucidates fundamental ideas – as most novels do not. You have created three-dimensional characters that are plausible, even if such of them as are historical may not have been born so in life. You move these in a great chess pattern

and, although the king survives, the reader knows he has been checkmated. The ironies, the paradoxes, the theological refinements, will all be appreciated.

With reason and candor Huebsch continued in this same letter, observing:

> [...] your critics will presumably point out anachronisms, at which you will smile! [...] Ideal, of course, for the film! What rich material, dramatic moments, confrontations, crises, monologues, and, oh, the spectacles: cathedral assemblages, bull-fight, battles, the funeral, to say nothing of the tender scenes of the Galiana! What a holiday for Hollywood! You may guess from the foregoing that I absorbed the book with full appreciation of its manifold merits. Generally I refrain from evaluating art by the comparative method, but I am ready to say – even remembering 'Erfolg,' 'Josephus,' and others – that this is your best. (Or is it as with the man who was asked which Brahms symphony he cared for most and answered, 'The one I heard last.') You labored greatly, and deserve the success that will come.

And in a P.P.S., as Huebsch termed it, the publisher posed the following question to his friend: 'The verses by [the Troubadour in England] Bertrand de Born [1140-1215] are too good. Did you write them?'

Equally significant remains Huebsch's letter of 22 April 1953 to Feuchtwanger:

> My impression of the whole [i.e., Rousseau work (*Narrenweisheit oder Tod und Verklärung des Jean-Jacques Rousseau*)] is that you have blended fiction and history no less successfully than in any of your novels and that you have combined *Wahrheit* and *Dichtung* so as to create first-rate entertainment while achieving your purpose of evaluating Rousseau and his contribution to social and political evolution.

In this same letter, we recognize that, true to his book philosophy, Huebsch was not necessarily publishing the work because he expected it to be a windfall. Huebsch articulated his expectations about the work cited above as follows:

> It is true that your main emphasis is on ideas yet here, as in your other works, the human interest is lively enough to hold even those readers who are indifferent to Rousseau's social and political thought. I do not predict a great sale in the United States but it will be a good sale and, what is more, it will ensure recognition of your increasing stature in letters.

In conclusion, this commentary has presented a sketch of Huebsch which hints at the remarkable career that he enjoyed and, at the same time, the unique personal and professional friendship that he shared with Lion Feuchtwanger. It has also offered some evidence of the unique association that Huebsch shared with Stefan Zweig and Franz Werfel. To be sure, Huebsch demonstrated extraordinary business practices and exhibited tremendous foresight.

Before Huebsch's association with the Viking Press or the émigré writers, i.e., when Huebsch published under his own name as B. W. Huebsch, Inc., the roster of writers which belonged to him was impressive.[44] Huebsch brought out the first American edition of D. H. Lawrence's *Sons and Lovers* and was the first publisher anywhere of James Joyce's *Portrait of the Artist as a Young Man*. Furthermore, whereas every other publisher had turned down, for example, Sherwood Anderson's *Winesburg, Ohio*, Huebsch recognized talent, accepted the work and became the first to publish this American classic. But Huebsch also could boast that his roster included figures such as Sylvia Townsend Warner, Harold Laski, Elizabeth Madox Roberts, Upton Sinclair, and Patrick White. Incidentally, the dramatic works of Gerhart Hauptmann appeared in the United States under the B. W. Huebsch imprint.

In closing, Marta Feuchtwanger's brief but most meaningful comments of 28 March 1963 to Ben Huebsch, who apparently had inquired if she would like to have the books her husband had sent to him, are remarkable:

> It would be a great satisfaction to me having your books, the books which Lion inscribed for you, in the library [at the University of Southern California]. Your name would be a part of Lion's Memorial. With great gratitude I would accept all those books you offered me. [...] As always, I admire your handwriting, as sure and clear as it was on the first day we met you. That is now more than thirty years ago. Please, take good care of yourself, I want to write many, many birthday cards to you. Please remember me to Mrs. Huebsch. Always yours, Marta F.

Notes

[1] Lion Feuchtwanger to Ben Huebsch, letter of 24 March 1930 (emphasis added).

[2] For permission to edit and publish these documents I sincerely thank the Lion Feuchtwanger Estate (University of Southern California at Los Angeles) as well as the Ben Huebsch Estate (New York). In particular, I am especially grateful to Marje Schuetze-Coburn, Curator and Director of the Feuchtwanger Archives, whose professionalism and assistance were so evident during my visits to the archives. No less special thanks are due to the archivists at the Library of Congress, D.C., whose Huebsch collection, aside from other valuable documents for this investigation, contains a considerable number of the Huebsch/Feuchtwanger letters. During many visits at the archives their exceptional assistance always was extended to me, and I am very honored to acknowledge their cooperation, too. I also thank Edith Weiß-Gerlach and Hans-Jörgen Gerlach (Berlin), Executor of the Heinrich Eduard Jacob Estate, for permitting me to meet with them, and to be a guest in their home on occasions. These H.E. Jacob documents, since October 1996 a part of the Deutsches Literaturarchiv at Marbach am Neckar, proved of much value in this study. Accordingly, I am grateful also to the various archivists at the Deutsches Literaturarchiv. I also will always be indebted to Frau Alice von Kahler (Princeton) and Frau Lucy Tal (New York). I dedicate this study to three cherished and dear friends and esteemed colleagues whose scholarship and individuality have genuinely impacted upon my own investigations: first, it remains an honor to express that the memory of Donald A. Prater pervades all of my scholarly writing; next that the exile studies of Wulf Koepke always have been for me genuinely inspiring; and, finally, with thanks and appreciation I acknowledge, too, the genuinely friendly advice and sincere encouragement of my long-time friend and colleague John M. Spalek. Finally, since the late 1980s I have been fortunate to enjoy the scholarly comradeship of Harald von Hofe who rightly is the acknowledged master of Lion Feuchtwanger studies. While any errors in this study are mine alone, my interaction with Professor von Hofe, as with the other individuals cited above, is considered a rare privilege which I am especially honored to mention here. The original orthography and punctuation of the documents have been retained; any editorial emendations are noted by square brackets.

[3] Wilhelm von Sternburg, *Lion Feuchtwanger: Ein deutsches Schriftstellerleben*, Berlin: Aufbau, 1994, p.20.

[4] Cf. András Sándor, 'Ein amerikanischer Verleger und die Exilautoren', in: John M. Spalek and Joseph Strelka, eds, *Deutsche Exilliteratur seit 1933. Bd. I: Kalifornien*, Bern: Francke, 1976, pp.117-34; and, for an engaging and equally pioneering essay, in the same volume, see: Wolf Koepke, 'Die Exilschriftsteller und der amerikanische Buchmarkt', pp.89-116.

[5] Wulf Köpke, 'Die würdige Greisin: Marta Feuchtwanger als Beispiel', *Exilforschung. Ein internationales Jahrbuch,* 7 (1989), 212-25 (here 220).

[6] Loc. cit.

[7] See Charles A. Madison, 'B. W. Huebsch & James Joyce', in: C.A.M., ed., *Irving to Irving: Author-Publisher Relations 1800-1974*, New York: R. R. Bowker, 1974, p.184.

[8] Ben W. Huebsch. Statement to Charles A. Madison, in: Madison, 'B. W. Huebsch & James Joyce', p.184.

[9] For a valuable perspective about 'The Publisher as Teacher' see the three studies which focus on Reclam's Universal-Bibliothek, Duden, and Langenscheidt in: *Die Unterrichtspraxis/Teaching German*, 28 (1995), 1, 1-18.

[10]In: *Saturday Review of Literature*, 2 July 1938, p.17.

[11] Loc. cit.

[12] Ben Huebsch, 'What has become of German literature?', in: *The English Journal*, 27 (1938), 627-37 (here 627). For an entirely different stance, consider the valuable position advanced by Sigrid Bock, 'Roman im Exil: Entstehungsbedingungen, Wirkungsabsichten und Wirkungsmöglichkeiten', in: Sigrid Bock and Manfred Hahn, eds, *Erfahrung Exil: Antifaschistische Romane 1933-1945. Analysen*, Berlin and Weimar: Aufbau, 1979, p.7 ff.

[13] Almost all the New York evening papers and morning papers acknowledged Adolph Huebsch's merits, reviewed the past acts of the deceased, and eulogized his every deed.

[14] Sarah Fraiman, *Judaism in the Works of Beer-Hofmann and Feuchtwange*r, Bern: Peter Lang, 1998, p.107.

[15] Irita Van Doren, 'About Ben Huebsch', in: Marshall A. Best, ed., *B. W. Huebsch. 1876-1964. A record of a meeting of his friends at the Grolier Club, New York City, on December 9, 1964*, private printing [Boston: Meriden Gravure, 1965], pp.13-14 (here p.13).

[16] Roberto Gilodi, 'Die unsichtbaren Fäden', in: *Verleger als Beruf: Siegfried Unseld zum fünfundsiebzigsten Geburtstag*, ed. Christoph Buchwald, Frankfurt am Main: Suhrkamp, 1999, pp.63-66 (here 63-64).

[17] 'Zu den unveröffentlichten "Gesprächen" Stefan Zweigs mit Ben Huebsch im Entscheidungsjahr 1933', in: Stefan Zweig, *Exil und Suche nach dem Weltfrieden*, ed. Mark H. Gelber and Klaus Zelewitz, Riverside: Ariadne, 1995, pp.279-94. See also my studies: 'Unpublished Letters between Franz Werfel, Alma Mahler Werfel and Ben Huebsch: 1941-1946', *Modern Austrian Literature*, 24 (1991), 2, 123-200. Special Werfel issue (with D. Daviau and J. Johns). Further, see my: 'The Struggle for Survival – From Hitler's Appointment to the

Nazi Book-Burnings: Some Unpublished Stefan Zweig Letters, with an Unpublished Manifesto', in: J. B. Berlin, J. Johns, and R. Lawson, eds, *Turn-of-the-Century Vienna and its Legacy: Essays in Honor of Donald G. Daviau*, Wien: Edition Atelier, 1993, pp.361-88. See also my study: 'Briefe aus Brasilien: Stefan Zweigs *Schachnovelle*', in: Ingrid Schwamborn, ed., *Die letzte Partie: Stefan Zweigs Leben und Werk in Brasilien, 1932-1942*, Bielefeld: Aisthesis, 1999, pp.245-64.

[18] Other invaluable sources remain Sándor, 'Ein amerikanischer Verleger und die Exil-autoren' and Koepke, 'Die Exilschriftsteller und der amerikanische Buchmarkt'. See note 4.

[19] At this point, we should direct attention to Hugo F. Garten's brilliant summary of the literary trends that took place during this period. To be sure, only with a firm grasp of Gar-ten's position can a profound understanding of the period even become possible. See: Hugo F. Garten, 'Main Trends in German literature today', *German Life & Letters*, 1 (1947), 44-53.

[20] Cf. Deborah Vietor-Engländer's admirable and indispensible 'Wetcheeks Welterfolg: Ein kritischer Forschungsbericht', in: *Lion Feuchtwanger: Materialien zu Leben und Werk*, ed. Wilhelm von Sternburg, Frankfurt am Main: Fischer, 1989, pp.312-35. Also the four-volume bibliography: Sandra H. Hawrylchak and John M. Spalek, eds, *Lion Feuchtwanger: A Bibliographic Handbook*, München: K. G. Sauer, 1998-2004. Of course study of Feucht-wanger demands consideration of not only the remarkable primary and secondary suggestions presented by Vietor-Engländer but also the Spalek/Hawrylchak model reference volumes. About this concern, see especially: Carol Paul-Merritt, 'The Reception of the German Writers in Exile by the American Liberal Press 1933-1945: Changes and Trends', in: John M. Spalek and Robert F. Bell, eds, *Exile: The Writer's Experience*, Chapel Hill: University of North Carolina Press, 1982, pp.95-118.

[21] Consideration of the similarities between Mann and Feuchtwanger proves rewarding. To be succinct, 'dem bürgerlichen Schriftsteller Feuchtwanger stellt sich ganz wie Thomas Mann die Auseinandersetzung mit dem Faschismus dar als selbstkritische Überprüfung der Grund-positionen bürgerlicher Kunst im Exil. Betroffen wird die Beerbbarkeit bürgerlicher Kunst-positionen durch den Faschismus analysiert; überprüft wird das Verhältnis von Kunst und Politik mit dem Ziel der Neuversicherung von Kunst als Organ humanistischer Weltaneig-nung und antifaschistischer Orientierung.' See Jan Hans und Lutz Winckler, 'Von der Selbst-verständigung des Künstlers in Krisenzeiten: Lion Feuchtwangers *Wartesaal-Trilogie*', in: *TEXT + KRITIK: Zeitschrift für Literatur*, H. 79/80 (1983), pp.28-48, esp. pp.43-44.

[22] H. E. Jacob's wife was Lucy Tal's cousin.

[23]See my study: 'In Exile: The Friendship and Unpublished Correspondence between Thomas Mann and Heinrich Eduard Jacob', in: *DVjs*, 64 (1990), 1, 172-87. See also my: 'Thomas Mann and Heinrich Eduard Jacob. Unpublished Letters about Haydn', *Germanisch-Romanische Monatsschrift*, 40 (1990), 2, 71-89. See also my: '"War unsre [KZ] Gefangenschaft ein Einzelfall, etwas Monströs-Zufälliges oder war sie die näturliche Folge natürlicher Gegeben-heiten?" – The Unpublished Exile Correspondence between Heinrich Eduard Jacob and Raoul Auernheimer (1939-1943)', *Germanisch-Romanische Monatsschrift*, 49 (1999), 2, 209-39. See also my '"Durch mich geht's ein zur Stadt der Schmerzerkorenen, / durch mich geht's ein zum ewiglichen Schmerz, [...] / Laßt, die ihr eingeht, alle Hoffnung fahren!" – The Unpublished Correspondence of Heinrich Eduard Jacob in KZ Dachau und Buchenwald

(1938-1939) (and unpublished letters with the German PEN-Club in London)', *Germanisch-Romanische Monatsschrift*, 49 (1999), 3, 307-31.

[24] George Steiner, 'A Kind of Survivor', in: G. S., *A Reader*, New York: Oxford University Press, 1984, pp.220-34 (here p.230).

[25] Lothar Kahn, *Insight and Action: The Life and Work of Lion Feuchtwanger*, Rutherford: Fairleigh Dickinson University Press, 1975, esp. pp.165-66.

[26] See Frederic Warburg, *All Authors are Equal: The Publishing Life of Frederic Warburg 1936-1971*, New York: St. Martin's, 1973, p.61.

[27] Lionel B. Steiman presents several excellent and invaluable explanations about Werfel's actions during these trying times. See, L.S., 'Franz Werfel – His Song in America', *Modern Austrian Literature*, 20 (1987), 3-4, pp.55-69. In a similar sense, Carl Steiner postulated: 'Of all the Jewish writers of Austrian descent who had the good fortune to escape Nazi persecution and the Holocaust, Franz Werfel not only achieved the greatest measure of success in American exile, but also left an indelible mark on the American consciousness.' In fact, Carl Steiner argues that *The Song of Bernadette* 'enabled him to vie successfully in popularity with the likes of Thomas Mann and Lion Feuchtwanger.' See: Carl Steiner, 'Showing the Way: Franz Werfel's American Legacy', *Modern Austrian Literature*, 20 (1987), 71-79 (esp. p.71).

[28] Joseph Pischel, *Lion Feuchtwanger: Versuch über Leben und Werk*, Leipzig: Reclam, 1976, pp.125-26.

[29] Harry Levin, *Refractions: Essays in Comparative Literature*, New York: Oxford University Press, 1966, p.62.

[30] Stefan Zweig, *Die Welt von Gestern: Erinnerungen eines Europäers*, Frankfurt am Main: Fischer, 1993, pp.7-13.

[31] Koepke, 'Die Exilschriftsteller und der amerikanische Buchmarkt', p.103.

[32] Terry Reisch, 'Franz Werfel: Waiting for His Time to Come', in: Wolfgang Elfe, James Hardin and Gunther Holst, eds, *The Fortunes of Writers in America: Studies in Literary Reception*, South Carolina: University of South Carolina Press, 1992, pp.185-210.

[33] The concept of dictation was of special interest for Feuchtwanger; cf. in this regard, Theodor W. Adorno: 'Das Diktat ermöglicht dem Schriftsteller, sich in den frühesten Phasen des Produktionsprozesses in die Position des Kritikers hineinzumanövrieren.' And 'dies dialektische Verfahren entspricht aber exakt der Disposition und Strategie des freischwebenden Intellektuellen L[ion] F[euchtwanger] [...].' See: Klaus Modick, 'L. F. als Produzent: Über die kuriosen, eigentümlichen, ja wunderlichen Methoden des Dr. Feuchtwanger', in: *TEXT + KRITIK*, (1983), pp.5-18.

[34] Charles Madison, *Book Publishing in America*, New York: McGraw-Hill, 1966, p.296.

[35] Kahn, *Insight and Action*, p.274.

[36] Lion Feuchtwanger, 'The Working Problems of the Writer in Exile', in: *Writers' Congress: The Proceedings of the Conference held in October 1943 under the sponsorship of the Hollywood Writers' Mobilization and the University of California*, Los Angeles: University of California Press, 1944, pp.345-49.

[37] As one might expect, Huebsch's Viking Press was not the only firm that suffered from a loss of top-flight translators. One would expect, in fact, that Thomas Mann's publications with the Alfred A. Knopf Publishing Company would have eliminated such annoying and distressing problems, yet this was hardly the case. In fact, Mann's works suffered greatly in terms of translation issues, and to this day there remains much controversy surrounding them. In this regard, cf. Jeffrey B. Berlin, 'On the Making of *The Magic Mountain*: The Unpublished Correspondence between Thomas Mann, Alfred A., Knopf, and H. T. Lowe-Porter', *Seminar: A Journal of Germanic Studies*, 28 (1992), 283-320; see also: Jeffrey B. Berlin, 'Thomas Mann's Unpublished Correspondence from 5 January 1936 to 3 May 1936 with Alfred A. Knopf and H. T. Lowe-Porter', *Euphorion: Zeitschrift für Literaturgeschichte*, 95 (2001), 197-210.

[38] Hilde Waldo was Feuchtwanger's secretary from October 1940, i.e., the date of his arrival in the United States until his death in 1958. Before her immigration to the United States, Hilde Waldo had spent much time in Great Britain, and, accordingly, was proficient in English. To a significant degree, she was responsible for many of the corrections. At the same time, we cannot disregard that Feuchtwanger did check each correction.

[39] Kahn, *Insight and Action*, p.273.

[40] Cf. William H. Gass, *Reading Rilke: Reflections on the Problems of Translation*, New York: Basic Books, 1999, see esp. pp.53 ff.

[41] George Steiner, *After Babel*, New York: Oxford, 1975, p.x.

[42] As noted, numerous perspectives could be considered here. For the sake of brevity, let us only speak once again about the matter which troubled him so greatly. On 14 May 1943, in a letter to Richard J. Walsh of the John Day Company in New York, Huebsch honestly stated: 'It is good news that an efficient translator from the German is available, The problem of getting the right people has given me violent headaches, and the job of reviewing the work of those who claim to be efficient translators has cost me so much time lately.'

[43] Martin Gumpert, *First Papers*, New York: Duell, Sloan and Pearce, 1941.

[44] As Huebsch has explained in his unpublished, typewritten oral history manuscript, archived at Columbia University, his merging with the Viking Press was an uncomplicated event. In 1925 Huebsch bought stock in the newly formed Viking Press and the Viking Press owners bought stock in B. W. Huebsch, Inc. This transaction, it should be noted, was completed before the Viking Press actually had published any books. As Huebsch viewed the matter, his two Viking Press business partners, namely Harold Guinzburg and George Oppenheimer, moved into his business, which was a going concern. (Oppenheimer 'pulled out a few years after we started because there came opportunities more in line with his own tastes and desires in the theatrical business – theatre, and then Hollywood'.) 'In a way', as Huebsch stated, '[the] Viking is really a continuation of [his] firm rather than a new one. Then, as Huebsch

reported, he 'stuck around long enough for [his] partners to get the hang of the business […].
He [= Huebsch] stayed until December' and then 'pulled up stakes and went abroad and
stayed there for a year' (Oral History Interview, pp.74-75).

GLOSSARY OF FEUCHTWANGER TITLES

Since Feuchtwanger's works have been referred to variously by their German or English titles in this volume, we give below a glossary of these titles. The glossary is taken from Sandra H. Hawrylchak and John M. Spalek (eds), *Lion Feuchtwanger: A Bibliographic Handbook/Lion Feuchtwanger: Ein bibliographisches Handbuch*, volume 2, Munich: K.G. Saur, 1999.

Die Brüder Lautensack	*Double, Double, Toil and Trouble*
Erfolg	*Success*
Exil	*Paris Gazette*
Der falsche Nero	*The Pretender*
Die Geschwister Oppenheim/ Die Geschwister Oppermann	*The Oppermanns*
Die Gesichte der Simone Machard	*The Visions of Simone Machard*
Goya oder Der arge Weg der Erkenntnis	*This is the Hour*
Das Haus der Desdemona	*The House of Desdemona*
Jefta und seine Tochter	*Jephta and His Daughter*
Der jüdische Krieg (*Josephus*, Bd. 1)	*Josephus*
Jud Süß	*Power* (US edition) *Jew Suess* (UK and US editions)
Spanische Ballade/Die Jüdin von Toledo	*Raquel, the Jewess of Toledo*
Moskau 1937	*Moscow 1937*
Narrenweisheit oder Tod und Verklärung des Jean-Jacques Rousseau	*'Tis Folly to Be Wise or Death and Transfiguration of Jean-Jacques Rousseau*
Simone	*Simone*
Der Tag wird kommen (*Josephus*, Bd. 3)	*Josephus and the Emperor* (US edition) *The Day Will Come* (UK edition)
Unholdes Frankreich/ Der Teufel in Frankreich	*The Devil in France*
Thomas Wendt/Neunzehnhundertachtzehn	*1918* (in the volume *Three Plays*)
Waffen für Amerika/ Die Füchse im Weinberg	*Proud Destiny*
Wahn oder Der Teufel in Boston	*The Devil in Boston*
Die Witwe Capet	*The Widow Capet*

INDEX

List of Contributors

Daniel Azuélos is Professor of German at the Université de Picardie-Jules Verne, Amiens, France. The author of a major study on *Aufbau*, the New York weekly, he has also published widely on exiles from Nazi Germany (Arnold Zweig, Lion Feuchtwanger, Hannah Arendt, Norbert Elias) as well as on Jakob Wasserman and Arthur Schnitzler. Forthcoming : *L'entrée en bourgeoisie des Juifs allemands ou le paradigme libéral, 1800-1930* (Presses universitaires de Paris-Sorbonne, 2005). azuelos.daniel@wanadoo.fr

Jeffrey B. Berlin is Professor Emeritus of Comparative Literature at Holy Family University (Philadelphia/USA). His principal interests are Modern European literature (1900-1945), literary history in the early 20th century in Great Britain and Germany/Austria, literary relations between American publishers and German/Austrian authors, life-writing, the Holocaust, the theory and practice of textual editing, especially epistolary documents, the German/Austrian émigré in Great Britain (1933-1945) as well as Schnitzler's *fin-de-siècle* Vienna. On editorial board of *Modern Austrian Literature* (1976-1999); member of Modern Language Association (MLA) International Bibliography Team (1981-1990); Schriftführer of Internationale Stefan Zweig-Gesellschaft (Universität Salzburg, 1992 to present). Many guest lectures in Europe and USA. Numerous scholarly publications, including articles, editions, monographs, introductions, and translations. JBB106@aol.com

Wulf Koepke, Distinguished Professor of German, emeritus, Texas A&M University, is the author of *Lion Feuchtwanger*, 1983, in the series of 'Autorenbücher', as well as a number of studies on Feuchtwanger. Koepke edited and co-edited several books on exile literature and wrote *The Reception of the Major Novels of Alfred Döblin*, 2003, as well as numerous studies on Döblin, Heinrich Mann, general problems of exile studies, and literature of the postwar years. Koepke is co-editor of the Yearbook *Exilforschung*. His other area of expertise is the late 18th century, in particular the works of Jean Paul Richter and Johann Gottfried Herder.

David Midgley is University Reader in German Literature and Culture, and Fellow of St John's College, Cambridge. He has published widely on German literary modernism, and his latest book, *Writing Weimar* (2000), is a broad-based study of the literature of the Weimar Republic in relation to its social and cultural context. drm7@joh.cam.ac.uk

Pól Ó Dochartaigh is Senior Lecturer in German at the University of Ulster. He is Chair of the Royal Irish Academy Committee for Modern Languages, Literary and Cultural Studies. His main research interests are in German, Jewish and Celtic literature and history. His recent publications include *Julius Pokorny, 1887-1970: Germans, Celts and Nationalism* (Dublin 2004) and *Germany since 1945* (Basingstoke & New York 2004). He is also editor of the *Feuchtwanger Newsletter*. p.odochartaigh@ulster.ac.uk

Arnold Pistiak is Lecturer in Comparative Literature at the University of Potsdam. His main research interests are in Heinrich Heine´s later poems (*Ich will das rote Sefchen küssen*) and prose (*Lutèce/Lutezia*). He has also published on Friedrich Hölderlin and Lion Feuchtwanger. pistiak@rz.uni-potsdam.de

Marje Schuetze-Coburn is Feuchtwanger Librarian and Associate Executive Director, Specialized Libraries and Archival Collections, at the University of Southern California in Los Angeles. Currently she serves as Secretary/ Treasurer of the International Feuchtwanger Society. schuetze@usc.edu

Alexander Stephan is Professor of German, Ohio Eminent Scholar, and Senior Fellow of the Mershon Center for the Study of International Security and Public Policy at Ohio State University. Previously he taught at Princeton University, the University of California at Los Angeles and in Florida. Major book publications: *Im Visier des FBI. Deutsche Exilschriftsteller in den Akten amerikanischer Geheimdienste* (Stuttgart, 1995, pb. Berlin, 1998, engl. as '*Communazis.' FBI Surveillance of German Emigré Writers*, New Haven, 2000), *Christa Wolf* (Munich, 4th, enl. and rev. ed. 1991), *Die deutsche Exilliteratur* (Munich, 1979), *Max Frisch* (Munich, 1983), *Anna Seghers im Exil* (Bonn, 1993), *Anna Seghers: 'Das siebte Kreuz'. Welt und Wirkung eines Romans* (Berlin, 1997); (eds.) *Peter Weiss. Die Ästhetik des Widerstands* (Frankfurt, 3rd ed. 1990), *Schreiben im Exil* (Bonn, 1985), *Exil. Literatur und die Künste nach 1933* (Bonn, 1990), *Christa Wolf. The Author's Dimension* (New York, 1993; London, 1993; Chicago, 1995), Ulrich Plenzdorf, Günter Kunert, Anna Seghers, and others, *The New Sufferings of Young W. and Other Short Stories from the German Democratic Republic* (New York, 1997), Uwe Johnson, *Speculations About Jakob and Other Writings* (New York, 2000), *'Rot=Braun'? Brecht Dialog 2000. Nationalsozialismus und Stalinismus bei Brecht und Zeitgenossen*, with Therese Hörnigk (Berlin, 2000), *Jeans, Rock und Vietnam. Amerikanische Kultur in der DDR*, with Therese Hörnigk, (Berlin, 2002), *A. Döblin, L. Feuchtwanger, A. Seghers, A. Zweig. Early 20th Century German Fiction* (New York, 2003), Anna Seghers, *Die Entscheidung. Roman.* Collected Works, vol. I, 7 (Berlin, 2003). Editor of the book series *Exil-Studien/Exile Studies*. Numerous contributions to radio and television in Germany and the USA on Bertolt Brecht, Marlene Dietrich, Anna Seghers, Thomas Mann and other topics; produced for German television a documentary film titled *Im Visier des FBI. Deutsche Autoren im US-Exil* (ARD, 1995). stephan.30@osu.edu

Ian Wallace is Emeritus Professor of German at the University of Bath. He founded *German Monitor* in 1979 and is its General Editor. Numerous publications on German literature and cultural politics. He is President of the International Feuchtwanger Society. His main research interests are in GDR literature and exile literature. i.wallace@virgin.net

Europa in *Grande Sertão: Veredas*
Grande Sertão: Veredas in Europa

Stefan Kutzenberger

Amsterdam/New York, NY 2005. 314 pp.
(Internationale Forschungen zur Allgemeinen und Vergleichenden
Literaturwissenschaft 85)

ISBN: 90-420-1605-1 € 65,-/US $ 91.-

Grande Sertão: Veredas ist einer der großen Romane der Moderne, der in seiner
Materie und Sprache dabei brasilianischer nicht sein könnte. Eigens nach
„Europa in *Grande Sertão: Veredas*" zu suchen, scheint deshalb ein gewagtes
Unternehmen. Stefan Kutzenberger zeigt jedoch, dass die europäische Tradition
diesem brasilianischen Nationalepos nicht nur einzelne Themen und Motive wie
Pakt und Teufel liefert, sondern dass auch die christliche Weltsicht Riobaldos aus
Europa stammt und dort vor allem aus der religiösen Philosophie Søren
Kierkegaards. An Hand dessen Theorie der Wiederholung soll Riobaldos ewige
Frage nach seiner Schuld endlich beantwortet werden.
Eine kurze Geschichte der Rezeption von João Guimarães Rosas Werk in
Deutschland und eine kritische Analyse der berühmten deutschen Übersetzung
von Curt Meyer-Clason zeichnen den Weg von „*Grande Sertão: Veredas* in
Europa", vor allem im deutschsprachigen Raum, nach. Der hier erstmals
veröffentlichte Briefwechsel zwischen Guimarães Rosa und dem Kiepenheuer &
Witsch Verlag schafft einen unmittelbaren Einblick in das Verlagswesen der 60er
Jahre, das mit einer nahezu unschuldigen Begeisterung auf der Suche nach dem
exotischen Lateinamerika war.

USA/Canada: One Rockefeller Plaza, Ste. 1420, New York, NY 10020,
Tel. (212) 265-6360, Call toll-free (U.S. only) 1-800-225-3998,
Fax (212) 265-6402
All other countries: Tijnmuiden 7, 1046 AK Amsterdam, The Netherlands
Tel. ++ 31 (0)20 611 48 21, Fax ++ 31 (0)20 447 29 79
Orders-queries@rodopi.nl www.rodopi.nl

Please note that the exchange rate is subject to fluctuations

Regionaler Kulturraum und intellektuelle Kommunikation vom Humanismus bis ins Zeitalter des Internet
Festschrift für Klaus Garber

Herausgegeben von Axel E. Walter

Amsterdam/New York, NY 2005. XI, 1030 pp. (Chloe 36)

ISBN: 90-420-1715-5   Bound   € 240,-/US $ 336.-

Anläßlich der Emeritierung von Prof. Dr. Dr. h.c. Klaus Garber entstand diese Festschrift, in der 38 Kolleginnen und Kollegen, Schülerinnen und Schüler aus dem In- und Ausland den bedeutenden Literaturwissenschaftler mit wissenschaftlichen Aufsätzen bedenken und ehren. Die hier versammelten Beiträge bieten zum thematischen Komplex „Regionaler Kulturraum und Intellektuelle Kommunikation", mit dem zentrale Forschungsgebiete Garbers wie insgesamt der internationalen Literaturwissenschaft berührt sind, neueste Forschungsergebnisse. Die Beiträge erschließen vielfach erstmals unbekannte Quellen und eröffnen unter den verschiedensten methodischen Ansätzen künftige Perspektiven für eine interdisziplinäre und kulturwissenschaftliche Forschung. Von den Anfängen der Frühen Neuzeit bis in die Moderne reicht das thematische Spektrum der eigens für diesen Band verfaßten Aufsätze.

Entstanden ist so eine Festschrift, die sich in ihrer thematischen Geschlossenheit und ihrer wissenschaftlichen Aktualität deutlich von den ansonsten vorgelegten Werken dieser Gattung akademischer Ehrenschriften abhebt.

USA/Canada: One Rockefeller Plaza, Ste. 1420, New York, NY 10020,
Tel. (212) 265-6360, Call toll-free (U.S. only) 1-800-225-3998,
Fax (212) 265-6402
All other countries: Tijnmuiden 7, 1046 AK Amsterdam, The Netherlands.
Tel. ++ 31 (0)20 611 48 21, Fax ++ 31 (0)20 447 29 79
Orders-queries@rodopi.nl   www.rodopi.nl
Please note that the exchange rate is subject to fluctuations

Philosophie, Gesellschaft und Bildung in Zeiten der Globalisierung

Herausgegeben von Hermann-Josef Scheidgen, Norbert Hintersteiner und Yoshiro Nakamura

Amsterdam/New York, NY 2005. 348 pp.
(Studien zur Interkulturellen Philosophie 15)

ISBN: 90-420-1785-6   € 70,-/US $ 98.-

Der Begriff „Globalisierung" wird zunehmend nicht nur in den Disziplinen der Ökonomie und der Kommunikationswissenschaft diskutiert, sondern auch in den Gesellschafts- und Erziehungswissenschaften sowie insbesondere in der Interkulturellen Philosophie. Der Diskurs über Globalisierung verläuft dabei teilweise analog demjenigen über Inter- und Multikulturalität.

Die Beiträge dieses Bandes geben ein breites Spektrum wieder. Sie reichen von der Konstatierung der Globalisierung als einer Rahmenbedingung, zu der man sich als Wissenschaftler reflexiv oder reaktiv zu verhalten habe, über die Analyse diverser Teilaspekte und über visionäre Einforderungen utopischer Globalisierungsauslegungen bis zur Negierung ihrer erkenntnistheoretischen Bedeutung. Das Gemeinsame dieser Vielfältigkeit ist die Bestimmung des Globalen als eines Szenarios der Begegnung.

USA/Canada: 906 Madison Avenue, Union, NJ 07083, USA.
Fax: (908) 206-0820 Call toll-free: 1-800-225-3998 (USA only)
All other countries: Tijnmuiden 7, 1046 AK Amsterdam, The Netherlands.
Tel. ++ 31 (0)20 611 48 21, Fax ++ 31 (0)20 447 29 79
Orders-queries@rodopi.nl   www.rodopi.nl
Please note that the exchange rate is subject to fluctuations